DISCARDED

D0008378

*The Statesmanship of*
# ABRAHAM LINCOLN

## *Also by Olivia Coolidge*

THE APPRENTICESHIP OF ABRAHAM LINCOLN

GREEK MYTHS

LEGENDS OF THE NORTH

THE TROJAN WAR

EGYPTIAN ADVENTURES

CROMWELL'S HEAD

ROMAN PEOPLE

WINSTON CHURCHILL AND THE STORY OF
TWO WORLD WARS

CAESAR'S GALLIC WAR

MEN OF ATHENS

MAKERS OF THE RED REVOLUTION

EDITH WHARTON, 1862–1937

PEOPLE IN PALESTINE

LIVES OF THE FAMOUS ROMANS

THE KING OF MEN

EUGENE O'NEILL

WOMEN'S RIGHTS

MARATHON LOOKS ON THE SEA

THE GOLDEN DAYS OF GREECE

GEORGE BERNARD SHAW

TOM PAINE, REVOLUTIONARY

THE MAID OF ARTEMIS

GANDHI

COME BY HERE

THE THREE LIVES OF JOSEPH CONRAD

TALES OF THE CRUSADES

# The Statesmanship of
# ABRAHAM LINCOLN

## by Olivia Coolidge

*Charles Scribner's Sons / New York*

Copyright © 1976 Olivia Coolidge

Library of Congress Cataloging in Publication Data


Coolidge, Olivia E.
    The statesmanship of Abraham Lincoln.

        Continues the author's The Apprenticeship of Abraham Lin-
coln.
        SUMMARY: A biography concentrating on the years during
which Abraham Lincoln served as President.
        1. Lincoln, Abraham, Pres. U.S., 1809–1865—Juvenile literature.
[1. Lincoln, Abraham, Pres. U.S., 1809–1865. 2. Presidents] I. Title.
E457.905.C66      973.7′092′4 [B] [92]      76–14863
ISBN 0–684–14677–0

1 3 5 7 9 11 13 15 17 19 H/C 20 18 16 14 12 10 8 6 4 2

Printed in the United States of America

# Contents

*Pictorial material follows page 128*

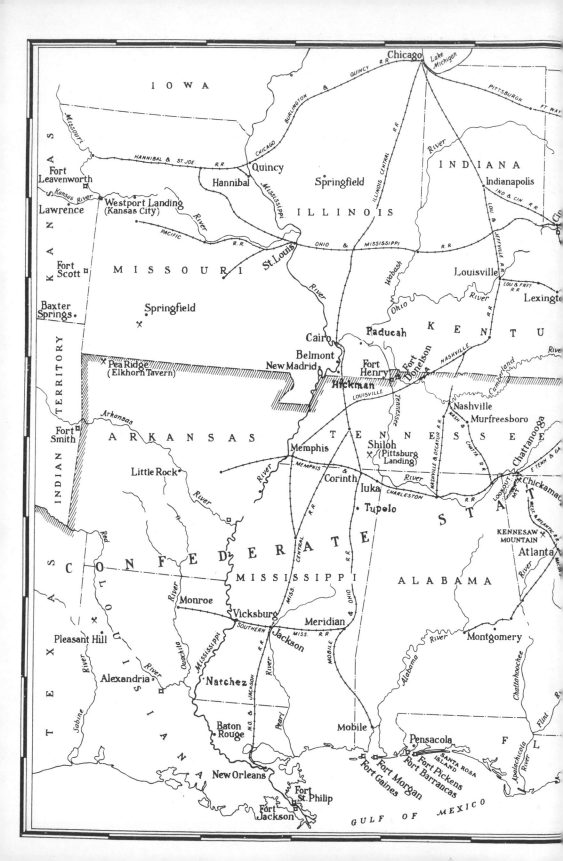

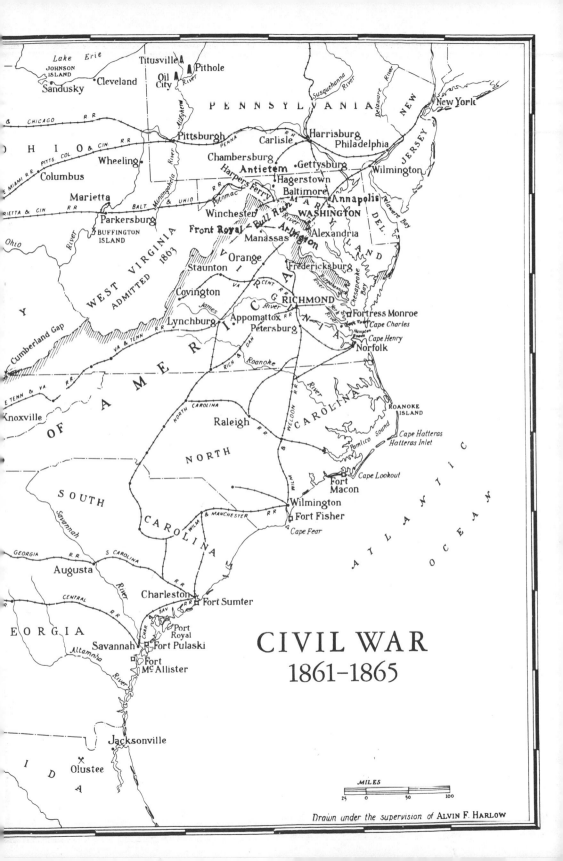

CIVIL WAR
1861–1865

*Drawn under the supervision of* ALVIN F. HARLOW

MILES

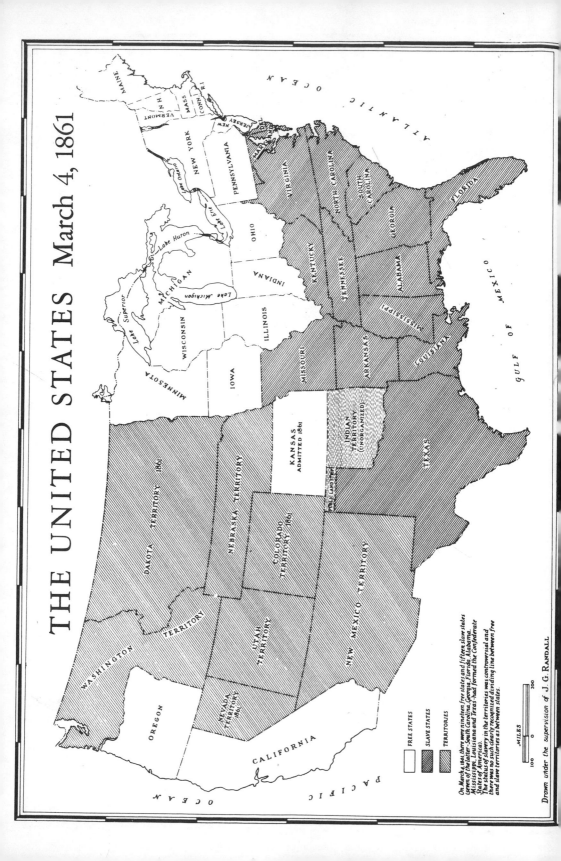

# THE UNITED STATES  March 4, 1861

MAINE

VERMONT

N.H.

MASS.

CONN. R.I.

NEW YORK

NEW JERSEY

PENNSYLVANIA

OHIO

INDIANA

ILLINOIS

MICHIGAN

WISCONSIN

IOWA

MINNESOTA

MISSOURI

KENTUCKY

VIRGINIA

NORTH CAROLINA

SOUTH CAROLINA

GEORGIA

TENNESSEE

ALABAMA

MISSISSIPPI

ARKANSAS

LOUISIANA

FLORIDA

TEXAS

KANSAS
ADMITTED
1861

INDIAN
TERRITORY
(UNORGANIZED)

NEBRASKA TERRITORY

DAKOTA TERRITORY 1861

COLORADO TERRITORY 1861

NEW MEXICO TERRITORY

UTAH TERRITORY

WASHINGTON TERRITORY

NEVADA TERRITORY 1861

OREGON

CALIFORNIA

ATLANTIC OCEAN

GULF OF MEXICO

PACIFIC OCEAN

Lake Superior

Lake Michigan

Lake Huron

Lake Erie

Lake Ontario

St. Lake

PUB. LAND STRIP

FREE STATES

SLAVE STATES

TERRITORIES

On March, 1861 there were nineteen free states and fifteen slave states
(seven of the latter--South Carolina, Georgia, Florida, Alabama,
Mississippi, Louisiana and Texas--had formed the Confederate
States of America).
The status of slavery in the territories was controversial and
there was no such clearly recognized dividing line between free
and slave territories as between states.

MILES

100    0         200

Drawn under the supervision of J. G. RANDALL.

# Introduction

THE INFLUENCE OF ABRAHAM LINCOLN did not end with his death because the Union which he refounded has endured and because many things which he said have lived after him. It is not easy for us to understand what sort of man Lincoln was in his lifetime because we see him at the high points of his career or his eloquence, and we tend to judge him by them. Indeed, this often happened to men who had known him well. Horace Greeley, editor of the New York *Tribune*, wrote some years after Lincoln's death: "There was probably no year of his life when he was not a wiser, cooler, and better man than he had been the year preceding." This agrees with what we instinctively feel, but during Lincoln's lifetime Horace Greeley by no means thought of him this way. On the contrary, Greeley frequently criticized Lincoln. As late in the war as 1864, Greeley despaired of victory with Lincoln as leader and Ulysses S. Grant as general. Nor was Greeley atypical. Edwin Stanton in the War Office, William Seward in indiscreet letters to American ministers abroad, radicals of Lincoln's own party in Congress, Peace Democrats, even War Democrats such as McClellan while commanding general

of the Army of the Potomac, all spoke of Lincoln at one
time or another without reverence and even with contempt.

We ought, therefore, in studying the life of Abraham
Lincoln to consider what his contemporaries did see in
him besides a kind, ugly man with plain manners who
wasted their time with funny stories, who came to his job
of President without knowing much about it, and who
made, as some thought, a good many mistakes. Some people learned to admire him or came to have reason to love
him. But they all saw him as what he primarily was, a
politician.

The Lincoln legend prefers to call him a statesman, implying that he rose above the spoils system, the personal
claims of friends for jobs, the bargaining for votes in return for favors. Yet Lincoln never made the least effort to
reform the political system of his country. He accepted the
fact that political power is gained by a party and that the
individual, no matter what his private convictions, has to
support the whole party platform. He knew that parties
were held together by jobs. Although he generally gave
some thought to the fitness of the candidate in paying off
political favors, he gave more to the question of whether
his congressional delegates would back him. In fact, the
political game was instinctive with Lincoln. One of his
most remarkable achievements was to keep together
through four years of war and many disasters a party with
no strong traditions, no personal devotion to himself, and
considerable elements which disagreed with him on policy. This is not a role for a superman, but for a manipula-
tor. Contemporaries were bound to call their leader wily
or weak, particularly when they failed to control him. He
made no claim to be a great man, and they were not likely
to think of him in those terms.

The people who learned to love and respect Lincoln
were those who saw less of him than did the politicians, the
big local bosses, or the editors of important newspapers.

To private people, ordinary voters or disfranchised women, Lincoln often did appear great—partly because such people look up to their leaders in times of crisis, and partly because he really thought of government, despite its mechanism, as being of and by the people. He spent, for instance, hours of his busy day seeing people—not just politicians—and called it his "bath in public opinion." He waited if possible to act until he felt the people were behind him. On Reconstruction after the South's defeat, he could not wait, but he did say that if his measures were not acceptable to the people as a whole, he would alter them. He not only saw the people, but talked to the people. His eloquence, so justly admired today, was used to make the basic issues of his policy clear to the people, to appeal to their common sense, their sense of justice, their old ties with the South.

It is this side of Lincoln which is generally remembered by admirers who think "politician" an uncomplimentary word. But it is well to reflect that he struggled through the war as a politician, not as a great statesman or a military genius. He was not upheld by the love and loyalty of a whole united people, even during the early days of the Civil War when the North expected a rapid victory. He was the unknown quantity then, the obscure man elected by a minority vote in a time of crisis. Later, as the war dragged on and as opinions hardened, his critics became vociferous and savage. It was not until late in 1863 that political leaders in his own party discovered to their surprise that the President could be a political asset.

At last came the end of the war with a great outburst of cheering, which might have been cheers for victory, for the prospect of revenge, for the end of bloodshed, for anything as much as for the President. Lincoln walked through the streets of Richmond, the only triumph which he seems to have desired. He held a Cabinet meeting to plan the reunion of the country in down-to-earth, practical ways. He was happy for the first time in years—and then he died, whereupon his countrymen chose to forget what they had thought about him and proclaimed him a great man. Time has confirmed this verdict, but there was never a moment in his life when he was made conscious of it. Would he laugh if he knew and tell a little story? Very probably.

# 1

## The Inauguration
## of a President

DURING THE FIRST TWO MONTHS OF 1861, Abraham Lincoln, waiting in Springfield, Illinois, for the moment when he would take office, had received no communication from James Buchanan, the President whom he was to succeed. The breakup of the Union, which had been a long time coming, was now taking place in haste, but the man who would have to deal with its consequences was not consulted. The underlying cause of the nation's division was simple enough: the conflict between the expanding rural South with its system of slave labor and the expanding industrial North, obtaining its workmen from an unending stream of immigrants from Europe. Much has been written about the ramifications of the quarrel which, though clear in essence, is extraordinarily complex in detail. Among the great puzzles of the time, the forces which elevated a homely Midwestern lawyer to the position of President-elect seemed so capricious that intelligent men could only hope that someone could be found to run the administration for him.

To understand why the times had produced such a President we have to realize that life in America was then in many ways duller than in Europe. The men of the New World had thrown off the superstitions of the Old, but had discarded with them the ancient festivals which marked the changes of the year, the colorful religious processions, the pageantry of royal courts, the more homely celebrations when the heir of a local great house came of age or got married. Spectator sports and mass entertainments lay fifty years ahead. Even religion in its raw, revivalist form was losing ground to sophistication and diversity of religious beliefs. Public festivals were chiefly provided by politics. In most years there was an election campaign at some level, involving the political clubs in planning conferences —agreeable in themselves—which eventually produced marches accompanied by brass bands, cheap gaudy uniforms, floats, torchlight processions, doggerel rhymes set to simple tunes, and receptions for the candidates or their representatives, who exchanged floods of oratory enlivened by personal remarks or yells from the crowd.

To add intensity to every conflict, there were a surprising number of prizes to be won. As there was no regular civil service—state, national, or local—civil employees, high or low, were appointed by the appropriate elected officials. Having no right of tenure, they were liable to be replaced if the opposition party was lucky enough to win the next election. Politics, though colorful, exciting, and more or less bloodless, was definitely battle.

From his watching position in Springfield, the speed with which the nation could split asunder was incomprehensible to Lincoln. He could not believe that the silent majority of the Deep South was not still faithful to the old ideals. Despite a long political career, he misunderstood the emotions which had been continuously aroused in the country.

By conviction Lincoln had been a member of the Whig Party, which had long battled with the Democrats for control of the government. Under the complex pressures of the early Fifties, the Whig Party had broken up, leaving many a would-be statesman without backing. Lincoln had concentrated on his legal practice, with the result that in 1860 his political career, which had consisted of several terms in the State Legislature and a single term in Congress, was ten years behind him. He was a lawyer in the Illinois state capital, a man of many friends and acquaintances, an excellent stump speaker, and an influential figure in state politics. But even his widely reported campaign against Stephen A. Douglas for the United States Senate in 1858 had not really brought him onto the national scene.

Meanwhile other Whig politicians, more active or more deeply committed, had allied themselves with movements which they hoped would keep them in power. There was, for example, the American Party—anti-immigrant and anti-Catholic. Those who favored it soon earned undying hatred from an increasing segment of the population. Other Whigs leaned toward the immigrants, but this also had its perils. Since the Irish generally voted Democratic, Whigs had to look for support among the Germans, who were generally abolitionists. Theirs was an extremist position loathed by many, even in the North.

As a result, when Germans, "Americans," Whigs, and even a number of northern Democrats formed the Republican Party in order to oppose the pro-slavery policy of the Democratic administration, every prominent Republican presidential possibility was hated by some large section of his own party. William H. Seward, leader of the Whigs, had as Governor of New York shown enlightened toleration to Catholics and was in consequence unacceptable to staunch "Americans." Senator Salmon P. Chase of Ohio was frankly an abolitionist. Everyone had his enemies inside the new party, with the single exception of the prudent man who had not held any office for the last decade and whose recent re-entry into political life was prompted by his opposition to the spread of slavery—the one sentiment which held these discordant interests together. The Fifties had been a period when enemies were easier to get and keep than friends. It was really remarkable that Lincoln had managed—at least in the North—to refrain from arousing any hatred.

This lack of enemies is perhaps the first sign that Lincoln had unexpected qualities and that the Republican National Convention of 1860 which had chosen him in this emergency had not been so misdirected as some thought. It is true that there must have been other obscure politicians who, out of timidity rather than tact, had managed to please everybody. But Lincoln was greater than they. In a period when all found it hard to define a position on slavery which was both firm and fair, Abraham Lincoln had outlined a middle position with remarkable clarity—and he had never been induced by his own eloquence or the frenzy of others to depart from it. Such discretion in such times argued a clear head and political gifts of a high degree. Few understood his qualities—and yet Lincoln had been more than the favorite son of the state which had happened to play host to the National Convention.

All this does not imply that the selection of Lincoln had been an act of deliberate wisdom unmixed with good luck. It merely suggests that the lucky man had needed to show some personal qualities without which even the best of luck would not have given him the nomination. Unfortunately, his personality, which would have been manifest in a modern presidential campaign, was rendered useless because it was the custom that a presidential candidate should not campaign in person. Thus the "best stump speaker in the West" sat at home while others spoke for him, and Lincoln had to be elected as a symbol—the "Railsplitter," or "Honest Abe," the log-cabin boy who had made good. In general people voted for the Republicans, not for Abraham Lincoln; and they did so not only because the spread of slavery had to be stopped, but because—if the Republicans won—they could initiate the biggest turnover of political jobs that had ever been heard of.

Of course the Republican Party was a totally northern

one and could not count on a single vote in the Deep South. Had the Democratic Party retained its national appeal, a Republican victory would have been impossible. But during the Presidency of James Buchanan, the division between a southern administration and the ablest Democrat in Congress, Stephen A. Douglas of Illinois, had widened hopelessly. Douglas, a prisoner of his own northern constituents, could only make gestures toward reconciliation. Southern leaders neither could nor would make any. In the Democratic National Convention, northern strength had been too great to prevent anyone except Douglas from being nominated, while southern opposition was too strong to allow him the necessary votes. The result had been two candidates, Douglas, who would get few votes in the south, and John C. Breckenridge, who would collect none in the north. In desperation, the middle states put up a candidate in the name of "Union" who was not likely to get too many southern or northern votes.

In these circumstances, if the Republicans could sink their differences and vote for a single candidate, they ought to win. It was easier to work for a symbol, a cause, and the tremendous prizes of office than it would have been to support a man whom one section or other had reason to detest. As a result the Republicans elected a President whom few of them knew. None suspected he would prove one of the greatest men ever chosen to that office. Yet Lincoln was not entirely a miracle, an act of God, a special favor to the nation. In a sense all great men are such, but there are reasons why they appear where they do. It is only that the confusion of the times had obscured what these were.

At the beginning of 1861, the President-elect had still not stepped onto the national stage. Lincoln's silence during the campaign, his inexperience, his caution, and the gulf between his party and Buchanan's had prevented him from making himself widely known. Daily in Springfield he received visitors for hours at a time, but though most of them wanted to talk about jobs, a surprising proportion simply walked in to stare. Who was this President? Was he as homely as people said? Did he mind a decent man who did not have anything much on his mind except just *looking* at him? He didn't? He needn't think himself better than anyone else, after all.

Such obscurity might seem all very well to the leaders of the Republican Party as long as they were out of power. But whereas a candidate might be a symbol, a President was a person who needed to be known by his supporters. Caution might suggest that a parade of Abraham Lincoln through the states which had elected him might anger the South and accelerate the breakup of the nation. But as the inauguration approached, the absolute necessity of introducing Lincoln to his supporters was obvious—and in a sense less dangerous because his inauguration itself would give greater offense. It was therefore arranged that he should take his time approaching Washington and that he should officially visit a number of states, including the important eastern ones of New York, New Jersey, and Pennsylvania, all of which had played a key role in his election.

The special train which steamed out of Springfield on February 11 to carry Abraham Lincoln on this triumphal tour was a model of contemporary ideas of railroad splendor. Upholstered lavishly in plush and decorated by an engraving of the Senate of 1850, it consisted of a bedroom, a day-coach, and a sleeping coach with reclining chairs for Lincoln's family and attendants. These last, besides relatives and important political friends, included John G. Nicolay, Lincoln's secretary, John M. Hay, Nicolay's assistant, and Elmer E. Ellsworth, a colorful young man who had studied law in Lincoln's office and for whom the President-elect felt an almost paternal affection. Another companion who sought advancement in Washington was Ward Lamon, a familiar friend from the Eighth Judicial Circuit who carried a banjo to while away the tedious hours of travel and a miscellaneous assortment of weapons intended to counter the threats to Lincoln's life which had been arriving by mail at Springfield. The War Office had supplied four military aides, while a large array of people was keeping watch on railroad crossings and whistle stops along the route. It was later rumored by a sensation-loving public that there had been an attempt to derail the train and that a live grenade had been discovered in the carriage.

Lincoln seems to have wished his wife and two younger children to go straight to Washington without accompanying him on his eleven-day trip. Many official receptions had been arranged, and there would be countless little speeches for him to make at five-minute stops in crowded stations. He had seldom taken Mary on his political tours; this one would be wearing; and she had been alarmed by the threats against him. Mary Lincoln, however, was in the flood tide of her personal triumph and was not disposed to forego any part of it. She did not leave Springfield with her husband, but joined the cortège in Indianapolis next day, having got her way, according to rumor, by a hysterical scene.

However this may be, though young Robert Lincoln was embarrassed by the glare of publicity, while his younger brothers, Willie and Tad, were in high spirits at the adventure, Mary Lincoln was exultant. Nineteen years earlier she had married the least acceptable of her suitors, a man of low origin, plebeian manners, and small means. Her attempts to make her husband presentable had been foiled by his determination to live plainly. Mary had been forced to raid his pocketbook for her necessities and had at times found nothing in it. Her pride had suffered by comparison with her three sisters in Springfield, all of whom had made more worldly matches than she. At last the hour of her triumph had arrived. Among the boxes corded up by Lincoln and addressed to the White House were several containing fine clothes bought by Mary on a shopping trip to New York. These were crinoline days when ladies' clothes were elaborate and expensive, and Mary was determined to show the hostesses of Washington that the new President's wife outshone them all. Unfortunately her New York visit had also disclosed to reporters that she was easily flattered and could be induced to make indiscreet remarks about politicians whom she saw as potential rivals to her husband.

Much had happened since the election, but Lincoln himself had achieved little. His Cabinet was still unformed at a time when seven states had already withdrawn from the Union. Even while Lincoln's train moved on its roundabout route to Washington, a similar train was bearing Jefferson Davis to Montgomery, Alabama, for his inauguration as President of the new Confederate States.

In Washington, President Buchanan, nearly seventy and ailing, had signally failed to cope with the secession crisis. Like Lincoln, he regarded himself as President of the whole country—but he had taken no practical steps to remain so. He had not published an immediate appeal for national loyalty, but had left it to Congress to set up committees to work out a compromise with the South. He had not even hastened to reorganize his Cabinet by excluding secessionist members, but had retained them in office during the two crucial months after Lincoln's election. His attitude had been that though secession was constitutionally wrong, he could not prevent it, since he had no right to resort to force. Consequently he had acquiesced with little protest in the seizure of United States customs houses, post offices, arsenals, and other possessions by the seceding states. In the case of South Carolina, he had merely given a conditional promise that he would not reinforce the forts commanding Charleston Harbor as long as the state left Federal properties alone.

Since this arrangement left the initiative to South Carolina, the forts would probably have fallen to secessionists without fuss had it not been for the action of Major Robert Anderson, selected to take charge expressly because he was a southerner. The major's garrison was stationed in Fort Moultrie, a crumbling structure which was indefensible from the landward side. Fort Sumter, though stronger, was still under construction and occupied only by a tiny detachment of soldiers to supervise the workmen. Less than a week after South Carolina officially seceded, Major Anderson neatly executed a secret transfer of his Moultrie garrison to Sumter, gaining possession of a stronghold which presented both Buchanan and the leaders of the newly independent state with a serious crisis.

South Carolina, which had proclaimed independence on December 20, lost no time in sending commissioners to demand the evacuation of Sumter. Left to himself, Buchanan would have preferred to give way, even though the Charleston arsenal, customs house, and post office as well as Forts Pinckney and Moultrie had been seized in reprisal for Major Anderson's maneuver. By the end of December, however, the President had been forced to strengthen his Cabinet by two determined Union men. What is more, John B. Floyd, his southern Secretary of War, was on the brink of resignation, following the discovery that, owing largely to his neglect, about a million dollars had been embezzled by his underlings. As Edwin M. Stanton, Buchanan's recently appointed pro-Union Attorney General, insisted, ". . . no Administration, much less this one, can afford to lose a million of money and a fort in the same week." This being only too true, Buchanan nerved himself to uphold Major Anderson's act, to refuse further recognition to the commissioners from South Carolina, and to set in motion plans for reinforcing Sumter. A light-draft steamer called the *Star of the West* was ordered south with troops and supplies. Since Jacob Thompson of Mississippi still headed the Department of the Interior, it is not surprising that he sent warning to South Carolina. Meanwhile, no orders were given to Anderson in Sumter. In consequence, when the *Star of the West* appeared off Charleston and lowered boats, she was fired on—while the

Sumter guns, lacking instructions, remained silent. The *Star of the West* was driven off, but Buchanan did not dare denounce the incident as an act of war. Major Anderson wrote fairly cheerfully about his stores and prospects, relieving the President from the necessity of doing anything in the last weeks of his term.

As Lincoln set out for Washington, his thoughts were not focused on Sumter, but on the even more immediate problem of how to form a government at all. The composition of his Cabinet had been a problem to him ever since his managers had won his nomination by promises of important positions to state leaders who could deliver votes. Lincoln had taken no direct part in their negotiations, though he had at least consented to them by sending a couple of friends to bargain with Indiana before the convention opened. Nominations, as he well knew, involved such arrangements. During the convention, however, he had panicked, fearing his committee might bind him by promises he could not keep. He accordingly sent a famous message from Springfield: "I authorize no bargains and will be bound by none." His horrified committee agreed to take no notice of what would have put an end to his chances. The result was that while the nomination of Honest Abe was widely proclaimed as the choice of the people uninfluenced by back-room deals, the successful candidate was complaining: "They have gambled on me all around, bought and sold me a hundred times. I cannot begin to fill the pledges made in my name."

The unfortunate truth was that Lincoln was just as much hampered by the nature of the Republican Party as he was by the promises which had bought his nomination. The Republicans had grown into a national party not much more than four years earlier, cemented together by anti-slavery and pro-northern feelings. Even on these subjects it contained every shade of opinion—from the abolitionist views of Salmon P. Chase of Ohio to the tolerance of ex-Democrats and even slave owners, who deplored the institution in principle and looked forward to its quietly withering away at some time in the future. In fact, the Republican Party was united less by common principles than by victory and the consequent prospect of jobs. If Lincoln excluded any of the major groups from high office, he ran the risk that the Republicans would split as the Democrats had done when Buchanan had excluded Douglas from his pro-southern administration. Pondering this problem in Springfield while "Ain't you glad you joined the Republicans?" echoed over the sound of marching feet or acted as chorus to a thousand election speeches, Lincoln quietly made decisions before the campaign was over. The day after he was elected he privately drew up a list of his projected Cabinet. Nearly four months later the names were almost identical, but negotiations to get the men he wanted remained unfinished.

The nub of Lincoln's problem was a man to whom he had made no commitments, namely his disappointed rival for the nomination, Senator William H. Seward of New York, acknowledged head of the defunct Whig Party which now formed the center and the majority of the victorious Republican Party. If Seward were to be brought into the Cabinet, he must be offered its most prestigious position, that of Secretary of State. But Seward and his chief backer, Thurlow Weed, political boss of New York, aspired to control far more than a mere Cabinet position. It seemed to them both that the inexperienced Lincoln would have to delegate the real power to somebody else—and to whom more fittingly than to Seward? Thus even before the election, Weed journeyed out to Springfield to make it clear that the price of support in New York was the selection of a Cabinet of old-time Whigs agreeable to Seward. Lincoln, who desperately needed the support of New York, made Weed no promises, but left him to suppose that his suggestions would have the force of commands, the more so as they were acceptable to the Illinois political leaders who had formed Lincoln's own committee at the Chicago convention.

Lincoln did obtain the support of New York, which was

crucial to his election, but Seward's chagrin at being nosed out for the nomination was so great that it was freely rumored he would decline a Cabinet office. Not wishing to provoke an abrupt refusal, Lincoln enlisted the help of Hannibal Hamlin, the Vice-President-elect, in sounding Seward out.

It seems very possible that Seward would indeed have refused the offer of a position which he openly professed he did not want if he had not been a patriot as well as a Republican. He saw the Union breaking to pieces, President Buchanan too weak to halt the process, and an ignorant railsplitter elected to replace him. Seward felt it his duty to save the Union, since he took for granted that no one else had sufficient authority to do so.

Unfortunately for Seward's plans, the new President had every intention of governing personally, the more so because Seward had a number of enemies, particularly in the south, where an indiscreet speech about an "irrepressible conflict" over slavery had been much resented. Lincoln was quick to counter any offense which might be caused by Seward's appointment by turning to his next-most-prominent rival for the Presidency, Bates of Missouri, whom he asked to be his Attorney General. Edward Bates, a distinguished Whig lawyer, was not in himself unacceptable to Seward, especially since he would be too old to compete for the Presidency in 1864. He came from a slave state, and his strength was in the border region not yet completely committed to North or South. He was in fact someone whom Seward himself might have chosen, more particularly as Bates shared the New Yorker's low opinion of Lincoln. The only ominous thing about the appointment was that Seward had not been consulted in advance.

Having enlisted his two chief rivals, Lincoln now considered politicians to whom promises had been made in his name at the convention. Prominant among these was Simon Cameron of Pennsylvania, who had offered his state's votes to Lincoln in return for a Cabinet position. The deal had been made without Lincoln's authority, but Lincoln's Illinois advisors insisted that Pennsylvania—almost as important to Republicans as New York—would never support the new administration unless the promise to Cameron was honored. Lincoln therefore saw Cameron and suggested either the Treasury or the War Office. Cameron, who preferred the Treasury, sought to consolidate his position by "leaking" the news. A strong opposition group from Pennsylvania thereupon descended upon Lincoln with so many facts and figures to Cameron's discredit that the President felt obliged to take back his offer. Cameron in his turn collected piles of recommendations which poured onto Lincoln's desk, almost overwhelming the unhappy Nicolay.

Seward's hands were personally clean, but he had never hesitated to profit from the crooked New York machine of Boss Weed. When Cameron sought to bolster his position by an alliance with the powers ruling New York, Seward thought far more about control of the Cabinet than about his ally's reputation. He felt particularly favorable to Cameron when news got about that Lincoln was now considering Chase of Ohio for the Treasury.

Salmon P. Chase was a handsome, intelligent, upright, ambitious lawyer-politician who had been Governor of Ohio—and in his own opinion was the best presidential candidate in 1860. He had waited for everyone to realize this fact and had been greatly disappointed when he was hardly even considered by the convention. It was, however, by the swing of a few votes from Ohio that Lincoln had won on the third ballot, so Chase's friends expected him to be rewarded. Politically Chase belonged to the radical, anti-slavery wing of the Republican Party, which took a belligerent attitude toward secession. There was no one less likely to defer to Seward than Chase, secure in his high opinion of his own merits, priggish about his honesty, and uncompromising on the great issue which was dividing the nation. In consequence, when Lincoln showed signs of considering Cameron for Secretary of War and Chase for the Treasury, Seward made it clear that he would not serve with a man so distasteful to him.

Since Seward's appointment as Secretary of State had already been announced, his resignation would have been a serious embarrassment. Lincoln put off the decision, but his other appointments came under Seward's scrutiny also, with similar results. There was little to be said for or against Caleb B. Smith of Indiana, who was to be Secretary of the Interior, as agreed at the convention. He was a lightweight for the job and easily manageable. It was the remaining two Cabinet appointments which offended Seward.

It had been understood that one Cabinet place should go to a New Englander, and there was also a tradition that the Vice President should select one member. Ostensibly Lincoln offered Hamlin the choice between Charles Francis Adams of Massachusetts and Gideon Welles of Connecticut for Secretary of the Navy. But when Hamlin inclined to Adams, who was a long-time personal friend of Seward's, Lincoln insisted that Welles was preferable because he was an ex-Democrat in a Cabinet that already had a full quota of ex-Whigs. Welles had not supported Lincoln at the convention, but his opposition to Seward had played a large part in weakening the strength of the New York Senator. In fact, Seward recognized him as one of those chiefly responsible for his failure to get the presidential nomination.

Deeply displeased to find Welles preferred to Adams, Seward was equally indignant about the selection of Montgomery Blair for Postmaster General. Montgomery's father, Francis P. Blair, had been one of Jackson's Kitchen Cabinet and had retired to Chevy Chase, Maryland, a good many years earlier, where he built a delightful mansion at a distance from Washington convenient for weekending politicians. Little went on in government that old man Blair did not know about; and though he was a firm supporter of the Union, his personal friends included men of every political persuasion. His son Montgomery dominated Maryland. His younger son Frank had moved to Missouri and made himself powerful there. Old Blair was ambitious for his sons, and all three worked together. It might be said that Seward objected to Welles as an enemy who had been preferred to his friend Adams. He looked on Chase as his most dominating rival, but on Montgomery Blair as an unscrupulous intriguer. He doubted whether he could save the Union with the aid of such colleagues and prepared to send in his resignation when the appointments were announced. He felt confident of his power to force Lincoln into line.

It turned out that Seward had mistaken his man. Lincoln journeyed to Washington and went through his inauguration without making any announcement of Cabinet offices save those of Seward and Bates. When Seward brought up the question of the others, Lincoln made it clear that if alterations were to be made in his proposed list, they would have to start at the top with Seward's resignation. Seward did offer to resign and would probably have insisted upon this if he had been given more time. But on the day after the inauguration, when President Lincoln had to send the names of his Cabinet officers to the Senate for confirmation, Seward could not bear to leave the management of the present terrible crisis to Chase—for he assumed that Lincoln would be dominated by Chase if not by him. He withdrew his resignation without suspecting that he had been outmaneuvered by a man stronger than himself who was even more determined to govern. The new President's expedient of including all his chief rivals in his Cabinet looked more like weakness than the political adroitness it actually was.

It was with this impending confrontation with Seward on his mind that Lincoln undertook the task of meeting and greeting his exuberant northern electors on his trip to Washington. At the smaller towns there were whistle stops where he came out on the back platform of his railroad coach to speak to cheering crowds who had put up decorations and saluted him with cannon. One of these last was discharged straight at the train in the excitement, bursting open a door and shattering three windows, but luckily injuring no one. When Lincoln had to alight for more formal receptions, public frenzy was uncontrollable. In Buffalo the pressure of the crowd at the station was so great that Major Hunter, one of Lincoln's escorts, dislocated his arm in a frantic struggle to open a lane to the presidential carriage. At every reception Lincoln had to shake hands with enormous queues of people, and he must have been thankful for the strength that years of axe-handling had built into his grip. He made no remarkable speeches, but was careful to strike a note of appreciation for each place he visited, to convey an easy confidence, and to welcome on equal terms his own supporters and those who had voted for rivals.

The Hudson River Railroad supplied a special car of its own to bring the President-elect to Manhattan. This was upholstered in "royal purple," carpeted with plush, painted with national emblems, festooned with red-white-and-blue, and spangled with stars. A quarter of a million people lined the route of his procession from the railroad station to the Astor House in Manhattan. Here another hand-shaking ordeal awaited Lincoln. The stopover was long enough to include a gala performance at the opera, which he attended in black gloves—a social gaffe. He found a moment to take Willie to Barnum's Museum, perhaps while Mary Lincoln was holding a reception, where she flirted with a fan and was archly playful toward the gentlemen who called upon her. Lincoln spoke at City Hall, where high and low crowded to see him in such numbers that coats were torn, hats lost, and crinolines demolished.

Editorial policy rather than a strict regard for fact dictated newspaper comments, but most found some-

thing to say about the simple manners of the President-
elect. "Abe is becoming more grave," wrote *Vanity Fair*,
tongue in cheek. "He don't construct as many jokes as
he did. He fears that he will get things mixed up if he
don't look out." The New York *World*, more appreciative, claimed that "Abraham Lincoln has won all our
hearts by the manly simplicity of his character." More
than one reporter thought little of Abe's oratorical
style, comparing it to his disadvantage with the elaborate flourishes of more fashionable speakers. Southern
editorials called him an ape, but described him as
though he were an ogre, distorting all he said into
threats against the South.

Leaving Manhattan, Lincoln made his tumultuous way
across New Jersey, stopping long enough in Trenton for
a banquet with the State Legislature. He had to leave before the meal was ended, but his hosts suffered "no loss of
spirits" by his early departure and did not break up until
their drunken renderings of "The Star-Spangled Banner"
had lost all harmony. Lincoln himself went on to Philadelphia, where he was greeted by a hundred thousand people
lining the route to his hotel.

His schedule called for a full morning in Philadelphia
the next day, which was Washington's Birthday, followed by a trip to the State Legislature at Harrisburg
in the afternoon. Here he would spend the night and
then proceed by train through Philadelphia and Baltimore to Washington. As the party arrived from Trenton, however, Norman B. Judd, the Illinois political
leader who was traveling with Lincoln, received an urgent message from Allan Pinkerton, most famous of private detectives. The one major city on Lincoln's route
which had extended no invitation to him was Baltimore,
chief city of slave-owning Maryland and home of many
who were violently pro-Southern. Unfortunately, the
railroad to Washington went through the town, arriving
at one station and leaving from another. Between these

two points it was customary to uncouple the railroad cars and harness horses to drag them right through the public streets. The danger of exposing Lincoln in this fashion might have been minimized by transferring him to a carriage surrounded by mounted men, but it could not be entirely removed. The Baltimore chief of police, a political opponent, was satisfied to say that the city was orderly and that routine precautions would be sufficient. Pinkerton, who had opened a business in Baltimore as cover for an investigation, was positive that murder had been planned and a group of gangsters chosen to execute it during the transfer. He had come to Philadelphia to urge Lincoln to cancel his Washington's Birthday engagements and set out for Washington twenty-four hours before he was expected.

Lincoln flatly refused to consider this proposition. He had taken little notice of the threats against his life which had poured into Springfield by mail or been published in Southern papers. He regarded his commitments in Pennsylvania as official and foresaw that he would give lasting offense if he did not honor them. But before he could set out for Harrisburg the following afternoon, he received another message. Young Frederick W. Seward had been sent up from Washington by his father to say that General Winfield Scott, Commander of the Army, had independently received news of a Baltimore plot from secret agents. By this time S. M. Felton, president of the railroad, had been drawn into the discussion. It was agreed that Lincoln, accompanied only by Pinkerton and Ward Lamon—the latter armed with a large pair of pistols, a slingshot, brass knuckles, and a bowie knife—should set out from Harrisburg that very night by special train. They would transfer in Philadelphia onto the regular night train for Washington, which would have to be delayed to wait for them. They would pass through Baltimore in the early hours of the morning, arriving in Washington shortly after six. Lincoln was reluctant to agree, foreseeing a loss of dignity when the papers got hold of the story. Since it was, however, his duty to take sensible precautions, he even consented to disguise his conspicuous appearance by an old overcoat and soft hat before getting aboard the special train. In Philadelphia the last part of the night train was reserved for an "invalid," whom station officials allowed to mount from the back of the carriage. A large package containing old newspapers was wrapped up and rushed to the conductor as a public explanation of the delay in setting out.

As a result of these arrangements, the trip proved uneventful, and Lincoln was welcomed in Washington by his old friend Elihu B. Washburne of Illinois. Senator Seward, who had also intended to be on the platform, overslept. Meanwhile, in Baltimore, fifteen thousand by no means friendly people, who had gathered to see Lincoln arrive on the day train, attempted to assault the Baltimore Republican Committee, which had come down as a group to welcome their leader. When Mrs. Lincoln and the children appeared without the President-elect, the crowd could only vent its disgust in booing.

Lincoln was perfectly right about the unfortunate results of his night journey. Baltimoreans indignantly protested that there had been no conspiracy and that their city was one of the most orderly in the country. Southern editors mocked Lincoln for having panicked in the face of imaginary danger, caricaturing him as disguised in a cloak and plaid Scotch cap. Much was said about his having left his wife and children to face a crowd which he had avoided himself. Even Northern editors felt that the new administration had made an undignified start. Perhaps the only advantage of the affair was that it allowed Lincoln to make his formal call on President Buchanan in decent privacy. Shortly thereafter he was ensconced on the second floor of Willard's hotel, protected only by the anteroom of his suite and a notice downstairs saying, "Positively no persons admitted to the halls above, other than guests of the house." Here Lincoln conducted last-minute negotiations about his Cabinet, while receiving calls from congressmen, from members of a peace conference promoted largely by the State of Virginia, from the Mayor of the District of Columbia, from the General-in-Chief, from former President Tyler, and President Buchanan. It goes without saying that he was also besieged by office seekers who had flocked to Washington in the thousands and jammed not only Willard's, but every passage or room to which they had access in the executive departments.

Winfield Scott, the General-in-Chief, was a veteran of the War of 1812, too fat and infirm to sit a horse and greatly preferring the comfort of his New York residence to the rigors of a Washington office. He was not, however, unmindful of his soldierly duty. He had seen to it that the formal counting of the Electoral College ballots had taken place in a city provided with sufficient troops to keep order. He had at his disposal no more than six hundred and fifty-three regular soldiers, since the tiny professional army of the United States was largely occupied in guarding far western frontiers. To make up for deficiencies, however, militia had been called up, drilled, and provided with uniforms and weapons. General Scott had feared that assassins might lurk among the spectators of the inaugural procession or that a band of armed raiders might ride over from Virginia. He had accordingly taken precautions against both, stationing sharpshooters on the rooftops all the way down Pennsylvania Avenue and siting guns to command the processional route as well as the approaches to the platform built over the East Capitol steps for the inauguration. Under this he had concealed fifty soldiers as an extra precaution. He had used his militia to line the route, stationed cavalry at crossroads, and surrounded the presidential carriage with a mounted escort which partially blocked it from view. Soon after twelve noon on March 4 a Republican procession enlivened with bands, uniforms, and decorations was backed up behind Willard's awaiting the moment when Buchanan and Lincoln would emerge together and climb into their six-horse open carriage.

It was a clear winter day, and rumors of violence had not deterred spectators. Every window or ledge capable of affording a view was packed with people, while the crowd in the street swept aside the militia several times and stopped the soldiers with whom General Scott had headed the procession. A determined assassin might easily have taken a shot at the President-elect. That no one did so may be attributed in part to the uselessness of the gesture, since Vice President Hamlin was even less acceptable to the South than Abraham Lincoln.

Arrived at the Capitol, Buchanan and Lincoln entered the Senate Chamber by means of a wooden tunnel which was part of Scott's security precautions. After the brief ceremony in which the Vice President was sworn in, the participants filed out onto the platform to face a crowd which was thought to number about twenty-five thousand. Senator Edward D. Baker of Oregon, the old friend after whom Lincoln's dead son had been named, made a brief introduction of the President-elect. Lincoln advanced to the lectern, as one account has it, still carrying his shiny new hat and gold-knobbed cane. As he tried to balance the hat on the lectern in order to put on his spectacles and lay down his papers, Stephen A. Douglas, who was sitting close behind, reached forward to take it and sat holding it while his rival spoke to the nation.

This tale is not authenticated, but it has some symbolic value. None of the four candidates in the presidential election had striven harder for national unity than Douglas. Despite his poor showing in the Electoral College, Douglas's popular vote had been second only to Lincoln's. The secession of the Deep South had actually increased his importance inside the Democratic Party by removing his bitterest opponents. Douglas, like Seward, intended not merely to support the inexperienced Lincoln, but to direct him. No President of a divided country could ignore the services the Little Giant might render. It remained to be seen whether he could manage the Lincoln puppet more ably than could Seward.

Lincoln stood with his back to the Capitol, now shorn of its wooden dome and crowned by a protruding crane which was to remain there for the better part of the next four years. The two marble wings of the building, which had been added since Lincoln was last in Washington, were not completely finished, so that blocks of marble, pieces of pillars for the colonnade, and wood for scaffolding were strewn around. Confronting him was a vast throng of people, many of whom had never seen their new President except in rough reproductions in the newspapers and who were discovering for the first time the effect of his new whiskers and the steel-rimmed spectacles he donned for reading. Great care had been taken with his appearance for the occasion. Nobody could say that Lincoln's black frock coat and trousers did not fit, that his waistcoat was not silk, his hat not new and glossy, his hands not respectably gloved. Unfortunately the style of his garments, though perfectly correct for the occasion, served to emphasize his narrow shoulders, his slightly stooping posture, and the abnormal length of his arms and legs. Everything about him appeared odd, including his high-pitched voice and uncultivated accent.

No speech of Lincoln's received more care in preparation than his First Inaugural. The original manuscript, already much worked over, had been set in type for him before he left Springfield. Since that time, though even his capacity for endless work had been severely taxed, he had submitted his speech to various critics, including Seward. By now the printed version had been cut up and pasted together with emendations intended to remove any possible shade of provocative language.

Lincoln's difficulty was that the main principles around which his inaugural was composed were strong and binding. Slavery was wrong and must not be extended. The recent election had shown that the strongest party in the country held this opinion, which Lincoln was therefore determined not to reverse. It was, however, his desire to put forward this resolution in an inoffensive way. He was eager to assure the South that he had no intention of interfering with slavery where it existed and that he was prepared to accept a constitutional amendment which would render it impossible for Congress to do so. He added a plea for calm reflection, reminding the seceding states that they were establishing a precedent which was bound to lead to further divisions later.

Lincoln's own position as Chief Executive was in similar fashion unalterable. His solemn oath to "preserve, protect and defend" the government of the United States gave him no authority to recognize secession. It was his duty to "hold, occupy and possess the property and places belonging to the government," but he was careful not to define these as forts, customs houses, or other particular spots, and had cut out any mention of his duty to repossess what had already been seized. Instead, he was quick to say that he planned no invasion and would not appoint Northern officials to exercise the functions of government in "certain sections" where local men refused to undertake them. Such an attempt would be so irritating and impractical that he thought it better to refrain from exercising his legal right.

None of the modifications which Lincoln introduced into his speech after leaving Springfield showed any yielding on his two basic points. The changes concerned the manner, rather than the matter, of his speech. Secession, which he had described as "treasonable," he now called "revolutionary." He referred more emphatically to peaceable solutions and to his determination not to initiate violence. He closed with an appeal to his "dissatisfied fellow-

countrymen," reminding them in high-flown language
whose mixed metaphors were suggested to him by Seward
that they had common ancestors and common traditions
about lives sacrificed to establish or to uphold their common republic. His own eloquence, more simple and natural, assured all southerners that "The government will not
assail *you*. You can have no conflict without being your-
selves the aggressors. . . . We are not enemies, but friends."
His anxiety to be perfectly plain about his intentions was
almost painful.

The oath of office was administered to Lincoln by old
Chief Justice Roger Taney, who four years earlier had
published the Dred Scott decision denying the right of
Congress to forbid slavery in the Territories. Taney's act
had contributed almost as much as any man's to the Republican protest which had led to Lincoln's election. Now his
bent, emaciated figure with his black robes flapping
around him made him an apt symbol of the southern leadership which had endured long past its prime and was
giving way. The ceremony was soon over. President Lincoln went down to take his place in the carriage with
former President Buchanan, coldly distant, seated on his
left.

The day was crowned by an inaugural ball at which
Mary Lincoln in a beautiful silk of her favorite blue received with her husband. Tickets were ten dollars each,
which excluded some of the weirdest eccentrics who had
come to Washington in hope of jobs. It was not considered
a very big occasion, since only about five thousand attended. Washington was to a great extent a southern city,
and many residents ignored the celebration. Nor was the
ball very gay in spite of champagne and the excellent Ma-
rine band. Mary Lincoln danced with Douglas, but the
new President was better at shaking hands than at this sort
of thing. In any case, the crowd had not come to dance but
to get a closer view of Lincoln, still a strange figure to
many. Luckily a lavish supper redeemed the occasion,

while many young people, including Robert Lincoln, stayed to have a good time long after President and Mrs. Lincoln had retired to their new residence, whose inconveniences were not so clear to them as they quite shortly would be.

# 2

## Sumter

THE NEW HEAD of a new party was President in Washington. Abraham Lincoln had not been seen in the nation's capital for more than ten years. His single term as a Congressman had been inglorious, and he had never served as Senator. He had never held an administrative post, and if the running of his private law firm was anything to go by, he had no organizing ability. Though widely acquainted with politicians, he knew few of the civil servants who carried on the work of the departments of state. Nor would it have helped him if he had, since they were all Democrats and must be replaced.

The rise to power of a new party had produced a scramble for jobs unprecedented even in the days of Andrew Jackson. Every Republican member of Congress had supporters to place in strategic positions. Newspaper editors followed the example set by Joseph Medill of the Chicago *Tribune* in picking a candidate for the Chicago post office who could be trusted to see that his subordinates pushed the sale of the *Tribune* all over the Northwest. Hotel lobbies in Washington were crawling with office seekers, and it was said some of them were hunting in gangs. George

Templeton Strong, a diarist with a sense of humor, recorded that the janitor of the Columbia College Law School had a fancy for a consulate in the Middle East. Strong professed himself glad to help, on the grounds that a man so inefficient at dealing with fires and boilers must surely have a genius for something else.

Many candidates came to see Lincoln in person; many more sent friends to plead their cause. The White House had most of the disadvantages of a palace without the size which might have compensated for them. The state rooms on the first floor were handsome, but too small for the President's formal receptions, which were traditionally open to the public. In consequence much damage was done to their furnishings, and their upkeep was a problem. The private quarters of the President's family were on the second floor, but so was his office, a suite of three rooms at the head of the main stair. Lines formed up this stair and across to Lincoln's anteroom, where his secretaries tried, not always successfully, to sort out those with important business from madmen and to give a special welcome to old friends. There was, it is true, a guard at the door; but the precautions which had surrounded Lincoln on Inauguration Day had been abandoned. If the President wished to go to his sitting room down the hall or even to his dining room for lunch, he had to emerge into the passage and run the gauntlet of people who thrust papers into his hand, blocked his path, or tugged at his coattails. It was the sheerest good fortune that none were armed.

Not all the President's time was taken up by office seekers, for his official engagements were time-consuming. Seward had the State Department draw up detailed instructions for the inexperienced President on how to receive the members of the diplomatic corps, how to dress on various occasions, when to hold his levees, how to behave at state dinners, and which guests must be invited as soon as possible. Much time had also to be spent on his mail, which was enormous and largely concerned with jobs. It is hardly surprising that people who had hoped for a more vigorous policy than Buchanan's were soon disappointed. Edwin M. Stanton, who had been the most forceful of Buchanan's last-minute Cabinet appointments, reported to his former employer: "Every day affords a proof of the absence of any settled policy or harmonious action in the administration." Chase, Blair, and Welles, he remarked, agreed on all questions and were invariably opposed by Seward, Bates, and Cameron. Smith, the lightweight, took both sides at once, while the President varied unpredictably. Horace Greeley of the New York *Tribune*, equally disillusioned, said the Lincoln government had no ideas in its collective head except the spoils of office and antagonism toward the South.

Such onlookers did Lincoln less than justice. It is true that many of his days were taken up with trivial matters, but the long nights were his own. The terrible situation of the country had been crystalized for him on his second day of office by a letter from Major Anderson, commander of Fort Sumter, announcing that he had no more than six weeks' provisions.

Since December 20 of the preceding year, when South Carolina had proclaimed her independence, Mississippi, Florida, Alabama, Georgia, Louisiana, and Texas had seceded. With South Carolina, these six other states formed a Confederacy, chose a President, and started to draw up a constitution. They also seized United States property within their borders. By the time of Lincoln's inauguration, only Sumter, Fort Pickens at Pensacola, Florida, and a couple of inconsiderable islands in rebel territory still flew the United States flag. Accordingly, when Lincoln announced his intention to "hold, occupy and possess the property and places belonging to the government," he was understood to have referred particularly to these forts. Yet only two days after his bold words, Lincoln was informed that Sumter must be reprovisioned or surrendered by April 15. The problem which Buchanan had left for him was uncomfortably urgent.

The details of the situation in Charleston were understood neither by Lincoln nor by his Cabinet advisors, unless possibly by Seward. Cabinet meetings throughout March were uneasy occasions on which members found little in common and showed small confidence in Lincoln. When Lincoln asked his Cabinet on March 15 for written opinions, Blair was the only one anxious to relieve Fort Sumter. The seceding states had acquired a considerable stock of munitions, some distinguished officers, and many professional soldiers from the United States Army. Fresh guns had been sited in Charleston, both to command Sumter and to beat off a relieving force. It seemed doubtful whether the fort could be supplied, though Gustavus Fox, Assistant Secretary of the Navy, was eager to try. General Scott, who had originally seen no difficulty in holding Sumter, now estimated that he needed twenty thousand soldiers to do it, which was a larger force than the entire United States Army, most of which was scattered in small contingents along the Mexican and western borders.

The difficulties of reprovisioning Sumter had become more formidable through Buchanan's delay. In addition, the political risks of such an action had grown enormously. An expedition against a greatly strengthened Charleston could result in nothing but war. At the moment there were only seven states in the Confederacy; but several more, including the all-important Virginia, were holding constitutional conventions. Virginia's inclined to another compromise in the state's historic tradition. But while the majority of the Virginia convention were unionist, nothing whatever would induce them to coerce their Southern neighbors. The outbreak of war would force the secession of Virginia—and no one knew how many other states would follow. War might isolate Washington, make Lincoln a prisoner, and break up the Union forever. No wonder all Cabinet members but Blair preferred the surrender of Sumter.

Lincoln inclined to the same view. Virginia was far more important to the Union than Sumter. On the other hand, only two days before reading Major Anderson's letter, Lincoln had given the nation a promise in happy ignorance of the fort's desperate position. The country was looking to him for leadership, and he had a principle to uphold which was the more important because so many forts and arsenals had already been lost. The lower South was talking a new language; and Lincoln, the almost unknown President, had to make it clear whether he accepted its right to do so. Actions speak louder than words, and what Lincoln did about Sumter would set the tone of his administration in a fashion which could not be done by inaugural promises.

It was characteristic of Lincoln's cautious mind that his first decision was to learn more about the situation in Charleston. He sent Gustavus Fox down to see Anderson, and a couple of his Illinois friends—one born in Charleston, the other in Virginia—to visit Charleston friends and talk with officials. Like many Northerners, Lincoln could not believe that the ancient loyalties which had bound men to the Union had vanished so quickly. He felt sure there were elements to which an appeal could be made.

From the moment that Anderson had taken over Sumter, the sight of the United States flag on an island in their harbor had caused intense irritation to the populace of Charleston. The Governor of South Carolina had wanted to attack the fort before Lincoln's inauguration, since he reasoned that Buchanan would fail to act, while Lincoln would hardly commence a war on account of an incident which had occurred under the previous administration. The formation of the Confederacy had caused a delay. The Confederate government at Montgomery did not wish to be dragged into war merely because Charleston was unable to put up with the sight of the United States flag for a few weeks. The formation of the new government took time, and the opportunity passed. It was not until the second week in March that the commissioners from South Carolina were replaced in Washington by three envoys from the Confederate States empowered to negotiate on all questions raised by the division of the country. These gentlemen applied to the Secretary of State for an appointment with the President in order to present him with their credentials.

The request was one which Seward could not possibly grant, since it would amount to a recognition of the Confederacy's independence. There was nothing, however, to prevent him from receiving messages through John A. Campbell of Alabama, at the moment an Associate Justice of the United States Supreme Court, who was waiting to join the Confederacy at the most convenient moment. Seward knew more about the Charleston situation than did President Lincoln, for he had not only been in Washington during the previous session of Congress, but had been informed of the inner workings of Buchanan's Cabinet by Edwin M. Stanton. He was completely convinced that the border states must be kept in the Union, in the hope that the Deep South would eventually discover that alone it was too small a unit for independent existence.

Unlike Lincoln, therefore, Seward already knew what ought to be done and felt bound to do it. Through Campbell he conveyed to the Confederate envoys an assurance that Sumter would be evacuated in a few days. When this did not occur, he explained through the same intermediary that questions of state could not be decided according to an exact timetable. The Southern negotiators informed their government—with perfect justification—that the Lincoln government had promised to surrender Sumter. No one realized that Seward's promise rested only on the assumption that Lincoln could pursue no other course.

The month of March went by without further action on Sumter because Lincoln was waiting for his emissaries' reports, which proved bleakly discouraging. Things were even worse than he realized because Ward Lamon, one of his two Illinois envoys, had spoken indiscreetly in Charleston of the need to surrender Sumter, not out of disloyalty toward his chief but because he could see no alternative, given the situation he found in South Carolina. But while the Confederacy regarded the surrender of Sumter as promised, anger at Lincoln's lack of a policy was growing within the Union. On March 28, General Scott made another appraisal of the situation, and called for giving up Fort Pickens at Pensacola as well as Fort Sumter. But when Lincoln again asked the Cabinet what he should do, Chase, Welles, and Blair were for reprovisioning Sumter, despite the risk of war, while Bates remarked that it must be relieved or evacuated soon, and Cameron said nothing. Only Seward and Smith spoke openly for surrender. Lincoln, who had called the Cabinet together less to decide on the matter than to clear the problem in his own mind, stayed awake all that night worrying over his decision.

To lose both Pickens and Sumter was not acceptable to Lincoln, who knew that the Union was looking to its President for leadership. If it found none, the cause of the United States would be lost even more certainly than if a war should force Virginia and the border states to take the Confederate side. Since, however, Sumter was strategically untenable, its loss might be accepted, provided that Pickens was promptly reinforced. Lincoln had already sent orders that troops which Buchanan had left lying off Pensacola on the *Sabine* should be landed at once. An expedition for reprovisioning and further strengthening Pickens was being assembled in New York under conditions which were supposed to be secret. On April 1, Lincoln ordered this expedition to set out and—just in case there should be a failure at Pickens—an expedition was to be assembled for Sumter.

Unfortunately, on April 6 when the Pickens expedition was still a good way from its goal, Lincoln made a discovery which he was to make more than once in the coming years. It was one thing to send an order, but quite another to have it carried out. President Buchanan had made an informal agreement with Florida that he would not land troops for Pickens so long as Florida made no attack. There was nothing binding on Lincoln in this arrangement, which was merely Buchanan's way of leaving another problem to his successor. However, the captain of the *Sabine* refused to land reinforcements for Pickens on the grounds that his country's word was pledged that he should not. Thus, Florida, well aware that a relief expedition had sailed from New York, could easily have anticipated its arrival by overpowering the tiny garrison.

If Sumter was to be saved instead of Pickens, its relieving expedition must sail from New York in a day or two, since Anderson would surrender if not reprovisioned by the fifteenth. In other words, if Lincoln now waited for certain news about Pickens, it would be too late to do anything for Sumter. The first indication that the new President was able to lead his country in this crisis was the order that he gave to sail for Sumter. Characteristically he tried to cover the boldness of his decision by a display of exaggerated caution. No troops or ammunition were to be landed unless resistance was made. To underline his peaceful intentions he sent a private envoy to the Governor of South Carolina in order to explain that he planned nothing but the peaceful landing of stores. It is clear today that after the promises of Seward—and probably in any case—Lincoln had no chance of avoiding a conflict. He may at the time have supposed that he had one, or he may have done what he could for the sake of the record. In either case he accepted a risk of war rather than a reversal of his stated policy, namely that the President of the United States would assert its rights as far as he was able.

The consequences of Lincoln's act—the loss of Virginia, Tennessee, Arkansas, and North Carolina—were so disastrous that it is easy to stress his lack of wisdom while making little of the principle on which he based his decision. It is, however, fair to say that the Confederacy was in a belligerent mood and had not only these four states to gain by provoking a quarrel, but Kentucky, Missouri, and

possibly Maryland and the city of Washington itself. Seward's policy might well have failed to save these states and failed also to rally the North. Unexpectedly the times had produced a President who, when he promised to "hold, occupy and possess the property and places belonging to the government," had meant what he said.

The Sumter expedition sailed as ordered, but not without a muddle which throws further light on the inexperience of Lincoln and on Seward's attempt to run the government. Welles, Secretary of the Navy, had designated the *Powhatan,* commanded by Captain Mercer, as the flagship of the fleet bound for Sumter. Seward, who was determined that Sumter must be abandoned, wished the powerful *Powhatan* sent down to Pickens. Accordingly he drew up an order transferring command of the ship to Captain Porter and ordering it to join the Pickens fleet. This paper he presented to Lincoln in a pile of others on State Department matters. Lincoln, busy with patronage problems and without experience of administration, signed it without reading it through. The *Powhatan* sailed for Pickens to the fury of Welles, who had discussed his arrangements with Lincoln beforehand. Apprised of what had happened, Lincoln could only say that he was at fault, as indeed he was. He ordered Seward to reverse the instructions, and Welles sent a steamer after Captain Porter with a message signed in his own name as Secretary of the Navy ordering him to return to New York and hand his ship over to Mercer. Porter, already in receipt of an order signed by the President, refused to obey the instructions of a mere member of the Cabinet. He went on his way with the Pickens expedition, leaving that designed for Sumter reduced by the transfer of its strongest vessel. The incident was of no importance to Sumter's fate or the outbreak of war, but it demonstrates how disorganized the Lincoln government was. Seward's pretensions were encouraged by the carelessness of a President whom few thought equal to his job.

The citizens of Charleston had put up reluctantly with the Confederate government's claim that the status of Fort

Sumter, like all outstanding questions, was a matter for negotiation with the United States government. They had been somewhat mollified by the arrival of a newly appointed Confederate general to take command. P. G. T. Beauregard, former Superintendent of West Point, was a colorful professional soldier exactly suited to the high tempers of the men of Charleston. Volunteers were soon hard at work siting cannon, piling up ammunition, and laboring on breastworks. Sumter was nothing but an unfinished fort on a small island surrounded on about two-thirds of its circumference by Charleston harbor and unapproachable on the seaward side save by ships of shallow draft. Charleston patriots thought it was almost a shame that Anderson might march out of there on April 15 without a gun being fired. Thus Lincoln's message about reprovisioning Sumter was as fatal as a match in a powder magazine. Beauregard did not open fire without consulting his government in Montgomery, but its leaders in their turn were angry at what they considered repudiation of Seward's definite promise. Everyone on the Southern side agreed on the issue, and there was nothing but protocol to cause delay. On April 11 an ultimatum was delivered to Major Anderson, demanding he evacuate the fort. Quite correctly Anderson replied that he would do so on the fifteenth, provided that he had not been relieved or received other orders. This answer was solemnly adjudged not good enough. At 3:20 A.M. on April 12 he was notified that fire would be opened on him in one hour.

The reduction of Fort Sumter took thirty hours, during which time the little garrison made almost no impression on the guns attacking it. No one was killed, but the fort was reduced to rubble, and there was no point in holding it any longer. Anderson was allowed to march out with colors flying and to go free together with his company and such private property as they could salvage. War might have begun, but Beauregard was still able to afford a chivalrous gesture.

Much has been written about the incident of Fort

Sumter, for although the South opened the conflict, it naturally claimed intolerable provocation. Southerners were convinced that Lincoln had been clever enough to provoke the Confederacy into firing the first shot of a war he was determined to have. It is true that even in those waiting months at Springfield Lincoln had privately let his supporters in Congress know that he would resist secession and regarded the extension of slavery as brought to an end by the people's decision in the November election. He would oppose any compromise which reopened that issue. There is no indication, however, that he was preparing for war.

In his handling of the Sumter crisis, we can fairly accuse Lincoln of being too ignorant of Southern feeling as a result of his long absence from Washington and isolation from Southern leaders. It might be maintained that he should have been willing to take the risk that Pickens would be relieved (as in fact it was) and should have let Sumter fall. It is obvious that he should have kept closer check on Seward, despite a thousand distractions. He does not, in fact, appear to have exercised judgment superior to that of everyone else. He does appear as a man who, having told his country what sort of leadership to look for, was determined to provide it. But the cautious temperament which warned him to avoid a clash if remotely possible is as characteristic of the man as his refusal to compromise on issues he thought vital. If there was to be war, the South would have to start it, but nothing suggests that Lincoln maneuvered for an outbreak.

# 3

# War Opens

NEWS OF THE BOMBARDMENT of Fort Sumter
appeared in the Washington papers some twenty-four
hours after it had opened. Lincoln, always slow to make up
his mind, had great ability to absorb sudden shocks without being thrown off balance, so that he went through that
Saturday, April 13, as though nothing had happened. Naturally he had foreseen the possibility of war. Since April 1
he had asked for daily reports from General Scott, who was
collecting the few hundred regular soldiers he could lay his
hands on and sponsoring the enrollment of local militia to
guard important government buildings. To make such
provisions for an emergency, however, was no more than
insurance. Lincoln did tell a Virginia delegation which
was scheduled to meet him that Saturday that he felt it
necessary to retake Sumter and possibly other forts in
Southern possession, but he added that military occupation of the seceded states was not his intention.

His considered policy was worked out in a series of
Cabinet meetings held on Sunday. It was beginning to
dawn on the members of that body that their President had
a mind of his own. Seward had sent Lincoln a memoran-

dum on April 1, stating that the government had not
adopted any definite line of action and must do so. He
recommended that it rise above internal squabbles by em-
broiling the country with Spain, France, Great Britain,
and Russia in an effort to drive these countries out of their
New World possessions. Such a crusade, he claimed,
would pull the country together, provided that its leader
was uncritically supported by both President and Cabinet
alike. As leader, Seward offered himself. In the light of our
present knowledge it is hard to read this appalling proposition with the patience that Seward's reputation deserves.
He had revived a suggestion long popular with Douglas,
but the Little Giant was too astute to press it on a divided
country whose seceded members were eager for foreign
aid and recognition. It was presumably with considerable
shock that Seward received a firm answer from Lincoln,
criticizing his plan and dismissing the problem of leadership in one blunt sentence: "I remark that if this must be
done, *I* must do it." Seward, however, was not vindictive
and truly had the interests of his country at heart. If he did
not entirely cease from meddling, he did begin to study
Lincoln and generously admitted a short while later that
"The President is the best man of us all."

On Sunday, April 14, momentous decisions were made
which affected the whole nature of the war. We do not
know which suggestions were originally Lincoln's—
which Cabinet members supported them and which opposed. It is more significant that they represented conclu-
sions which laid a tremendous responsibility on Lincoln.
As President, he did not have the constitutional power to
declare war. Congress had just adjourned and was not
scheduled to reconvene until December. A weaker President would have recalled it at once and caused much confusion thereby, for Congress as it then existed was a body in
turmoil. Representatives from Virginia and other slave
states would never hear of coercion being applied to those
who had seceded. Quarrels which would have arisen might

have forced Kentucky, Missouri, and even Maryland to join the South. Quick action would in any case have been impossible. Thus the first decision Lincoln made was to act without Congress for the present, falling back on a statute of 1795 which empowered the President to call the militia of the states into Federal service if the laws of the United States were resisted by "combinations too powerful to be suppressed in the ordinary course of judicial proceedings." It was true that this power of the President lapsed thirty days after the opening of Congress—and that the country would certainly demand an emergency session between April and December. Accordingly, Lincoln summoned a special session for July 4 and drafted the militia for three months which, allowing for delays in local recruitment, should still send everyone home by about August 1. Thus in asking for three-month volunteers, Lincoln was not expressing any view on the probable duration of the emergency, nor in calling for a total of seventy-five thousand was he making any estimate of the numbers he might need. He was asking for as many as the War Department could conceivably supply. States had their own militia equipment, but tents, medical supplies, food, and transport would be needed as well as extra arms and ammunition. The regular army was only thirteen thousand, while the arsenals in which its supplies were stored had passed in many cases into secessionist hands.

On Monday, April 15, a proclamation drafted the day before was made public, and telegrams were sent out to the state governors, demanding from each his quota of militia. Support from the North was enthusiastic. Loyal unionists there had watched their country fall apart with anxious gloom which had seemed like apathy because there was nothing for them to rally around. They now jumped so eagerly at the chance of action that the country seemed transformed. Democrats were quick to volunteer as well as Republicans because Douglas, reserving the right to differ with Lincoln on other issues, was entirely at one with him on the need to save the Union. Traveling out to Illinois, Douglas made a couple of great speeches to his loyal followers there but—worn out by his exertions in the presidential campaign—proved physically unequal to further effort. He died in early June, but not until he had rallied his supporters behind Lincoln. Northern volunteers came forward in such numbers that the harassed Secretary of War could not accept them all.

Far different was the effect of Lincoln's proclamation in the border slave states. Virginia's hitherto unionist convention passed a secession ordinance within two days, subject only to a referendum certain to confirm it. Tennessee, Arkansas, and North Carolina soon followed. The Governor of Kentucky indignantly refused militia for the wicked purpose of coercing sister states. In Missouri, Maryland, and Delaware strong Southern factions threatened to increase the power of the South and paralyzed Northern efforts to pursue the war.

The Confederate government had already made considerable preparations for war. Beauregard commanded an army of seven thousand in Charleston, and agents were purchasing arms from abroad. But Governor Andrew of Massachusetts had likewise read the signs of the times. Since the first of the year he had been re-equipping his militia and compiling a roster of men who could be called quickly into service. The Sixth Massachusetts regiment was consequently ready to be dispatched to Washington within a few days. On the Friday after Sumter it arrived in Baltimore prepared to make the crossing from one depot to the other through the center of the city.

Maryland was a slave state and Baltimore a southern town. Governor Hicks was a Union man, and wealthy citizens were aware that they depended on Northern trade; but there were many secessionists, particularly among the rowdy elements of the population. A few hundred volunteers from Pennsylvania had already been hooted at and stoned as they passed through the city. The

Sixth Massachusetts, well-armed and businesslike, aroused stronger resentment. Obstructions were piled in front of its cars; and when the men descended to march through the streets, their progress degenerated into a running fight. They arrived in Washington with four men killed and thirty-one wounded, leaving a larger number of Baltimoreans on the field of battle. The Mayor and police chief, hastily deciding that no more troops could be brought through Baltimore, ordered the destruction of the railroad bridges leading into the town from the north. Thus on Saturday morning, one week after the news of Sumter appeared in the papers, Washington found itself cut off from northern reinforcements, newspapers, and even letters. Twenty-four hours later, the telegraph office in Baltimore was seized by secessionists, and no northern news whatever reached the capital for some days.

Panic mounted in Washington. The Republican takeover of jobs was not complete, and many persons employed by the government were known to be disloyal. Others were suspected, for every man's decision was a highly personal one. On April 18, one day after the Virginia ordinance of secession, which had yet to be confirmed by referendum, Colonel Robert E. Lee rode into Washington to confer with General Scott, whose favorite officer he was. Lee also had an appointment with that old intriguer Francis P. Blair, who was empowered by the President to make him an unofficial offer of high command. Lee was a devoted professional soldier who had spent his entire career in Federal service, disliked slavery, and did not believe that a state had the right to secede from the Union. Yet he refused the flattering offer, sent in his resignation, and— before it even had time to take effect—accepted command of the forces of Virginia. If Lee could act in such a way, there was no telling how any border-state man would interpret his duty.

Southern papers which trickled into Washington revealed a belligerent response to Lincoln's call for militia.

Since the Confederate government had understood that
Sumter's surrender had been promised, it leaped to the
conclusion that Lincoln was seeking an excuse for all-out
war. "On to Washington!" cried Southern editors, pointing out that Beauregard's army was now free to move
north and claiming that Virginia could raise an army almost overnight. Washington was unfortified and topo-
graphically indefensible except by an army established on
the heights of Arlington across the Potomac. The Sixth
Massachusetts and local militia were inadequate for this
job. The professional army and navy men, still fewer in
numbers, were paralyzed by the defection of many officers.
Families hastened to leave town, either from a desire to go
south while they still could or from fear of being caught
by a Southern invasion.

    On no one was anxiety a greater burden than on the
President. The breaking of the Baltimore bridges had been
countered by an arrangement to transport Northern
troops by steamer from Perryville on the Susquehanna to
Annapolis, which was connected to the capital by a branch
line. News shortly came in that the Seventh New York, the
Eighth Massachusetts, and some Rhode Island troops were
off Annapolis. The inhabitants of that town, however,
even more Southern-minded than Baltimore, had sabo-
taged the engines and torn up the tracks as far as Annapolis
Junction on the main line twenty miles away from Washington. It was not easy to move raw militia troops on foot,
especially over hostile country. The Eighth Massachusetts,
moreover, was commanded by Benjamin Butler, a difficult
politician now turned soldier who could be relied on to
obstruct any rivals wishing to get to Washington first.
General Scott, who had not so much as a cavalry squadron
to send out and gather news, was forced to rely on scouts
based at Annapolis Junction, who collected as much rumor
as truth from the countryside.

    In his usual way the President made a jest of his troubles,
telling some of the wounded men of the Sixth Massachu-

setts: "I don't believe there is any North. The Seventh
Regiment is a myth. Rhode Island is not known in our
geography any longer. *You* are the only Northern realities." But in the privacy of his White House office, his
secretaries, Nicolay and Hay, saw him stare out of the
window at the Potomac, up which it was thought reinforcements might appear, as he repeated to himself: "Why
don't they come! Why don't they come!" Even more dis-
turbingly, Lincoln's very senses deceived him. He distinctly heard cannon fire and looked around him, only to
perceive that no one else had done so. Not trusting himself
to speak of the matter, he walked out of the White House
to see what was going on. There was no unusual activity
in the half-empty town, where everybody had his private
concerns. Lincoln crossed the bridge of the Washington
canal and turned down the "island," which is southwest
Washington today. Unnoticed he traversed the whole
length of it as far as the United States Arsenal, which was
located at the junction of the Potomac and the West
Branch. The arsenal doors were open and unguarded so
that anyone, it appeared, might help himself. There was no
gunfire, however, and no agitation. The President walked
silently back to the White House.

The Washington panic was only of six days' duration.
Despite breakdowns in commissariat, the intrigues of General Butler, and the torn-up Annapolis lines, the troops got
through. They had mechanics among them; and a competent engineer named Andrew Carnegie arrived to take
charge of repairs. Two weeks after fire was opened on
Sumter the New York Seventh paraded proudly down
Pennsylvania Avenue, soon followed by the Eighth Massachusetts and the Rhode Islanders. The city was saved.

Lincoln, acting with firmness and dispatch, now moved
to secure Maryland, which was essential if Washington
was to remain the nation's capital. Governor Hicks, unable
to prevent the Maryland Legislature from assembling, was
persuaded to summon it to meet in Frederick rather than

in secessionist Annapolis. Along the vital railroad lines connecting Washington with the north Lincoln supplied guard troops and suspended habeas corpus. This ancient basis of civil law gives magistrates the right to require that any man arrested be produced in court and a case made out against him. Under the martial law with which Lincoln replaced it, people might be imprisoned for display of Confederate emblems, for disloyal articles, or even for sermons. John Merryman, recruiting a company to go south and fight for the Confederacy, was thrown into jail. Chief Justice Taney issued a writ to bring Merryman to trial, but found himself blocked by the general in command. Taney cited the officer for contempt, but was powerless to do more than proclaim that the President had no right to suspend habeas corpus. Lincoln boldly disagreed, pointing out that the Constitution provided for martial law in cases of rebellion or invasion. Since Maryland at the moment was neither in rebellion nor invaded, he added that he saw no reason to let all the laws of the country be destroyed because one might not be violated in a limited area. Merryman stayed in jail; and the State of Maryland, to the disgust of a proportion of its citizens, stayed in the Union. The Baltimore bridges were soon repaired, and many more regiments came rolling down from the north. Washington, which had so lately longed for troops, soon faced fresh problems in playing host to a large, disorganized army.

# 4

## Bull Run

CONGRESS CONVENED on July 4, 1861, in special session to listen to a message from the President detailing the affair of Sumter and the steps he had since taken. It is a fairly long message, and there is not a word about slavery in it. The issue of the Civil War to Lincoln was purely one of democracy. Could a republic which had been founded to express the will of the people survive the opposition of a strong minority? A failure of the American experiment would argue that democratic government had an incurable weakness, for America was unique. The monarchies of Europe, even including that of England, rested on basic assumptions different from those expressed in the United States Constitution.

It is interesting to see how unhesitatingly Lincoln, elected by about 40 percent of the popular vote, identified himself with the will of the people. By July, 1861, he could in fact claim to be a majority leader because Douglas was dead and had left his followers nobody else to look to. It was not, however, the support of a majority which justified Lincoln's position, but the constitutionality of his election. Those who did not like the working of the Constitution must try to amend it. Knowing that the South did not possess the power to do this, Lincoln demanded that it submit to what it could not alter. His strength as a national leader lay in his unbending resolution on this point and his ability to concentrate attention on the single issue which was vital. He told Congress he had acted at Fort Sumter in defense of the Union, forced to attempt the fort's relief lest the people imagine that he dare not assert the nation's right to do so.

Another important claim in Lincoln's message to Congress was that he had needed to show the world that the United States intended to remain a single unit. Only two weeks before Sumter, Lincoln's Secretary of State had been urging him to quarrel with the most powerful nations in Europe. Men's chaotic emotions, their previous lines of policy, their mistaken reliance on Union feeling in the South, all clouded their thinking. Yet Lincoln, though inexperienced in international affairs and without previous contacts among the foreign envoys in Washington, had been able to pick out the point of real importance from Cabinet discussions on the subject, namely that he must encourage, not weaken his friends abroad. The importance of this policy was emphasized in April when Lincoln, in response to a threat of Southern privateering, proclaimed a blockade of Confederate ports. Unless England, the world's greatest naval power, would respect his right to do this, the cause of the United States was probably lost.

By July 4 when Lincoln reported to Congress, war preparations had gone forward at such a galloping pace that neither side had waited for formalities which would until recently have been a matter of course. Virginia's constitutional convention had passed its secession ordinance on April 17, subject to confirmation by a referendum on May 23. Without waiting for the popular vote, the Virginia Legislature had sent delegates to the Confederate Congress and had accepted the transfer of the Southern capital to Richmond. Recruiting had begun, and arrange-

ments had been made to admit Beauregard from South
Carolina with an army which was being rapidly swollen
by contingents from other seceded states. The arsenal at
Harpers Ferry had been seized, and much equipment
transferred to Richmond. A race for the Norfolk Navy
Yard was won by Virginia, whose forces found the installations imperfectly destroyed and gained possession of the
damaged *Merrimac,* one of the most modern vessels of the
United States Navy.

While Virginia hastened to act before voting, President
Lincoln did not hesitate to respond without waiting for
authority from Congress. At the beginning of May, per-
ceiving that popular feeling was behind him, he called for
forty-two thousand three-year volunteers and, greatly daring, enlarged the ranks of the permanent army and navy.
By July 4, he was ready to ask Congress for four hundred
thousand men and four hundred million dollars. Some of
these men were already available, since the War Department had not cut off volunteering when the number of
forty-two thousand volunteers had been reached. Armies
in Washington and elsewhere were rapidly assuming an
organized form under recognized commanders. Almost
none of Lincoln's acts lay strictly within his constitutional
powers, but by leaving initiative to the enemy, he was able
to justify what he had done in response.

In pursuance of this policy, Lincoln had been careful not
to move Federal forces into Virginia until after the state-
wide referendum. He had reinforced Fortress Monroe,
commanding the entrance to the Chesapeake Bay, and had
sent an expedition which came too late to save Norfolk.
These places, however, had been Federal property. The
outposts of Lee's army were permitted to establish themselves on the Arlington Heights overlooking the Potomac,
where they were close enough to have shelled Washington
if they had possessed the guns. Over the Marshall House,
Alexandria's hotel, the Confederate flag was clearly visible
through Washington telescopes, indicating that the navi-

gation of the river would be threatened if Lee could fortify
the decrepit port. Not until the morning after Virginia's
referendum did the Union army cross the river under command of an elderly lawyer, Charles W. Sandford, who had
headed the New York militia. It will never be known what
the inexperienced troops would have done if they had met
opposition, since Lee's forces were not large enough to
fight. The Federal army camped unopposed and began
work on fortifications.

While the militia marched over the bridges to Arlington,
the New York Fire Zouaves under Colonel Elmer E. Ellsworth were being ferried across in two steamers to seize
Alexandria. The Zouaves were named and dressed in imi-
tation of French elite troops who wore North African
baggy trousers, short jackets, and fezzes. They had been
recruited by Ellsworth from the ranks of the New York
Fire Department; and they had already made themselves a
name for being tough, rowdy, and devoted to their colonel.
Ellsworth, the fiery little man in his early twenties who
had joined the Lincolns on their trip to Washington, had
done so with the intention of starting a military career.
The claim of his Zouaves to be crack troops had been
recognized by their selection for the Alexandria assignment. They found the town undefended, but the inhabitants sullen. Ellsworth ran into the Marshall House, over
which the Confederate flag still floated, and hauled the flag
down. He was descending the stairs with it bundled in his
arms when the innkeeper shot him dead at point-blank
range, the first casualty of the Union invasion of Virginia.

Elmer Ellsworth was not just any officer who had made
a rash move and been killed, but a romantic figure, head of
the conspicuous Zouaves, who so adored him that it was
difficult to restrain them from burning Alexandria in revenge for his death. He was also connected by close personal ties with the President's family. His body lay in state
at the White House; Mary Lincoln placed his portrait surrounded by a laurel wreath in his coffin; the President's

carriage followed his Zouaves in the funeral procession. In consequence, Ellsworth briefly became a national symbol of the young men about to die. The North indulged in an orgy of sentimental regrets which was only too quickly to be replaced by the realities of mourning. It was significant that among those who had loved Ellsworth was the President, who had so lately been an unknown politician and was so rapidly becoming a national symbol. In an age when sentiment counted for much, it seemed peculiarly fitting that Lincoln should be among the first to mourn. It was one of several moments when chance seemed to single him out for a special role.

All these events and many others had happened before the opening of the emergency session of Congress, presenting that body with two main facts to consider. Should this be an all-out war with every Northern resource thrown into the struggle? If so, what sort of a war was it going to be? On the first question the feeling of the country was strongly affirmative and was reflected in Congress. The second was already governed by the course of events. It was right for Lincoln to present the quarrel as a test of political democracy, since only on this principle would Northerners and slave-holding border states be able to unite. But the actual course of a war is not necessarily decided by its basic assumptions. The question of slavery in the seceded states became an issue from the moment that Federal forces occupied Virginia soil.

Benjamin Butler, the self-willed and indiscreet politician who had come down with the three-months' men from Massachusetts, had already raised an uproar by moving his troops from the railroad junction they were guarding to a spot which threatened Baltimore. This arbitrary act jeopardized the improving relations between Washington and Maryland. General Butler was hastily transferred to Fort Monroe which, though Federal property, was in Virginia. In late May three Negro slaves appeared at the Fort. They belonged to a Southern officer who had been

using them to dig entrenchments for Confederate cannon.
The owner demanded them back under the provisions of
the Fugitive Slave Law which, according to Northern theory, still applied to the whole country. Butler, however,
replied that if Virginia claimed to be a foreign state, she
could not simultaneously demand the protection of United
States laws. He kept the slaves and set them to work on his
own entrenchments. Pretty soon General Butler was har-
boring a refugee camp of about nine hundred Negroes. He
defined them as "contraband of war," or in other words
property being used by their owners in aid of a rebellion.
But if they were property, whose property were they now?
Not Butler's certainly. Not the Federal government's,
since it had no intention of becoming a slave owner. To
return them to their angry masters after the war was un-
thinkable. The situation was further complicated by the
drift of Negroes from Washington or Maryland into the
encampments of the Army of the Potomac. The problem
grew greatly in scale later in the summer as Federal expeditions took possession of the barren strips of land and
offshore islands from Hatteras to Port Royal in order to
interrupt communications between Confederate states by
sea and intercept cutters unloading supplies from larger
ships in barren creeks. Hatteras Creek and in particular
Port Royal contained plantations whose white owners had
fled, leaving behind them the Negro population. General
Butler, who was with the expedition, found uses for these
people.

To the majority of Congress, as to Lincoln, the war was
not about slavery, yet slave labor helped the Southern war
effort. The Constitution permitted the property of traitors
to be sequestered, but only during their own lifetime. This
was all very well when it involved land or cattle. It did not
seem applicable to human beings.

Neither Congress nor Lincoln had wanted this problem,
especially as border slave states were vital to the Union.
The best that Congress could do was to draw a strict dis-

tinction between slaves who were actually used by Confederate armies and those who simply belonged to Southern owners. It was not a distinction which could in practice be observed in the swelling camps of the "contrabands," but for the moment it had to suffice. It provided Lincoln and other moderate men with an urgent reason for settling the quarrel between the states before major parts of the South were overrun.

Lincoln's original call-up of the militia had set a pattern for the new army of the United States which was beginning to take shape. The soldiers digging in on the Arlington Heights had been recruited in their own states and had elected their captains or enrolled in companies which individuals were raising. Majors, colonels, even generals were state-appointed, subject to confirmation by the War Department. In other words, this amateur army was separate from the regular one and only influenced by it insofar as some of its officers were West Point men who had retired from the service to take up more lucrative positions in civilian life. Lincoln's decision to act through the states had been a sound political one. Nevertheless, a man who makes a military decision for political reasons cannot expect it to have a purely military effect. The army defending Washington was a motley crowd commanded by officers who knew little more than their men about making war.

These disadvantages of Lincoln's army were increased by his political choice for Secretary of War. Simon Cameron had been given the office because he was judged too corrupt for the Treasury and too influential to be left out of the Cabinet. Though the Secretary of War was traditionally an important official, his responsibilities in peacetime were not vast. Caught up in the sudden expansion of war before even routine patronage questions had been settled, Cameron found himself the target of army contractors, politicians who wanted to turn soldier, and literally thousands of men asking for appointments. The War Office, already a haven for Cameron's political cronies, gained suddenly an almost unlimited power of doing favors. It was soon apparent that military profiteering and wastage were going to be enormous factors in this war.

If Lincoln understood these difficulties, he so far gave no sign. Never an administrator, his policy was to leave the practical details of departments to those in charge. He had plenty of problems of his own on the highest level, centering mainly on his ignorance of military matters and the drawbacks of Winfield Scott, General-in-Chief of the Army.

Scott was too old and infirm for active service and, if the truth were to be told, no longer fit to direct a war. On the other hand, he was the country's foremost soldier and the only officer who had commanded a body of men large enough to be called an army. His immediate subordinates in active service were all old men because in the small peacetime army all officers above the rank of major were usually old. Younger men had had little experience under war conditions. Even Robert E. Lee, though now middle-aged, had never commanded more than three hundred men in combat. It was inevitable that Scott should press the claims of his elderly officers and that the politicians should feel dubious about them. Eventually the command of the Army of the Potomac, which could not indefinitely be left in the hands of an aging New York lawyer, was given to a protégé of Salmon P. Chase, passing over the aged Colonel Mansfield who was recommended by Scott. Major Irvin McDowell of the regular army was forty-three years old and consequently without significant experience of command. On the other hand, he had spent some time in France making a study of the army of that military charlatan Napoleon III. McDowell was an intelligent man who had done well in his profession, but had not the born commander's gift of impressing his personality on those whom he led. With some pains he assembled a staff which had qualifications for learning its expanded duties in such fields as commissary, engineering, ordnance, or medical needs. He did not, however, appoint a chief of staff or second in command. Since the United States had no staff college, officers lacked the theory as well as the practice of handling armies.

By the time congressmen began to arrive in Washington for the special session, McDowell had spent a few weeks organizing the army on the Potomac. The Sixth Massachusetts and the other early regiments were already talking about going home. Since their three-months' service was nearly up, and they had found soldiering boring, uncomfortable, and dirty, most of them felt that it was time someone else relieved them. Congress, however, thought militia with two-and-a-half-months' training in their duties ought to be used before they were replaced by greenhorns. Lincoln was not the only politician to perceive that a speedy end of the war would not only save bloodshed, but would solve complications about the future of slavery. Furthermore, there was still a feeling that the Confederate states were not so unanimous about secession as they sounded and would not fight with determination. The recent transfer of the Confederate capital to Richmond put the center of the rebellion nearly within McDowell's grasp. Congressmen who came to Washington with these ideas in mind were greatly encouraged by a grand parade of twenty New York regiments which were still on the northern side of the river. This was only about a third of all the regiments which composed the Washington army, and yet to the spectators half the nation's young men seemed on the march.

For all these reasons, even before Congress opened, there was pressure for action which the President could not ignore. General Scott, on the other hand, shared with McDowell and all the officers of the regular army a poor opinion of militia. The equipment of each regiment was different from that of the next; they had no idea of concerted action and little of military obedience; artillery, cavalry, and transport were insufficient. In any case, wars were won, Scott thought, by strategy and not by gallantry. He was hoping to start a great movement down the Mississippi to cut the Confederacy in half, while at the same time strangling it by blockading its coastline and seizing New Orleans. Unfortunately Scott was never in good enough physical shape to defend his opinion effectively against the many who were demanding speedy action. His advice was in part discounted because he was a Virginian and had no appetite for fighting over that settled and civilized country, only to leave wounds there which would not soon heal.

President Lincoln and his Cabinet were concerned lest the states lose enthusiasm for enlisting troops which were not used. The three-months' men, returning home disgruntled with military life, could cause a reaction against the war. Naturally politicians were more sensitive to such difficulties than to those of military logistics. General McDowell, so lately a mere major, had not sufficient confidence in himself to refuse to do what he was ordered. When instructed to attack Beauregard in Manassas, McDowell was ready to draw up a plan—if not in confidence, at least with reasonable hope of success. The consequence was that even before Congress had officially assembled, McDowell was given the order to advance. Scott, though vexed at the interference of politicians, did not feel it his duty to resign when he was overruled. His grand strategy involved preparations for several months before it could be put into action, and in the meantime, there was a clamor for the letting of blood. Scott shrugged his shoulders, accepting the orders of the Commander-in-Chief.

McDowell's plan was to march for Manassas in three columns with a total force of about thirty thousand against some twenty-five thousand under Beauregard. Success depended on the ability of General Patterson, then in the neighborhood of Harpers Ferry, to prevent Confederate General Joseph E. Johnston, who had fallen back from that place, from reinforcing the army at Manassas. It was unfortunate that McDowell did not get started as soon as he had intended and that some of the three-months' men were actually pulled out as the army moved. To Lincoln, completely inexperienced in war, these last-minute hitches probably resembled his own militia experience in the Black Hawk War when he was in his twenties. That tiny war had been successful, and Lincoln had no reason to suppose that the army men did not know their job. His confidence was reinforced by news of victory in West Virginia under General McClellan.

On Thursday, July 18, reports came in of fighting which turned out to be a preliminary skirmish in which the Union troops had been routed. The inexperienced army, exhausted by marching in the heat, had discarded equipment and thrown away or devoured the reserve rations which it carried in its knapsacks. There were, however, some Confederate prisoners who were presently brought into Washington, together with a reassuring message from General McDowell, asserting that he was completing arrangements to fight on Sunday near Bull Run. The news sent a thrill of excitement through Washington. Numerous noncombatants were eager to have a view of the first real battle on American soil since the Revolution. They included congressmen; the pioneer photographer Mathew Brady; William Howard Russell, war correspondent for the London *Times;* and adventurous ladies complete with escorts, carriages, spyglasses, and expensive picnic equipment.

The excitement in Washington was infectious but reassuring. None of those who streamed out to see the show had any expectation that they would be in danger. Lincoln, though necessarily anxious, could listen to the rumbling of guns without special alarm. Unofficial telegrams started coming in from people who could see little but dust and smoke. The President read them and, fidgeting for the real news, paid a visit to General Scott at his headquarters, where he found the old veteran taking an afternoon nap. Ever courteous, the general aroused himself to reassure the

President—and went back again to finish his sleep. Some
while later favorable reports were received, and Lincoln
felt able to order his carriage for his regular afternoon
drive. He was still not back at six o'clock when Mr. Seward
called at the White House, haggard with the news of disaster. Nicolay and Hay knew nothing except that there had
been reports of victory. "Tell no one," Seward said. "That
is not true. The battle is lost. The telegraph says that
McDowell is in full retreat and calls on General Scott to
save the capital. . . ."

The President and the Cabinet gathered in haste at
Scott's headquarters, where orderlies ran in with telegrams as they were received from the War Department.
Every report seemed worse than the last. McDowell had
hoped to fall back on Centerville, but was not able to make
a stand there. He spoke of holding Fairfax, but finally
announced that he was retreating to the Potomac. The
troops would not re-form and it was up to those left behind
in Washington to save it. About eight o'clock the first
spectators to leave the scene of battle came in with early
afternoon news of Federal success. They were soon followed by people in greater disarray. By midnight there
were accounts of running soldiers, discarded weapons,
smashed carriages, all the mad panic of defeat mixed up
with picnic parties. Some of those returning went to the
White House, where Lincoln received them stretched on
a couch in his office. He listened without comment while
they told him how the three-months' men had run away,
the civilian teamsters had panicked, volunteer officers had
deserted their commands. All night he heard such reports,
while crowds stood in the street waiting for news and
expecting the sound of Confederate guns approaching the
city.

Not till dawn did the army really begin to straggle in,
weaponless, footsore, and bedraggled, gathering in crowds
around the liquor stores to get refreshment. Many of the
men were hatless, coatless, shoeless. They had walked over

forty miles in thirty-six hours and fought a battle as well, so that they collapsed in doorways, propped themselves against lamp posts, lay in the gutters. Officers slept on their horses as they rode.

Now and again a regiment came by in battle order, but the best of the troops had nearly all been halted across the Potomac, leaving the Long Bridge over the river to be choked all Monday and Tuesday by supply wagons, ambulances, and country carts carrying those unable to walk. By this time it was clear that Beauregard's army was in too much confusion for pursuit. Washington citizens were handing out food or helping with the wounded. Scott was trying to round up officers who had taken refuge in comfortable hotels. He sent out mounted patrols to collect stragglers. Friends and relatives of combatants flocked into Washington, adding to the confusion with their attempts to find wounded men.

Everybody was angry and disillusioned, furious with Patterson, who had not prevented Johnston from reinforcing Beauregard, indignant with McDowell, contemptuous of the militia and especially of the officers who had deserted their men. General Scott received his share of criticism and lost his temper, blaming himself as the greatest coward in America for having allowed the politicians to talk him into a battle against his judgment. A serious conflict loomed between the government and the professional military men.

All these experiences were part of Lincoln's initiation into the complex problems of a civilian Commander-in-Chief in a large-scale war. It was a measure of his competence for the job that he was not completely shattered and was able to perceive that the Union was by no means overthrown. There was great public indignation, but the flood of three-year volunteers increased rather than diminished. Soldiers were ready to do the job, but demanded commanders who would not make mistakes in using them. Scott's reputation was seriously damaged, though the im-

possibility of replacing him by anyone with a quarter of his
experience left him in control for the present. Patterson,
who had let Johnston get away to reinforce Beauregard,
had to be dismissed. He was in any case a militia general
and as such clearly out of favor. McDowell, on re-examina-
tion, turned out not to have done so badly. He had nearly
won his battle. Parts of his army had fought well, and the
Confederates had been left in too much confusion for pursuit. All the same he had lost, and some of the reasons lay
at his door.

McDowell was a competent soldier and was later to become an excellent corps commander, but he was never
again commanding general. The President desperately
needed a new figure with a new relationship to himself.
There could be no question of ordering the next commander to plan a battle in a hurry. The army, and behind the
army the mass of the public, demanded a general who
could make volunteers into soldiers, and who would know
how to use an army as efficiently as the surgeon uses his
knife.

# 5

# Lincoln and the
# Politics of War

CLOSE BEHIND THE FRONT LINES in Washington,
Abraham Lincoln had learned in the summer of 1861 how
little he and the people whom he led understood about
battles. But at a time when so much was happening, political judgment was needed as desperately as military skill.
From the outbreak of the contest Lincoln had seen the
importance of keeping border states within the Union. He
had lost Virginia, but had saved Maryland. Further west,
Missouri and Kentucky appeared to face both ways, while
each in its own fashion was essential to the success of
Union strategy.

Kentucky, settled largely by Virginians, had preserved
a sense of kinship with the Old Dominion, even though
communications were shortly interrupted by the uprising
which resulted in the formation of unionist West Virginia.
When Kentucky Governor Beriah Magoffin had refused
Lincoln's call for militia, he had done so less out of sympa-
thy with secession than because of a feeling very general
in Kentucky that the Confederacy, even if wrong, must be
left in peace. From the military point of view, Kentucky
was crucial to the Union, since the state commanded the

south bank of the Ohio, whence it could strangle eastern trade with Missouri and the upper Mississippi Valley. "Kentucky gone," wrote Lincoln, "we cannot hold Missouri, nor, as I think, Maryland. These all against us, and the job on our hands is too large for us. We would as well consent to separation at once, including the surrender of the capital." Fortunately in 1861 Lincoln's diplomacy exactly suited this situation. He made no demands, but listened patiently to Kentucky deputations, whether hostile or friendly, assuring all that he had no plans to send Federal troops into the state. If Kentucky wished to remain neutral, the government would leave her alone as long as she obeyed Federal law. In the haphazard fashion of those times, Kentucky elections fell in June, 1861. Not until the results were in, returning nine Union candidates out of ten with a popular majority of almost twice the pro-Southern vote, did Lincoln breathe easily. It had not been accidental that he did not summon Congress to meet until after these crucial elections.

While he handled Kentucky with tact, Lincoln did not privately neglect his personal contacts in the state, including for instance Joshua Speed, one of his most intimate friends before his marriage, who was now influential there. Federals and Confederates both set up camps for Kentucky recruits across the border, each ready to invade if the other side did so. Both smuggled arms into the state for their partisans. The Kentucky State Guard, which had been called together to protect neutrality, was known to be Southern in feeling. Inevitably a Home Guard of Union volunteers set up a camp of their own not far from the state capital. Governor Magoffin protested to Lincoln, who assured him that the Home Guard was composed of native Kentuckians who had a fancy to camp in their own territory and presented no outside menace. A Kentucky state senator wrote to the President to protest the presence of Federal forces at Cairo, Illinois, just across the Ohio River. Lincoln told his secretary to reply that the President would consider the question, but he could not refrain from instructing him to add that the President would "never have ordered the troops complained of, had he known that Cairo was in your senatorial district."

As long as Kentucky remained neutral, Lincoln had little reason to do more than maneuver for position in the event that conditions changed. He could not get at the Southern forces across the state, but they were equally cut off from him. Traffic went unimpeded down the Ohio, and Federal forces could concentrate on the problems of Missouri.

As the only Midwestern slave state north of the old Compromise of 1850 line, Missouri was surrounded on three sides by free states. The violence which Missourians had sponsored in Kansas under the Kansas-Nebraska law of 1854 had demonstrated the strength of pro-slavery feeling. The failure to make a slave state out of Kansas was only a few years old, and it still rankled. On the other hand, the city of St. Louis was a great trading port, attracting settlers from the anti-slavery north, including many Germans, who generally were abolitionists. Thus while feelings in Kentucky were middle-of-the-road, the divisions in Missouri were extreme.

The chief faction leaders in Missouri were Claiborne Jackson, the Governor, who wanted to take the state into the Confederacy, and Frank Blair, brother of Lincoln's Postmaster General. Jackson called out the state militia, which was Southern in sentiment, and sent secretly to the Confederacy for cannon, hoping to seize the arsenal in St. Louis and, strengthened by its arms and equipment, stage a Confederate coup. Frank Blair, working through Nathaniel Lyon, a fiery, red-haired officer in the regular army, recruited forces from among Union sympathizers, smuggled in arms, and managed to defeat the more leisurely plot of Jackson. After several clashes, the Confederate forces retreated south to the state border, leaving Missouri, for the moment at least, in Federal hands.

Strategically Missouri was nearly as important to Lincoln as Kentucky because of the focal position of St. Louis. Without Missouri the small force which was at present based on Cairo would never grow strong enough to push down the Mississippi and cut the Confederacy in half. To plan such a campaign, the Federal government needed a commander of greater stature than an obscure army captain like Nathaniel Lyon. Lincoln's choice was guided by Frank Blair, who perceived that in the West a general was needed who would command respect from Western governors. This must not be some jumped-up West Point major like McDowell, but a strong political figure. Blair's recommendation was John C. Frémont, who had been the Republican candidate for President in 1856 and who had gained national fame for daring explorations in the Far West.

Frémont took up his duties in St. Louis on July 25 with the rank of Major General, and it must be admitted that he found himself in an impossible situation. Theoretically his main task was to prepare the expedition which was to open up the Mississippi. He found at his disposal twenty-three thousand troops, most of whom were three-months' men shortly due to go home. The governors of the Western states were eager to send him fresh recruits, but he lacked arms, uniforms, transport, and money. Missouri, even including St. Louis, was full of rebels, while a real guerrilla war was going on in the western part of the state. Confederate armies, whose size his scouts exaggerated, were standing poised in Arkansas and Tennessee. Frémont had to guard the railroads running southwest from St. Louis; to hold St. Louis itself and Jefferson City; and to strengthen Cairo, the focal point for the Mississippi campaign. Nathaniel Lyon, now facing more than twice his own numbers in southwest Missouri, appealed urgently for aid, but Frémont found no troops to spare. Lyon was defeated and killed in a fierce little battle against hopeless odds which should have opened Missouri to the Confederates. Luckily for both Frémont and Lincoln, Confederate leaders in those parts were amateurs also and did not follow up their victory.

Probably Frank Blair was right in supposing that a distinguished politician would fit better into the command of the West than a regular soldier of no previous importance. His mistake had been in supposing that Frémont had the qualities needed. The new general set up headquarters in St. Louis and collected a staff composed of men who had received some military training outside the ranks of the regular army. These were largely revolutionaries from Hungary, Germany, or elsewhere, trained in the smart, heel-clicking regiments of central Europe. One of their duties was to protect their commander from the casual interruptions which Lincoln was always so ready to welcome. Backwoods soldiers with a grievance did not like being put off by flashy staff officers with foreign accents. Frémont was unpopular not only with the common soldiers, but also with their leaders, who did not soon forget the fate of Nathaniel Lyon.

Despite these difficulties, Frémont was a man of considerable talents, not incapable of keeping his eye on essentials, one of which was to reinforce the vital garrison of Cairo. For commander he chose a man who was indeed a West Pointer, but was unpopular with the establishment. Ulysses S. Grant had been forced to resign from the army for drinking, and had since made no success of civilian life. Frémont found him efficient, liked him the better for being out of favor, and in choosing him made one of the important appointments of the war. Unluckily, this was about Frémont's only good selection. Devoid of business sense and needing every kind of military supply, he turned for assistance to friends from California, too many of whom were not above chicanery. Headquarters deals were soon an open scandal, leading to a quarrel with Frank Blair and his Washington connections.

Beset with problems on every side, Frémont's reaction

was to assert himself. He proclaimed martial law throughout Missouri, ordering that men found with weapons in their hands should be court-martialed and shot. The personal property of all citizens who took up arms against the United States should be forfeit. Their slaves, if they had any, should be freed. Only after this proclamation had been printed did he send a copy to Lincoln.

Lincoln lost no time in writing to Frémont that court-martialing and shooting were out of the question, since they would at once provoke reprisals. No executions were to be ordered without permission from Washington in each individual case. Even more importantly, Frémont should follow the guidance of Congress in his treatment of slaves. Those actually used by the Confederate armies might be treated as "contraband" and employed by the Federals. Others must be left as they were. No other policy was possible if any of the border slave states were to remain loyal. Kentucky in particular would immediately be lost if Frémont did not modify his order.

Frémont replied with a refusal. His proclamation, he argued, was as much a method of waging war as was a battle, and it therefore fell within his province. If Lincoln as Commander-in-Chief publicly gave him an order, he must of course obey—but he did not feel obliged to respect a private letter which merely urged him to retract. To explain his reasons, he sent his wife, Jessie, to argue with Lincoln.

Evidently Frémont and the President were already waging different wars. Lincoln had never threatened the domestic institutions of the Southern states, content to hope that slavery would eventually wither away. In response, Southerners had pointed out that even if Lincoln was not himself an abolitionist, he headed a party in which there were many. They questioned not merely Lincoln's goodwill, but his actual power to preserve and protect their human property. Frémont was doing his best to justify these fears.

Lincoln was in the right, not merely because of his better understanding of the vital border states, but because the treatment of slavery in the South was a political problem involving the nature of the war and the fate of the Union. Such decisions were for the President and Congress to make, not for a single general to settle because they might bolster his position in Missouri.

Lincoln acted promptly. He issued a public order to Frémont to cancel his proclamation. It was followed by Postmaster General Blair, sent to talk with the general and find out what was going wrong in Missouri. Jessie Frémont, overenthusiastic in support of her husband and far too familiar with his official job for Lincoln's liking, arrived at the White House with the intention of lecturing the President on matters about which she assumed he had not reflected deeply. She was given a freezing reception, and her eloquence suggested that Frémont was seeking favor with abolitionists for private political reasons.

The crisis stirred up by Frémont came at the end of August and the early part of September. What Kentucky would have done if the state had been given sufficient time to work up indignation will never be known. On September 3, however, a Confederate army from Tennessee crossed the Kentucky border to occupy Hickman and Columbus in order to plant heavy guns on the bluffs overlooking the Mississippi. General Polk, who had ordered the movement, was aware that it must swing Kentucky into the Federal camp—but he was afraid Grant's forces in Cairo would come downriver and capture Columbus before his own people could do so. The invasion prompted Grant to seize Paducah, a Kentucky township of great strategic importance on the Ohio. Kentucky, so recently neutral, dissolved into factions. Friends and relatives who were not far apart in political thinking now went their different ways, making choices which were perhaps more painful because they had hoped to avoid them.

All in all, it may be said that by the fall of 1861 Lincoln's diplomacy had been more successful than his generals' campaigns. Grant in Cairo had been efficient. In West Virginia, small bodies of troops under McClellan had fought spirited actions. The expeditions to Hatteras Creek and Port Royal had tightened the blockade. Such undertakings, however, involved small armies compared to those of McDowell, which had ended in the disaster of Bull Run, and Frémont, who was bound eventually to be edged out in favor of a more suitable general. But Maryland, Kentucky, and Missouri were in Federal hands and—generally speaking—the war was still about secession rather than slavery. Lincoln, taking an informal poll of opinion from all who visited him, still held to the one issue on which all were agreed.

Hardly had the crises in Missouri and Kentucky been settled, at least temporarily, than a crisis of an entirely different kind required from Lincoln great powers of self-control and cool judgment. Captain Wilkes, commander of one of the Federal ships of war which were trying to enforce the Southern blockade, intercepted the British mail steamer *Trent*, running from Havana to England, and removed James Mason of Virginia and John Slidell of Louisiana, appointed by Jefferson Davis as Confederate envoys to Great Britain and France. Wilkes brought his prisoners into Hampton Roads on November 15, and the news spread rapidly over the nation.

Mason and Slidell were well-known politicians who had taken a prominent part in persuading their states to secede. Their capture was an important event, and Captain Wilkes found himself a national hero. The British, on the other hand, receiving the news some twelve days later when the *Trent* arrived in London, were affronted to the point of frenzy by this interference with the freedom of the seas. A few politicians may have wryly reflected that in the War of 1812 it had been America who protested at the seizure of British naval deserters from American ships and England who asserted her right to take them. But the situation in

1861 was serious, not funny. War hysteria made some Americans ready to take on the whole world and lose their country. Some British people were beginning to resent Northern industrial competition, while others were big purchasers of Southern cotton. There were many friends of the South in England and more who were willing to see the too-powerful American republic break into fragments. If slavery had not been banned in British dominions and generally regarded as barbaric in Europe, it is difficult to be certain that England would have remained neutral. Thus the fury of the English at the insult offered them by the *Trent* affair was no mere trifle. It was supported by a very dangerous minority who would be glad of an excuse to break up the Union.

A few facts and a few men averted war. The Atlantic cable had not yet been laid, so that diplomatic exchanges could go no faster than steamers could cross the Atlantic. This gave tempers time to cool. Charles Francis Adams, Lincoln's ambassador, imperturbably refused to make pronouncements until he knew his government's case, but lost no time in warning Seward what the results of obstinacy would be. Albert, the Prince Consort, who really decided what Queen Victoria would do, saw the folly of war. When a belligerent ultimatum drawn up by the British Cabinet appeared on the royal desk, the Prince was sickening for typhoid, which was to kill him two weeks later. On the last working day of his life he suggested alterations which would enable America to give way without undue humiliation. President Lincoln perceived that the country must release Mason and Slidell, not only because the Union could not win a war against the South allied with Britain, but also because America could not without a certain awkwardness uphold in 1861 what she had denied in 1812. By releasing the two Confederate envoys, America remained consistent and might make it awkward for Britain to reverse her position once more. Luckily it was not necessary for the Lincoln government to apologize to Britain, since

Captain Wilkes had acted without orders. All the same, the Mason-Slidell incident was a bitter pill for Lincoln to swallow because the country needed a success, however minor, and because he himself had approved the capture before he understood what it must mean. The Wilkes affair was soon forgotten by a nation busy with a major war, but the fruits of Lincoln's diplomacy endured. The Confederate envoys were never recognized, scored no official successes, and eventually returned home in despair.

# 6

# Little Mac

ONE OF THE ADVANTAGES which Lincoln possessed
as a war leader was a strong physique. A sleepless night
after Bull Run, which would have paralyzed his predeces-
sor, did not prevent him from deciding the very next day
on a new commander. Since Frémont in Missouri was
already causing problems, it was natural that Lincoln's
attention should be drawn to George B. McClellan who,
with headquarters in Cincinnati, controlled the operations
of Ohio, Indiana, Illinois, and the western parts of Virginia
and Pennsylvania. Action had been going on in West Virginia, where McClellan's forces had won a clear victory
only ten days before Bull Run. It is true that the numbers
of men engaged had been small and that the successes of
the campaign had actually been achieved by subordinate
commanders. But McClellan had left Cincinnati to lead his
troops in person and had claimed full credit for the results,
which was duly accorded to him by the War Department
and the press, neither of which had sent trained observers
with him.

George B. McClellan was a personable young man in his
mid-thirties, a West Point graduate just old enough to have

taken part in the Mexican War, where he had distinguished himself for bravery. In 1855, General Scott had
appointed him one of three officers sent to Europe to ob-
serve the lessons of the Crimean War. It is doubtful
whether the Americans were able to learn much from the
blunders of the combatants, but they also toured Europe,
visiting forts and installations in various countries. On his
return, Captain McClellan designed a cavalry saddle
which was adopted by the army. This mild distinction
might have led to further promotion had he not shortly
resigned to become chief engineer of the Illinois Central
Railroad.

Traveling around in the execution of his job, McClellan
became acquainted with Abraham Lincoln, who not only
used the railroad extensively on circuit or during political
campaigns, but was the holder of a free pass as one of the
railroad's lawyers. No friendship sprang up between the
two men, partly no doubt because the ambitious young
engineer did not bother to look beyond Lincoln's homely
dress and manners, but partly because they had different
political views. During the Lincoln-Douglas debates of
1858, Douglas was permitted to hire a special car and hitch
a cannon onto his train in order to fire salutes when he
pulled into a station. Whether or not McClellan had any
hand in arranging this favor, he certainly rode with Douglas from time to time, giving the impression that the railroad as a corporate group preferred the Little Giant to its
own lawyer traveling in the day-coach. Shortly afterwards,
McClellan moved to Cincinnati to become vice president
and later president of the Ohio and Mississippi Railroad.
He was thus in a perfect position to take command in Ohio
when the war broke out, and he was appointed Major
General by that state. His success in West Virginia was the
immediate cause of his selection to replace McDowell, but
his acquaintance with Lincoln in Illinois had probably
recommended him further. McClellan was an energetic
young man of small stature, good-looking, and with great

personal magnetism. His abilities were all on show and were considerable. Less than twenty-four hours after McDowell's defeat, Lincoln wired McClellan to turn over his command to someone else and come to Washington at once.

Few soldiers in their thirties have been summoned to rescue their country from disaster. Unfortunately McClellan's inner weakness was vanity, and the situation went to his head. Within twenty-four hours of his arrival he wrote to his wife: "I seem to have become the power of the land. I almost think that was I to win one whole success now I could become dictator or anything else that might please me—but nothing of that kind would please me—*therefore I won't be Dictator.*" Fortified by this virtuous refusal, he flung himself into the task of getting the army back into shape. It was unexpectedly easy, not merely because McClellan was a fine organizer, but also because the army itself was sorting things out. The straggling soldiers in the streets had nowhere to go but to their units. Militia officers who had taken refuge in comfortable hotels were only too anxious to resign their commands. The three-months' men were ready to go home; the three-year men were pouring in; the fortifications across the Potomac were held by steady troops, while the Confederates lacked ammunition and supplies for making an attack. Since for the moment problems lay in Washington rather than in the front lines, it was not unreasonable for McClellan to set up headquarters in town, through which he rode daily in full uniform, escorted by a flamboyant staff. This conduct, which had been resented in Frémont, caught the fancy of the soldiers on the Potomac. McClellan looked well on horseback and made boastful pronouncements with éclat. Bull Run had brought a reaction against the free-and-easy ways of militia troops. Three-year recruits, eager to become soldiers, did not claim to be as good as their general. McClellan was visible everywhere, getting credit for new supplies from the War Department; basic training carried out by McDow-

ell and other subordinate commanders; better junior officers, appointed not elected; and further improvements in
the fortifications. Meanwhile his self-confidence and
youthful energy enabled him to assert authority as against
the Commander-in-Chief, the General-in-Chief, and the
Secretary of War, all compromised by the miscalculations
which had produced Bull Run.

Since the new commander was expected to make military decisions, it was not surprising that he was shortly at
loggerheads with General Scott. Having been summoned
to take charge of an army, McClellan emphasized its role,
presenting a war plan which reduced Scott's strangling
operation to a defensive holding on the outer periphery of
the Confederacy while an enormous, well-trained army,
lavishly equipped and led by himself, would end the war
by taking Richmond. The enemy capital, so temptingly
near, offered an opportunity to get out of a long war, thus
avoiding irrevocable decisions about slavery. McClellan
soon found supporters in Congress, which was still sitting.
From the moment of his arrival he had been encouraged
by Lincoln to bypass the General-in-Chief and go straight
to the top. The President would never have made such a
mistake in a purely political situation, but he was fum-
blingly conscious that military affairs took place in a different world from the one he was used to.

Out of McClellan's vanity and Lincoln's indiscretion a
quarrel between McClellan and Scott rapidly developed. It
seemed these warriors could never agree on any point.
McClellan, for instance, was a perfectionist, one of that
difficult breed which waits to act until every contingency
has been provided for. This led him to exaggerate enemy
forces and minimize his own, to dismiss the army's entrenchments as inadequate, and to talk dramatically about
a threat to the safety of Washington which he alone could
avert—and then only if his slightest wish was immediately
granted. He had no patience with Scott's infirmities or
with his inability to see the situation in quite such a lurid

light. "He understands nothing, appreciates nothing," wrote the young general to his wife about the old one.

Scott for his part had little confidence in the brash opinions of a young man who had been a mere captain until the war jumped him up to Major General. Aware, however, that he was too old for his job and had not the physical strength for a quarrel with McClellan, Scott merely held out to prevent the young man from becoming his successor. He had his own eye on Henry W. Halleck, a scholarly officer who had written a popular military manual. Halleck, unfortunately, was in California, while McClellan was on the spot consolidating his position by large dinner parties which included political figures. When it became necessary to remove Frémont from St. Louis, Lincoln needed Halleck for that job, since there were not many experienced officers available. Hard-pressed on every side, Scott insisted on resigning, though he paid tribute to the distinguished kindness and courtesy of Lincoln, together with his patriotism, lack of prejudice, activity, and perseverance. The political backgrounds of Lincoln and Scott, their temperaments, careers, and breeding had been totally different; but each could recognize distinction in the other.

McClellan, backed by a powerful faction in Congress, was by now the only possible successor to Scott. Lincoln offered the appointment somewhat dubiously, speaking of the dual responsibility of being an army commander and General-in-Chief. McClellan reassured him in almost jaunty fashion, claiming confidently, "I can do it all." Thus on a pitch-dark, rainy morning in November the new General-in-Chief went out with his staff and a squadron of cavalry to see the old general off at the railroad station. To his wife he moralized on the pathetic spectacle of Scott's departure in language which served to emphasize his own triumph. The curtain was up, and he stood full in the center, no doubt of his success even entering his mind.

Cameron at the War Department proved an even easier target than Scott. Despite corruption so rampant that it was fast becoming a public scandal, the Secretary's achievements had been considerable. He had multiplied the forces of the country many times over, had directed the soldiers to definite theaters of war, and had armed, uniformed, and equipped them in a style which the Confederates were never to match. McClellan did not wish to remove Cameron from his job, but rather to put an end to general orders issued by the War Department which affected the army as a whole, including himself. He began to publish his own orders to cover administrative problems, while Cameron—open to much criticism and also compromised by the fiasco of Bull Run—did nothing to stop him. Thus the four men in active charge of the war were very shortly reduced to two—Lincoln and McClellan.

In his initial dealings with McClellan, Lincoln had too readily hoped for the commander he was later to find in General Grant, namely a man who could work out a strategy, lead an army, and win a war. Though as President he felt obliged to make judgments on both McClellan and his plans, he was in no hurry to criticize either. He welcomed his general with relief and took on himself a good deal of the burden of keeping in touch with him, ambling over to pay a call instead of requesting the busy general to wait on him. This habit soon became tiresome to McClellan, who was reorganizing an army while exercising supervision over commanders in areas as far distant as Missouri. He was also making contact with politicians who were not by any means the President's friends. Prominent among these was that brilliant Pittsburgh lawyer, Edwin M. Stanton, a Democrat like McClellan and Attorney General in the last months of Buchanan's administration.

Stanton, like the young General-in-Chief of the Army, had had some contact with Lincoln in the 1850s which had not left a favorable impression on him. Retained by the Illinois firm of Walter Manny in a famous commercial case, Stanton had met Lincoln in court as the local lawyer

engaged to support him. He had taken one outraged look
at the peculiar figure clad in a long, loose coat marked with
stains of perspiration and crumpled by all the vicissitudes
of life on the judicial circuit and had refused to associate
with such an ape. Lincoln had taken his insulting rejection
without protest and had stayed three days to listen to the
case with the object of finding out whether high-priced
Eastern lawyers were as good as they claimed to be. He had
come to the conclusion that they were and had confided to
a friend that he was going home to make a more thorough
study of law.

Evidently it had been a shock to Stanton to meet this
uncouth provincial lawyer as President of the United
States a few years later. Unlike Lincoln, Stanton was a man
who pursued vendettas and had a considerable taste for
intrigue. As a member of Buchanan's Cabinet he had privately passed information to Seward, taking for granted
that the New York Senator was the future leader of the
Lincoln administration. He had joined Southerners in
Washington in jeering at Lincoln, and even after six
months of war was accustomed to refer to him as "the
original gorilla." Such being McClellan's choice of a
friend, it is not surprising to hear him say in those revealing letters to his wife that he had taken refuge in Stanton's
house "to dodge all enemies in the shape of browsing Presidents, etc."

Stanton and McClellan came together because they were
both Democrats who had greeted the election of Lincoln
as a political disaster. It was less excusable for the General-
in-Chief to seek intimacy with the extreme radical faction
of Republicans in Congress. Such men, lukewarm about
Lincoln because of his toleration of slavery in the Southern
states and his conciliatory attitude toward rebels, were
anxious to push the war in a spirit of vengeance. Their
only common ground with McClellan was that both parties had profited from Bull Run and both sought power.

If Lincoln thought that his commander was keeping

strange company, he said nothing about it and continued to show every sign of confidence in him. One evening, however, he called on McClellan, accompanied by Seward and presidential secretary John Hay. Lincoln was told that the general was attending the wedding of a young man on his staff. Hearing that he was expected home shortly, the President decided to wait and was ushered into one of the downstairs rooms leading off the front hall. Presently the general arrived and Lincoln heard him being informed that the President was waiting to see him. McClellan made an inaudible reply and went upstairs, presumably to wash his hands. He did not reappear. After a considerable delay a servant was sent to find him and returned with the information that he had gone to bed. It was possible to suppose that McClellan had been the worse for too much champagne, but even on those grounds the insult was not excusable. Lincoln showed no sign of personal resentment then or in the future, but he did appreciate that it was not right to expose the President to such treatment. From that time, whenever he needed to see the general, he sent for McClellan. Relations, though outwardly cordial, were less intimate thereafter.

Even before Scott retired, the country was looking for action. Confederate General Joseph E. Johnston had moved forward to Fairfax after Bull Run and had actually planted an outpost on Munson's Hill, less than ten miles from Washington. This was a considerable inconvenience to Federal troops covering the Potomac and an insult as well. McClellan gave no orders to clear the enemy out, and a reconnaissance raid undertaken without instructions by Colonel Taylor of the Third New Jersey Volunteers was not pushed home. At the end of September, 1861, when the Confederates withdrew of their own accord, it was discovered that there had been no entrenchments and that the cannon which had protected the lines were logs painted black. The news caused considerable uproar, but McClellan gave no signs of being anxious to redeem his reputation. He was still talking of the "great battle in front of us," but the only one he was actually waging was his battle with General Scott. His appraisal of the military situation was gloomy. He had managed to multiply the Confederate forces by five, claiming that Johnston had a hundred and fifty thousand men around Centerville, while he, McClellan, though in command of more than that number, had little over seventy-five thousand in hand for an advance. Newspaper analysts alternately besought their readers to be patient or prophesied startling events in the near future; but instead of receiving news of action, the expectant public was informed that the soldiers were building log huts inside their entrenchments to winter in.

Congress, which had adjourned its special session, reassembled in the regular way in December and gave such emphatic voice to discontent that Bates, Lincoln's elderly Attorney General, spoke to the President in no uncertain terms about his duty to know what sort of army he had and what his generals intended. This was all very well for Bates to say; but Lincoln had already written to Halleck, his general in Missouri, and also to Buell, commanding in Kentucky, and had been answered that they were making preparations, but apparently with no idea of taking the offensive soon and no understanding of each other's problems. The United States Navy, it is true, was planning an expedition against New Orleans which was to be supported by a military force, but this was not intended to set out before spring. McClellan confided no plans to the President and shortly took to his bed with an attack of typhoid, paralyzing not only the Army of the Potomac, but also the office of the General-in-Chief. At his wits' end, Lincoln appealed to Montgomery Meigs, the Quartermaster-General, saying: "General, what shall I do? The people are impatient; Chase has no money, and he tells me he can raise no more; the General of the Army has typhoid fever. The bottom is out of the tub. What shall I do?"

Meigs suggested Lincoln consult McClellan's chief

subordinates, and a conference took place in the White House between them and Cabinet members. It had the effect of hastening the recovery of McClellan and inducing him to disclose a plan for moving on Richmond by way of the Yorktown Peninsula instead of making a frontal attack on Johnston's forces around Manassas. This was at least progress, though Lincoln raised pertinent objections, asking whether the movement would not consume more money and time while giving no better prospect of success than a direct attack. It would also be more difficult to extricate the army in case of defeat, he pointed out. His comments reveal that Lincoln's inspired common sense was beginning to give him a good general grasp of strategy and of the problems that came within his range. He left it to McClellan, for instance, to claim, mistakenly, that the Peninsula roads were better and the terrain more suitable for campaigning. Lincoln's objections had no weight with the general, and it is useless to inquire after the event which one was right. Lincoln gave his consent to McClellan's plan because it was impossible for him to insist that the general act on a scheme which he did not believe in. Unfortunately the President was not convinced by the arguments mustered in favor of the Peninsular campaign, so that his support of McClellan lacked conviction.

This rift between Lincoln and his top general developed at a moment when newspapers and politicians were wondering openly whether McClellan were not too ardent a Democrat to press the war. Congress, angered by the unfortunate results of a skirmish between Federal and Confederate troops across the Potomac, had appointed a committee of both Houses to inquire into the conduct of the war. This committee, dominated by the radical faction of the Republican Party, saw the struggle in terms of an abolitionist crusade and adopted as its heroes men of the type of Frémont, recently removed from St. Louis on account of his anti-slavery manifesto. The temporary alliance between the radicals and McClellan had lasted long enough to make the latter General-in-Chief, but was rapidly being broken up by McClellan's insistence that his army was still not ready to move. Generals Buell and Halleck in the West were also professional soldiers who were reluctant to make an advance. Politicians and newspaper strategists, silenced for a time by Bull Run, soon began to say that West Point men saw war as a game of maneuvers to be played against their classmates in command of the Southern armies. Rising discontent brought pressure on Lincoln, who was well aware that the army depended on volunteers and that the Treasury could not raise money if the business community lost faith in the way the war was run.

By the time that Congress assembled in December, 1861, critics had found a focus in a fierce attack on Cameron. Nobody trusted him, and the soaring profits of contractors had become a public scandal. Lincoln was politically shrewd enough to replace the War Secretary with a Democrat, thus strengthening his presidential claim to lead the supporters of Douglas as well as his own. Doubtless, however, because he expected disapproval, Lincoln did not consult the Cabinet as a whole before offering the position to Edwin M. Stanton, who had insulted him, who had encouraged McClellan to despise him, and who called Lincoln "the original gorilla." Ever since the beginning of the Lincoln administration, Stanton had ingratiated himself with all those who, though supporting the war, disliked the President. He was in consequence acceptable to Wade of Ohio, Chandler of Michigan, Julian of Indiana, and the other radicals who dominated the Congressional Committee on the Conduct of the War. It seems probable that Stanton had also gained the support of Seward, who still looked on his colleagues as junior officers and interfered a good deal with affairs outside his department. He was agreeable to Chase, the strong anti-slavery man in the Cabinet, who looked on himself as Lincoln's successor. So close was Stanton's relationship with McClellan that he actually asked the general whether he should accept Lincoln's offer and was encouraged to do so because McClellan thought it would be most helpful to have a really firm friend in the War Department.

McClellan's illusion lasted little more than a week. Stanton's low opinion of Lincoln was genuine, but his friendships were only useful to give him the power that he craved. The new Secretary of War was not a firm friend to anyone but himself. He was, however, a devoted defender of the Union, and an incorruptible man with an almost unlimited capacity for work. He lost no time in taking over all functions which he considered properly his. From the beginning, Lincoln had a casual attitude toward his Cabinet, not even bothering at first to set a regular time for its meetings. Seward's meddling with affairs outside his department had seemed helpful in the emergency, especially because of the defects of Cameron. The censorship of news reports had gravitated somehow to the Department of State. Similarly, the General-in-Chief possessed the military telegraph office through which reports from generals came in. Stanton lost no time in transferring both to the War Department, choosing a moment when McClellan was absent to seize the telegraph records and install them on the second floor of the War Office. From here Secretary Stanton issued only what news he considered suitable to generals, newspapers, or politicians. It is true that the President had unlimited right of access, but even he had no telegraph in the executive mansion. It accordingly became Lincoln's practice to walk over to the War Department in order to look at telegrams as they came in, crossing the White House grounds by a public footpath leading to a side door of the War Department, an unpretentious building on Seventeenth Street. Since the path wound between bushes and trees, and Lincoln strolled down it unprotected at any hour of the day or night, he was urged to have a guard of soldiers, but resisted the notion as a restraint on his liberty quite foreign to his nature.

A serious cause of friction with McClellan was that Stanton was not disposed to recognize the claim of the General-in-Chief to issue orders which Stanton considered the prerogative of the War Department. Moreover, the general's unwillingness to take the offensive was the last quality with which Stanton was prepared to sympathize. The new Secretary of War had no more military experience than Lincoln, but he would not admit that abilities which had served him so well in law and politics were insufficient for managing a war. He did not aspire to lead armies, but he thought he knew pretty well how they ought to be directed.

Whether under Stanton's influence or in response to congressional pressure, Lincoln was induced to publish a formal order to all armies to move on the enemy on Washington's Birthday, 1862. Nothing came of this attempt to force a campaign to develop. McClellan's movement to the Yorktown Peninsula would take more time, while the western armies set things in motion as soon as possible. In January, General Thomas, commanding a division of Buell's army, won a decisive little victory in Kentucky which opened the road to Tennessee and exposed Confederate weakness along the Cumberland and Tennessee rivers. General Halleck in St. Louis was by no means an admirer of that Frémont appointee, Ulysses Grant, still commanding in Cairo—but he did suggest that Grant, in cooperation with gunboats under Flag Officer Foote, might see what he could do about capturing Fort Henry, the Confederate stronghold on the Tennessee. Grant and Foote found Fort Henry easy prey and moved across to the Cumberland in hopes of capturing Fort Donelson as well. This proved a harder nut to crack, but Grant was successful, electrifying the country by his reply to a request for terms: "No terms except an unconditional and immediate surrender can be accepted. I propose to move immediately upon your works."

These stirring victories, as welcome to the Union as rain

after a drought, contrasted with the failure of McClellan, who had undertaken to drive the enemy from the upper Potomac, where the Confederates still controlled a section of the Baltimore and Ohio Railroad. The general's plans depended on a pontoon bridge which was to rest on barges built lower downstream and towed up into position. No sooner was the movement begun than it was discovered that these barges were six inches too long to pass through the locks of the Potomac. The advance had to be abandoned, and Lincoln lost his temper for one of the few times in his life, telling General Marcy, McClellan's Chief of Staff, that if he had wished to know whether a boat would go through a hole or a lock, common sense should have taught him to go and measure it.

His exasperation was fortified by that of Stanton, who had emphasized the deficiencies of McClellan by a ringing message of congratulation to Grant. Lincoln was thus encouraged to criticize McClellan's plan to shift his army to the Peninsula by way of Annapolis instead of forcing the Confederates to abandon their blockade of the lower Potomac. Lincoln said that the march to Annapolis would look like a confession of weakness which would not be understood by the country at large. When a majority of McClellan's division leaders sustained their general at a council of war, the President interfered further, publishing a general order which divided the Army of the Potomac into five corps and appointed as their generals four officers who had shared his own point of view and only one who had upheld McClellan. This was distinctly hard on McClellan, who had for some time been resisting the formation of army corps because his senior division commanders were generals like McDowell whom he had not appointed himself. Lincoln followed up this blow by another general order forbidding the army to depart without leaving behind it a force which not only McClellan, but also the corps commanders, considered adequate for the defense of Washington.

The very day after publication of this last order, Confederate General Joseph E. Johnston relinquished his blockade of the lower Potomac as part of a movement evacuating his lines and falling back across the Rappahannock. McClellan, whose reluctance to make a frontal attack had led him to exaggerate the enemy's strength, was compelled to march out and occupy Centerville, where observers found more painted logs and indications that Johnston's numbers were far inferior to his own. Lincoln took advantage of McClellan's absence from Washington to relieve him of his post as General-in-Chief, giving as his reason the fact that a general in command of an army advancing upon Richmond was in no position to supervise other theaters of war. No new General-in-Chief was appointed for the present, and generals were instructed to report to the War Department. Top decisions would be made by Lincoln himself—after consultation with the Secretary of War.

To do him justice, Edwin M. Stanton did not propose to direct armies without some military advice. Looking around for a general who had never reported to McClellan as General-in-Chief, he summoned to Washington Ethan Allen Hitchcock, a semi-invalid retired general who was grandson and namesake of a Revolutionary hero. Hitchcock, who had never been greatly interested in his profession, had for years devoted himself to peculiar studies, such as an attempt to prove that Shakespeare, Dante, and the authors of the four Gospels had written in very far-fetched imagery about a philosophy of religion which was, to say the least, invisible in their works to the ordinary reader. Willing to do his best for the Union, though puzzled that he had anything to offer, Hitchcock accepted the position of military advisor to Lincoln and Stanton.

Unhappily for the general's peace of mind, the Secretary of War, who allowed himself no time for recreation and very little for sleep, suffered intensely from frayed nerves and would at intervals delight his enemies by losing all sense of proportion. The simple-minded Hitchcock was appalled to be suddenly offered command of the Army of the Potomac. "I am uncomfortable," he wrote in his diary, recording the unwelcome proposal. He was horrified by confidential revelations from Stanton that McClellan was an outright traitor to the Union cause and further distressed by an interview with Lincoln during which the President said that he was being urged to remove McClellan from command. In the circumstances, even offering advice was too much for Hitchcock's health. But when the elderly general sent in his resignation, Stanton implored him to remain because his departure would ruin the Secretary of War. Hitchcock burned his resignation, but soon confided to his diary that his advice was not taken and his salary was a waste of public money. Luckily his physical condition deteriorated so rapidly that he had to be given a leave of absence, which stretched out for six months, during which time Lincoln and Stanton found expert advice elsewhere.

This ridiculous episode reflects serious doubts, fostered by the radicals in Congress, whether McClellan really wished to win the war. He had only, his critics said, to depart for the Yorktown Peninsula, leaving Washington unprotected. Stonewall Jackson, in command of an army in the Shenandoah Valley, would come up and take the town. Its fall would be followed by French and English recognition of the Confederacy. Against their open opposition, it would be impossible for the Union to succeed. No serious historian really suspects that this was McClellan's intention, but it is at least fair to say that the general's vanity had led him to insist on a plan of his own choosing and to demand that every decision affecting it be left in his hands. It is useless to argue that if Lincoln had sustained his general, McClellan would have taken Richmond, sparing the country three more years of war and most of the tragedy of the Reconstruction era. Whatever Lincoln did in that spring of 1862 had to be imperfect because his general, his Secretary of War, and the most influential committee of Congress were incapable of working together. Since the final responsibility was his, he had to consider the fact that the war could be lost by the taking of Washington, whereas it would not necessarily be won by the taking of Richmond.

Unfortunately for McClellan, his virtues as an organizer and his failures as a commander both tended to produce the same result. The larger and better-equipped his army became, and the more he lost reputation, the stronger grew the pressure to use parts of his force for operations which bore little relation to a speedy end to the war. The size of the army to be left on the upper Potomac covering Jackson in the Shenandoah Valley was not decided by McClellan. Its general, Banks, a radical favorite, was not made subject to McClellan's orders. Another operation very much on the President's mind was an attempt to deliver the Union supporters of East Tennessee from Confederate occupation. This Appalachian district resembled West Virginia, which it adjoined, and was an area where slavery had never flourished. Frémont, very much a radical hero, could get into no trouble over slavery there and could be given a German division from McClellan's army because most Germans were abolitionists. Besides, if Frémont chose to turn on Stonewall Jackson, he and Banks might have the Confederates between a pair of pincers.

The council of war held at Lincoln's insistence to decide on the minimum force to cover Washington had agreed that the Potomac forts should be garrisoned and that a covering force of twenty-five thousand good troops was also required. Unfortunately, there were several ways of doing the necessary arithmetic. McClellan counted the army of Banks as the major portion of the twenty-five thousand. This force, though it covered the Shenandoah Valley, was in no position to protect the capital from an attack by Confederate General Joseph E. Johnston from the direction of the Rappahannock. McClellan contended that Johnston must withdraw to cover Richmond; but until he did so, there could be no certainty that he would not simply decide to take Washington instead. By the time that Lincoln and Stanton had discovered how McClellan's arrangements worked in practice, the general had moved with three-quarters of his army to the Peninsula, expecting the final corps, that of McDowell, to follow at once. His sense of betrayal can be imagined when McDowell's corps was retained by Lincoln's order and removed from his command. It is true that he had about three times the enemy's numbers; but—relying on exaggerated gross totals collected for him by the detective Allan Pinkerton—McClellan failed to perceive that, just as his own gross totals were widely different from his numbers present for duty, Confederate lists bore little relation to the men actually in the line.

In practice, McClellan's notion of warfare was to prepare such overwhelming strength that the enemy would fall back without a pitched battle. What he said, however, was more belligerent. When he came up against the enemy line at Yorktown on April 4, he reported, "I expect to fight tomorrow." What he actually did was to send for his siege train and spend four weeks siting his guns and writing that he needed McDowell's corps. By the time the Confederates retired from the position, he had received one division from McDowell containing about twelve thousand men, for whom at the moment he had no use. He notified Stanton that he was now in possession of Yorktown, that his success had been brilliant, and that he would push the enemy to the wall. In fact, he was not organized for pursuit, and rains were beginning to turn the Peninsular roads into mud.

Lincoln and Stanton, far more energetic than their commander, had made up McDowell's loss of a division by transferring to him one from Banks—relying on the army of Frémont, which was now assembling in the mountains, to tie down Stonewall Jackson by threatening his flank. No sooner was Yorktown taken than the civilian directors of the war perceived that Norfolk was now untenable by the Confederates. They came down in person to Fortress Monroe to arrange an expedition with General Wool, who was in command there. Finding themselves about thirty miles from McClellan, they invited him to come down for a discussion. He replied that he could not be spared for an instant. In other words, their chief general was hardly on speaking terms with the Secretary of War and highly suspicious of the Commander-in-Chief.

Despite his very considerable interference with the plans of McClellan, Lincoln was genuinely anxious for his success. Early in April he had written to the general: "I beg to assure you that I have never written to you, or spoken to you, in greater kindness of feeling than now, nor with a fuller purpose to sustain you, so far as in my most anxious judgment I consistently can. *But you must act.*" This pleading tone reveals not only the pressures on Lincoln, but his knowledge that the general might imagine his Commander-in-Chief hoped he would fail or was even conspiring to bring his failure about.

McClellan's distrust of the government, though in part justified, had developed out of his own character during his long delay in Washington. Despite his refusal to become dictator, he had acted less as the servant of the government than as its would-be master. When Stephen A. Douglas had died and his followers had rallied to support the Union, they had not forgotten that they belonged to the party which had long held the North and South together. In general, Democrats wanted to fight in order to show the South that it could not maintain a separate existence. Their aim, however, was not clear-cut victory, but the basis for a new compromise. It was natural for McClellan to defend Washington, but to doubt whether a smashing victory or a long occupation of northern Virginia would persuade the South to return to its former status as partner in a federal union. McClellan's desire to avoid a battle and to take Richmond by demonstrating his overwhelming strength made sense politically as well as being congenial to his nature. As strategy, however, such a course could only have been adopted by a man disposed to ignore the increasing bitterness created by the war, as well as the speed with which military operations in the South were eroding slavery. Lincoln had shown far more realism in his message to Congress of January, 1862, which asked for resolutions promising support of any plan a state might offer to free its slaves in return for compensation. He hoped that reason might prevail in this matter because buying freedom for the Negro at almost any price would be cheaper than paying for a war. Unfortunately slave states had no use for the Negro when freed and did not feel that compensation would solve this problem.

Far more extreme than the position of Lincoln was that of men, North or South, who perceived the conflict as a total war whose only possible endings were triumph or extinction. Simple characters like Robert E. Lee saw the war in this way. Northern radicals, with whom Stanton was soon allied, held similar opinions. Resisting such views, McClellan in the course of creating an army had gathered about him congenial officers. His Chief of Staff, General Marcy, was also his father-in-law. Dislike of the government seeped down through the Army of the Potomac from the top, becoming a factor in the promotion of younger officers. The enthusiasm of private soldiers, which had been deliberately whipped up to build morale into the army, took on a political point of view from the mere process of their being so long in Washington without major attrition or replacement. To the soldiers, Little Mac was their general, and his difficulties were caused by government interference.

It was easy for McClellan to play on his army's suspicions of the government in order to find excuses for his own management of the Peninsular campaign. The absence of McDowell's corps was a fruitful grievance. By the time the Federal army was established on the Chick-

alhominy, a few miles from Richmond, the Confederates
had perforce evacuated their lines on the Rappahannock
and concentrated them in front of their capital. Lincoln
and Stanton moved McDowell forward to Fredericksburg,
only fifty-five miles north of Richmond, and gave permission for him to march south and fall on Joseph E. Johnston's flank. McDowell was even to come once more under
McClellan's command, with the sole proviso that he should
not be moved from a position from which he could return
to Washington in an emergency. Far from being grateful,
McClellan wrote to his wife: "Those hounds in Washington are after me again. Stanton is without exception the
vilest man I ever knew or heard of."

McDowell's movement south, which had been slightly
delayed by the arrival of Shields's division transferred to
him from Banks's army in the Shenandoah Valley, was
scheduled for May 24. On the twenty-third, however,
alarming news came in to Washington. Stonewall Jackson,
reinforced to about sixteen thousand men, had marched
down the Shenandoah Valley and, by getting his army
over a rugged pass in Massanutten Mountain, had appeared on the eastern side of it instead of the western,
where Banks awaited him in Strasburg. So completely had
he escaped out of Banks's vision that the first notice of his
movement was his fierce attack on Front Royal, situated at
the junction of the two branches of the Shenandoah and
their parallel valleys. Front Royal, held only by a thousand
troops, had no chance. Jackson obtained prisoners and
booty, together with an opportunity to cut across onto the
turnpike north of Strasburg, which connected Banks to
Winchester, the depot for his army.

Banks, who had only about eight thousand men left with
him after sending detachments to garrison Front Royal
and reinforce McDowell, did the only possible thing. He
retired at a speed which nearly resembled precipitous
flight. He got away and managed to cross the Potomac, but
it was a close run which left his little army exhausted.

Jackson, moving toward Harpers Ferry, was suddenly within striking distance of Washington with no army barring the way.

Jackson's raid gave Lincoln and Stanton a chance to maneuver with armies which they had previously placed on the map, and it is instructive to see how they acted after the first moments of panic were over. The defense of the capital itself proved fairly easy. The army of Banks was not demoralized by fear of the enemy, but because it had been given no chance to turn on him. Jackson was not in sufficient strength to break through to the city, the more so as his men were ragged and shoeless after their tremendous march and, though he had captured great quantities of supplies, these were not necessarily tailored to his needs. He was in haste to retreat, while Lincoln and Stanton were determined that he should not get away. Their theory of war, exactly contrary to McClellan's, consisted of the notion that the enemy's army—not his lines, his capital, or his supplies—was the true target. Immediately they sent word to McDowell to cancel his southern movement and march with all speed to Strasburg so that if possible he might intercept Jackson's retreat, or at any rate pursue him up the Shenandoah Valley turnpike. To make sure that he understood the urgency of the movement, Secretary of the Treasury Chase, McDowell's particular friend and patron, traveled out from Washington to explain the position. Shields's division, which had just finished the tedious march from Strasburg to join McDowell, was started back at once, while another division followed as soon as the road was clear of Shields's troops. Shields himself was taken back to Washington for a fuller appreciation of the news received by the War Department, while the routine details of getting his men on the road were left to his subordinates.

The meeting which presumably took place in the War Department between Lincoln and Shields had a strange background. Shields, a fierce little Irish Democrat who had opposed Lincoln politically many years back, had been lampooned in some comical letters signed "Aunt Becca" which had appeared in the *Springfield Journal.* Pinning these on Lincoln, Shields had challenged him to a duel, not realizing that the most offensive of the series had been composed by a pair of giggling girls, one of whom was Mary Todd, whom Lincoln hoped to marry. The duel was staved off, and Shields shortly thereafter left Illinois to make his career elsewhere—but the War Between the States had a way of turning up people in unexpected guises. The problem now presented to Shields was, as McDowell aptly put it, one of legs. Could the legs of the Federals outstrip those of the men who marched with Jackson?

While these preparations were going on in Washington and Fredericksburg, another message went out from the War Department instructing Frémont to march for Harrisonburg at the head of the Shenandoah Valley—so that if Jackson were to slip through the Strasburg trap, he could be hustled along the Valley turnpike with McDowell's men hard at his heels, only to be faced at the upper end by Frémont's men astride his avenue of escape. Frémont was fifty miles from Harrisonburg in a small mountain town called Franklin, where he was still trying to organize his army. The roads in every direction were bad, but they were worst toward Harrisonburg, where Jackson had done some work to make them impassable. It would be easier, Frémont thought, to move on Strasburg, though this was a great deal further from him and two days' march nearer to Jackson. Apparently, however, Frémont was not thinking in terms of destroying Jackson, but of rescuing Banks, to whom Strasburg was nearer than Harrisonburg. Accordingly, Frémont made up his mind to use his own judgment, wired the War Department that he was setting out at once, and plunged north instead of south, moving along mountain roads which were not served by telegraph, so that for the next few days his contacts involved sending or receiving messages from distant places. He did not have his men nearly so well in hand as Shields or McDowell, or enough sense of urgency to explain the "question of legs" to them. In addition he encountered terrible rains which turned the unpaved roads into watercourses soon churned by the army into mud. The upshot was that both he and Shields were late at Strasburg. Jackson, though escaping only by the skin of his teeth, made good speed up the Valley turnpike, blowing bridges behind him, while the Shenandoah, swollen by recent rains, held back his pursuers. Attempts to cut him off foundered on muddy side roads, and Lincoln and Stanton called off pursuit. The armies were getting too far from Washington and also from McClellan, still encamped across the Chickahominy.

Lincoln and Stanton had demonstrated that around Washington and where they understood the terrain, they could direct armies. They had no recourse, however, against the arbitrary decisions of a man like Frémont. This weakness was likely to increase with the distance between themselves and the generals in receipt of their orders. Evidently there were two problems for the Commander-in-Chief, namely what orders to send out and how to get them executed. It was, in fact, expedient to have a General-in-Chief whose expert judgment would in itself have weight with distant commanders. This could hardly be McClellan, who was still on the Chickahominy after an inconclusive battle which, though he did not yet know it, had tipped the scales against him. The Confederate General Joseph E. Johnston had been wounded, and as his replacement Jefferson Davis had appointed Robert E. Lee.

# 7

## The Lincolns
## in the White House

So quickly had the Sumter crisis arisen and so dire had its consequences been that it is hard to keep in mind the fact that Lincoln, his wife, Mary, and his two younger sons had moved into the White House only a few weeks before the outbreak of war. To Willie and Tad the whole situation was great fun. They had the run of a large house, the attention of guards, cooks, gardeners, and other servants, subject only to the supervision of tutors whom they found it fairly easy to get rid of. Tad shortly acquired a pair of goats and a goat cart. Nobody objected if he drove it indoors or harnessed his team to a chair and let it drag him through the state reception rooms. No doubt the damage caused by a pair of goats seemed trivial beside the depredations of people at the President's receptions, who spat tobacco juice on the floor, cut lace out of the curtains for pincushion covers, or even removed squares of carpet for souvenirs. The boys' father, though he never objected when they burst into his office, was too busy to concern himself with what they did. Their mother, more aware that they lacked control, was struggling with personal frustrations. Tad and Willie had everything for the asking, from goat carts to cookies in the kitchen. It would be too much to say that they were popular with busy servants or with visitors to the White House, but they had their father's unaffected manner and chatted merrily with everyone.

Very different was the situation of Mary Lincoln, who had come to Washington with a number of preconceived notions. She had determined that it was proper for her to lead the world of fashion, to establish a salon, and to influence her husband, whom she thought too tolerant for his own good. Well-educated and brought up to consider herself a member of one of the first families in her hometown, it never occurred to her that her manners were provincial, even if her learning was not. Nor had she reckoned with the malice of newspapers unfavorable to Lincoln and eager to criticize his family. Least of all had she expected the competition of a lady who had cherished hopes of being mistress of the White House. Kate Chase, daughter of the Secretary of the Treasury, was a much younger woman than Mary Lincoln, a recognized beauty, and just as ambitious for her father as he was for himself. Kate had acted as hostess for Salmon P. Chase when he had been Governor of Ohio and was already familiar with many political figures. Mary, on the other hand, was too anxious to please, too pretentious, and far too easily offended. She liked flattery and did not know how to make friends with people who were not prepared to offer it.

The outbreak of war, if anything, strengthened Mary Lincoln's resolve to become a notable hostess, since it gave her an additional motive for backing her husband and keeping the Presidency in the public eye. Besides, the division of the country had been a personal tragedy for her, since her numerous Kentucky family was secessionist. Nothing could impair her loyalty to her husband, but it was hard to be abandoned by those on whose affection she had counted. Her reaction was to play her chosen part more magnificently than ever. Lincoln was too busy to

discourage her aspirations and even sympathized with
them after a fashion. Always punctilious in discharging his
ceremonial duties, he spent much time reviewing troops,
receiving visitors, holding regular levees, and presiding at
state dinners. He was proud of his wife's social poise and
seems to have listened to complaints, if she made any, with
an absent ear.

The furnishings of the White House were in a disgrace-
ful condition, in part because Buchanan had been a bache-
lor and careless about domestic matters, and partly because
the sovereign people felt it their privilege to do what damage they pleased to the national possessions. Congress before adjourning had been forced to make provision for a
complete refurbishing and had appropriated the enormous
sum of twenty thousand dollars, which was at Mary Lincoln's disposal to spend as she pleased. Lincoln's salary of
twenty-five thousand dollars already seemed astronomical
to a woman who had kept house on far less in Springfield
and was no longer paying household expenses. It is not
surprising that money went to Mary's head, but it is certainly shocking to find her console herself for every frus-
tration by spending.

Not until May was Mary able to go to New York, but
her excitement seems only to have mounted with the delay.
Shopkeepers were anxious to give her credit, and the thrill
of buying enabled her to ignore sarcastic comments in the
press. Eleven hundred dollars did not seem too much for
a dinner service of Haviland china emblazoned with the
arms of the United States. Indeed, she could not resist a
second set with her own initials, which she did not put
down to Lincoln's account, but to the nation's. Fine lace
curtains, custom-made carpets, extravagant hand-printed
wallpaper were irresistible. Amid so many domestic pur-
chases a few clothes for herself seemed necessary. Protest-
ing economy, Mrs. Lincoln paid a thousand dollars for a
cashmere shawl. Back in Washington with the agreeable
prospect of more such expeditions to Philadelphia or New

York, Mary hired workmen to modernize and repair the White House. Closed stoves gave better heat than open fireplaces. Gaslight replaced candles. The endless task of expressing her taste down to the smallest detail went on for months. Bills came in slowly, and Mary had soon lost all sense of proportion. Lincoln, who ought to have checked her, hardly noticed his surroundings and had no idea what luxuries cost. If he gave Mary's expenditures a thought, he merely supposed that twenty thousand dollars was an inexhaustible sum, far more than she needed or would know how to use. He had money troubles of his own, but they were concerned with arming, clothing, feeding, and paying armies of men.

By the end of 1861 when the bills were in, it was revealed to Mary that she had overspent by about seven thousand dollars. In panic she appealed to the Commissioner of Public Buildings to tell Lincoln that appropriations were always overrun and that things cost much more than he might expect. In tears she begged the Commissioner to help her out of this difficulty, which she swore would be her last. The Commissioner went to the President and found him both furious and bewildered. "It would stink in the nostrils of the American People," Lincoln exploded, "to have it said that the President of the United States had approved a bill overrunning an appropriation for *flub dubs*, when the soldiers cannot get blankets." He would pay the debt out of his own pocket, he insisted. As for the White House, it was furnished well enough when they moved in —better than any house they had ever lived in. Brought up in a log cabin, Lincoln was honestly unable to see that the state of the White House furnishings had mattered.

Lincoln did not pay out of his own pocket, and it would be interesting to know what arguments were employed to persuade him not to do so. The sum was buried in an appropriations bill in the next session and paid by the nation, presumably to avoid scandal. We also do not know what Lincoln said to his wife on this occasion. It did not put an end to her spending, however, which had by now become a mania. It merely drove her debts underground, forcing Mary into dubious maneuvers, such as discharging White House servants and then demanding that their salaries be paid to herself. These led to scenes with Lincoln's secretaries, who soon dubbed her "the Hell-cat." When confidential agents talk thus about the wife of their employer, troubles have arisen which sooner or later the husband cannot ignore.

Almost equally awkward was Mary Lincoln's failure to make friends among what she thought of as her social set. Critical, jealous, and demanding among her equals, she found it easier to talk to her housekeeper or her dressmaker, a mulatto called Elizabeth Keckley. There were male servants also with whom she became on confidential terms. These did not readily give offense and were happy to smooth over her little difficulties. Insensibly she fell into the power of John Watt, head groundsman at the White House, who was known to be corrupt and had been on the verge of dismissal before the Lincolns arrived. How to get rid of Watt became a problem, particularly since he had indiscreet letters from Mary Lincoln in his possession. He, however, was a servant, vulnerable to a careful mixture of threats and promises. The adventurers who attended Mrs. Lincoln's salons, taking her measure, and using her for their own ends, were more disturbing. She had apparently, save in the single case of Abraham Lincoln, no judgment of character. She trusted people whose reputation was not good and who were ready to turn on her the instant she ceased to be of use. Though extremely, and often astutely, critical of those who had not sought her favor, she was unable to look objectively at anyone she liked. Increasingly she became a target for gossip.

It is greatly to the credit of Mary Lincoln that in the midst of all her difficulties she never lost sight of the fact that her husband was bearing an almost intolerable burden which she was able by judicious management to lighten.

He enjoyed quiet evenings with his family and perhaps an intimate friend. Telling his little stories and laughing heartily when he came to the point, he forgot the Presidency for a moment or two and seemed to relax. He was late to meals. He did not mind what he ate. He hurried away to keep an appointment. Yet by unremitting, conscious effort over the years Mary Lincoln was of enormous help to him. She did not boast of it, nor did he make a particular show of his affection. By both, however, the bond was deeply felt and never broken.

Early in 1862, about the time of Mary's financial difficulties, she had also managed to involve herself in a nasty little scandal. James Gordon Bennett's paper, the New York *Herald,* had printed part of Lincoln's January message to Congress before it had been delivered. Congressional investigation pinned the blame on a so-called Chevalier Wikoff, who was one of the more dubious members of Mary's circle and also acted as a paid spy for the New York *Herald.* Wikoff admitted guilt, but went to prison for contempt of Congress rather than name his informant, who was widely believed to have been Mary Lincoln. Her reputation was officially saved by John Watt, her favorite White House servant, who stated that he had read the document left lying on Lincoln's desk and, being blessed with almost total recall, had been able to repeat large sections of it verbatim to Wikoff. The affair blew over, but not without a rumor that Lincoln had gone to the Capitol in person to implore the Republicans on the Judiciary Committee to keep his wife's name out of the scandal.

Whether this was true or not, there is no doubt that Mary's conduct was troublesome to her husband. Lincoln genuinely appreciated his wife's devotion and was proud of her social poise, but he had not the time or the interest in women's affairs to give her guidance. Probably he never had been able to control her hysterical outbursts and had failed to perceive that under these eruptions lay something dark and terrible. There seems no doubt that Mary felt many tensions which she did not know how to control; but her nature, to some extent at least, was resilient. Early in 1862, with these unpleasant episodes behind her, she was able to concentrate on realizing her social ambitions. The redecoration of the White House was now finished. Her court of flatterers gave her needed reassurance. It was time to put an end once and for all to the pretensions of Miss Kate Chase, whom she had seen with her own eyes holding unofficial court at the President's receptions. Mary sent out invitation cards for a select party of five hundred at the White House on February 5. At any time this occasion would have received a bad press because all social functions at the White House except for the formal state dinners were traditionally open to the public. Naturally people who had not received invitation cards were indignant, and hurt feelings were only partially assuaged by Lincoln who, remarking peaceably that he did not "fancy" the "pass business," insisted on some extra cards being sent out.

Further than this he would not interfere. Mary Lincoln, whose mail was sifted for her and who preferred reading the fulsome flatteries of the New York *Herald* to anything more astringent, probably never saw the response of Senator Ben Wade of Ohio to her invitation. "Are the President and Mrs. Lincoln aware that there is a civil war? If they are not, Mr. and Mrs. Wade are, and for that reason decline to participate in feasting and dancing." Senator Wade, very powerful in Congress, was one of the leaders of the Committee on the Conduct of the War, which was making political trouble for Mary's husband.

In single-minded pursuit of her ambition, Mary Lincoln gave point to the Senator's criticism by plunging once more into insane extravagance. The best caterer in New York came down with a great retinue of confectioners and cooks to toil for days producing huge sugary centerpieces and preparing elaborate dishes which demanded nearly a ton of game and ham, not to mention gallons of whipped-cream desserts and champagne punch. In deference to Queen Victoria, now in mourning for the death of the Prince Consort, Mary determined to dress in black and white. There was nothing else to suggest mourning in her low-cut white satin dress spread out over a wide crinoline and shaped into a train behind. It was lavishly trimmed with black lace; artificial flowers in black and white adorned her headdress and formed a corsage. Mary liked to display her plump white arms and shoulders with a freedom which critics thought unsuitable for a woman over forty. It seems to have been on this occasion that, when his wife paraded for him, Lincoln gave an appreciative whistle. "Phew! Our cat has a long tail tonight." He added gently, "Mother, it is my opinion, if some of that tail was nearer the head, it would be in better style." Mary, who had taught him all he ever knew about feminine apparel, was unlikely to spare a thought for her husband's criticism.

People grumbled, but they came to Mary's party, which went off in tremendous style. Her pleasure at her success was spoiled by anxiety over eleven-year-old Willie, who had come down with a fever. There was nothing feigned about the deep devotion of Lincoln and his wife to their boys, and both parents left their guests several times in the evening to visit Willie. In the ensuing days Mary lost interest in the repercussions of her famous party as Willie grew seriously and then dangerously ill. It seems most probable that he had caught typhoid like the General-in-Chief of the army and that both were victims of defective Washington drains. Presently Tad also sickened, but never became as ill as his brother. On February 20 a gray-faced Lincoln came into the office where his secretaries were working to tell them in stricken tones that Willie was dead.

Willie Lincoln was buried on a cold February morning in 1862, about the time when, according to the President's official order, the Federal armies were supposed to be advancing. Mary Lincoln was too prostrated to attend the funeral, and Tad had wept himself into a relapse. Neither parent ever completely recovered from the loss of Willie, who was the most promising of their four boys and the most like his father. In particular, Mary, who had already lost one son in Springfield and had taken it badly, had not the inner strength to bear this second blow. Gone was every social ambition. She received no one, made no appearances in public, and was too overcome to console little Tad for the loss of a brother who had been his constant companion. Her oldest sister, Elizabeth Edwards, always sensible of family claims, was persuaded to come on a long visit from Springfield to bear Mary company; but even Elizabeth could make little impression. She went home, and a nurse took her place. At this time Mary was not on good terms with her two other Springfield sisters, and the rest of her family was Confederate. She had a brother, three half-brothers, and three brothers-in-law in the Confederate forces. Thus to her grief for Willie was added from time to time official tidings of the deaths of young men whom she could not openly mourn. Half-sisters, who might on former occasions have given her comfort, were cut off even from letter-writing. Her only consolation was a new friend, Mrs. Stanton, who, poor woman, had buried six children.

Mary did make attempts to pull herself together for the sake of her husband, but she saw him so little and at such irregular intervals that the effort too often died away. The measure of his anxiety for her may be seen by his taking her one day to the window and pointing out the insane asylum, saying gently: "Mother, do you see that large white building on the hill younder? Try and control your grief, or it will drive you mad, and we may have to send you there."

In her desperation Mary turned for consolation to spiritualism, which was at the time in fashion. She began to visit séances in search of assurance that Willie was still within her reach. This involved her with several more dubious characters, one at least of whom attempted black-mail. After various mediums had been exposed, her belief in spiritualism died away; but she still refused to accept the death of Willie as final. Nearly two years after his death she told one of her sisters that Willie came to stand by the foot of her bed every night with the same adorable smile as ever. With him came Eddie, who had died before Willie was born, or Alex, her red-headed youngest brother, who was killed in the Confederate forces at Baton Rouge.

During the hectic spring and summer of 1862, Lincoln could do little more than provide a nurse-companion for his wife. Poor Tad, who received small consolation from his mother, attached himself to his father with all the vehemence of an impulsive nature. He would burst into Lincoln's office at all hours of the day and at night would refuse to go to bed without him. He would sit in the President's arms through interminable meetings and fall asleep on his shoulder. Most people did not know what to make of Tad with his unintelligible speech, his inability to read or dress himself, and his highly original powers of getting into mischief. Lincoln, however, expressed his grief for Willie by pouring out on Tad all the love and attention, and even all the toys, he would like to have given to Willie. That iron man Stanton, who had lost so many children of his own, was quite melted by Lincoln's devotion to his son and gave the boy a commission in the army so that he could call himself a "real" soldier.

In religion Lincoln had been something of a sceptic, so that in Springfield days he babysat while Mary went to church. Strangely enough, while Mary's religious beliefs told her no more than that Willie was still alive somewhere and consequently within reach, Lincoln turned to the Bible for consolation. He never perhaps formulated what he found there in terms of Christian doctrine, but he did derive from it a faith in God which he found it natural to express in biblical terms.

It was not of course possible for Lincoln, no matter how

deeply he mourned his son, to go into seclusion. Nor did
he plunge into harder work. He resumed, as he had to do,
the order of his days, which was already making him a
highly visible President. Even before Willie died, the
American people in what remained of the United States
had become used to the notion that Abraham Lincoln was
their President. It would be too much to say he was popular, especially in Washington, where criticism focused on
the inertia of Federal armies; but even those who had no
high opinion of his abilities had come to realize that Lincoln was the head of his own administration. Moreover,
though unpretentious in his private life, Lincoln was indefatigable in such duties as taking the salute at military
reviews or visiting the troops in their encampments. White
House receptions, open to anyone who cared to shake the
President's hand, went on uninterrupted, just as though no
war existed. Naturally the concentration of a tremendous
army in and around Washington meant that an unusually
wide range of people saw and heard the President on various occasions. He was in addition surprisingly easy of
access in his private office. After the initial queues of
would-be civil servants had presented their credentials,
they were replaced by men seeking army commissions, a
furlough for someone needed at home, or a permit to buy
cotton. Widows of soldiers who wanted to go back to their
parents sought permits to enter the Confederacy.
Wounded soldiers, relatives of prisoners, people in trouble
of one sort or another flocked to Washington or sent representatives. Edwin M. Stanton also held audience daily—
but Stanton found it easy to say "No."

Statistically it might seem impossible that personal contacts could familiarize so large a country with its President. Indeed, it actually was impossible, even allowing for
Lincoln's conspicuous appearance and unusual personality. It stands to reason that, like all Presidents, Lincoln was
chiefly known through what newspapers reported. Nevertheless, the remarkable thing about his contacts is the enor-

mous amount of time he devoted to them, behaving as though he really had leisure to meet people. He paid for this effort in fatigue. Inaugurated at fifty-two, Lincoln was a young man as Presidents go, and a man of strong physique which he abused recklessly during his years in office.

# 8

## A Critical Summer

BY EARLY SUMMER, 1862, the Union seemed on
the edge of victory. New Orleans had been taken and advances made up the Mississippi. A hitherto undistin-
guished general named John Pope took Island Number
Ten in a pincer movement down the river. It was true that
Ulysses Grant had suffered a near-defeat at Shiloh, which
horrified the nation on account of its casualty list; but even
Shiloh proved of more profit than loss to the Union forces.
Meanwhile McClellan, advancing slowly, but at least without check, was five miles from Richmond. Unexpectedly,
however, he was attacked by Lee toward the end of June
and driven back fifteen miles during seven days of furious
battle, losing his base on the Pamunkey together with the
railroad which might have hauled his siege guns into position. It is true that the Army of the Potomac fought desperately, inflicting some twenty thousand casualties. McClellan successfully transferred his army and supply base to
Harrison's Landing on the James River, but Richmond
was no longer within his immediate grasp. The low-lying
country of the Yorktown Peninsula suggested danger of
malaria or dysentery during the summer.

This serious reverse was put down by McClellan to the absence of McDowell's corps, which had gone off chasing Jackson. From his new position on the James he wrote that, given reinforcements of fifty, no, a hundred thousand, he would still take Richmond. He thought the Confederate forces double his own, though the truth was he had not been outnumbered but outgeneraled. At the same time, Jackson's raid up the Shenandoah Valley had convinced Lincoln and Stanton that Washington could not be defended by three separate armies, each with preoccupations and tasks of its own. They were busy constructing a Union Army of Northern Virginia out of the scattered forces of Frémont, Banks, and McDowell and had appointed John Pope, the hero of Island Number Ten, to command it. In consequence Lincoln insisted that there were few fresh troops available and that the numbers McClellan demanded were out of the question.

J. G. Randall, one of Lincoln's most profound modern critics, deplores his judgment in not putting all his eggs into McClellan's basket. The general's view was that an attack on Richmond would draw Confederate forces away from Washington and that Union forces were better employed fighting on the Peninsula than in standing guard in front of the capital. Even supposing, however, that McClellan's view was correct, he had made the grave mistake of confusing the ideal with the possible. He had demanded that Lincoln, his Cabinet, and the Congress defer to his judgment. At the time when he did so, he had created an army but had never yet used it in battle. He had never commanded more than a few thousand men under battle conditions and was known to have failed to get all these forces into action. If in these circumstances he insisted on a strategic move which would risk Washington if he proved wrong, he should have been prepared to undertake it with limited forces.

McClellan's performance during the Seven Days in command of the largest army put under one general in the history of the country had not been impressive to those in Washington who read his dispatches. It is true that Lincoln and Stanton had not been shown the last two sentences of his message after his defeat of June 27: "If I save this army now, I tell you plainly that I owe no thanks to you or any other persons in Washington. You have done your best to sacrifice this army." But even without these unforgivable words, McClellan's telegrams had not been those of a general in command of his nerves. "Success of yesterday complete," he wired on June 26. The next day he reported: "I have lost this battle because my force was too small. I again repeat that I am not responsible. . . ." Two days later he wired: "If none of us escape, we shall at least have done honor to the country. I shall do my best to save the army. Send more gunboats." In fairness, McClellan's acts were wiser than his words, and his army was transferred to a safe base on the James at Harrison's Landing. The only question was, would he or could he once more advance upon Richmond? By making his usual appeal for large reinforcements, he implied that he would not move. Accordingly Lincoln went down on July 8 to visit the army, primed with a list of questions for McClellan and his senior commanders.

This visit of Lincoln's merely deepened misunderstanding between the President and the general. One wonders why Lincoln made it, seeing that he had already appointed Halleck as General-in-Chief and seemed anxious to let him decide about McClellan. McClellan, always suspicious of political interference, must have intensely disliked Lincoln's questioning of his subordinates. Furthermore, the general made his own contribution to misunderstanding by handing the President a memorandum on the conduct of the war which was political, rather than military in nature. McClellan has been hotly attacked and equally hotly defended for pressing his advice on the President at this juncture. We have no evidence to tell us whether Lincoln himself thought this letter an impertinence, since he read it through and put it in his pocket without comment. In a general way McClellan was defending what had been Lincoln's official policy, maintaining that the war was about the Union and not against slavery, that the rebel South should not be outraged by offers of freedom to runaway slaves or by requisitions of goods from civilians. Rebel states should be reconciled, not conquered. McClellan did not hesitate to say that many of his soldiers had no enthusiasm for all-out war. Privately he was beginning to console himself for his own defeat by supposing that victory would have put power into the hands of politicians anxious to dictate severe terms.

It is really not important to decide whether McClellan's advice to Lincoln was or was not impertinent. The point is that it was ill-timed. It could not escape the notice of so astute a politician as Lincoln that 1862 was an election year, a convenient moment for a man who might seek the Presidency two years later to put forth certain feelers. Nor was he unlikely to have seen that a general whose staff incautiously urged him to save the country from incompetent politicians might be the very man to have presidential ambitions. Furthermore, only five days after he had pocketed McClellan's letter stating that the war was not about slavery and that the army would not fight to destroy it, Lincoln spoke for the first time to Seward and Welles about freeing the slaves in rebel states by proclamation in virtue of his powers as Commander-in-Chief. In preparing to depart so far from his original position, he was bound to note that General McClellan held opposite views.

Despite the worsening of his relations with McClellan, Lincoln allowed Halleck to make up his mind about the Army of the Potomac when he arrived in Washington some weeks later. Halleck went down himself to talk to McClellan, who told him that the Confederates in front of Richmond numbered two hundred thousand. Halleck had no information on this subject, but he could hardly avoid seeing that McClellan, if he were right, could not take the offensive. If, on the other hand, McClellan were wildly wrong, his competence was seriously in question. Not surprisingly, Halleck issued an order for McClellan to withdraw his troops entirely.

McClellan had chiefly himself to blame, but he did not see it that way. Aware that his political enemies had done their best to discredit him by fair means or foul, he put every reverse down to their influence. His former friend Stanton was the especial object of his hatred, and he compared him most unfavorably with Judas Iscariot. To his wife he wrote wildly about going to Washington with his "large military family" to seek justice. Apparently he had no real intention of doing so, but showed no dislike of similar talk among his staff. General Ambrose Burnside, who had been ordered to reinforce Pope's Army of Northern Virginia, made a visit to McClellan at the very moment when the latter was conferring with Halleck. Sitting outside the general's quarters, he heard the staff declare that the army ought to march on Washington to "clear out those fellows." Burnside got to his feet and said, "I don't know what you fellows call this talk, but I call it treason, by God!" Burnside considered himself a personal friend of McClellan's, but perhaps his forthright words were reported. At all events, just before McClellan left the Peninsula, he wrote to his wife, "I believe I have triumphed!! Just received a telegram from Halleck stating that Pope and Burnside are hard pressed." He was actually delighted at the possible defeat of his own colleagues.

Lincoln's appointment of Henry W. Halleck as the new General-in-Chief had been made at the recommendation of General Scott, whom the President had recently visited in his retirement. In view of continued successes in the West, it was natural for Lincoln to feel that there were better generals there. Halleck, who had taken over Frémont's job in Missouri at a time of confusion and weakness, had restored order and given direction to the successful movements of Pope and Grant. Eventually he had taken the field in person, and though his advance had been very much in the McClellan tradition, he had redeemed himself by taking Corinth, his immediate objective. One happy result of his removal to Washington was not deliberate. Grant, who had for some time been tied down by what amounted to garrison duties, was his logical successor.

Halleck's decision to withdraw McClellan from the Peninsula gave the initiative to Lee who, in front of Richmond, could move more rapidly against Pope than McClellan could to reinforce Pope. Strategically therefore it was important for McClellan to keep up pressure on Richmond, while at the same time hastening the withdrawal of some units. He did neither of these things. What chiefly concerned him was his own position when he reached his new headquarters at Aquia Creek on the Potomac. As ex-General-in-Chief he would not serve under Pope and bitterly resented the detachment of any part of his army. It was Halleck's duty to insist that the two generals cooperate against Lee. He could have done so by taking the field himself, reducing both Pope and McClellan to subordinate commanders. Unfortunately Halleck, to whom Lincoln wished to leave the situation, proved a theoretical soldier, too timid and indecisive for responsibility. Pope, reluctantly reinforced and inadequately supported, was defeated by Lee and Jackson on the old battlefield of Bull Run.

It is no disgrace to Pope that he was a lesser general than Lee or Jackson, but some of his difficulties were his own fault. He had not made himself popular with his army, which consisted of detachments made at one time or another from the Army of the Potomac. He subsequently complained that his corps commanders were sowing dissension to the point of not carrying out his orders. Fitz-John Porter, McClellan's favorite corps commander, had taken no part in the battle and was later court-martialed, though strictly speaking he had been within his rights. As for McClellan, Lincoln was correct in saying that he had done his best to insure that Pope would fail.

The defeat of the Second Battle of Bull Run faced Lincoln with one of the more difficult decisions of his career. Once more the battle had been so near Washington that the retreat, the wounded, and the confusion were seen in the capital directly. It was clear that the army had obeyed Pope unwillingly and that his defeat had destroyed any chance of his gaining the confidence of his men. Meanwhile Lee, whose view of war was an aggressive one, was preparing to invade Maryland. Confederate opinion was that Maryland citizens would rise if a victorious Southern army appeared within their borders. Lee hoped that by bringing with him arms and equipment, he would gain as many new recruits as he needed. Suddenly victory seemed within the grasp of the South. The ever-present fear that France and England would support a Southern success gave peculiar danger to the situation. What, then, should Lincoln do? If Halleck had risen to the occasion, he might have taken command, but his incompetence in crises was now as clear as the defeat of Pope at Second Bull Run. The army would fight for McClellan, but could McClellan beat Lee? Even if he could do so, was it wise to reinstate a general so difficult to control and one who deliberately had brought about the defeat of another commander?

Stanton had his own view on McClellan, namely that he did not even wish to wage outright war. The Secretary proceeded, therefore, to draw up a memorandum from Cabinet members, demanding that Lincoln should not reappoint McClellan to command. Welles, Secretary of the Navy, refused to sign on the grounds that the Cabinet's function was to advise the President, not to dictate to the Commander-in-Chief. Seward, ducking the issue altogether, chose this time for a visit to New York. On the other hand, Chase, representative of the radicals; Montgomery Blair, who had a brother in the army; and even Bates supported Stanton's manifesto. In fact, it seemed possible that the whole government would collapse unless

Lincoln gave way on McClellan. The general's opponents, however, had one weakness: there was no alternative commander on whom they were agreed. Nor were they, for all their political experience, a match for Lincoln when it came to a question of maneuver. Despite a very painful Cabinet meeting, the ultimatum which Stanton had prepared fell flat. McClellan was confirmed in command because the army, Lincoln insisted, would fight for no one else. Incidentally, the right of the Commander-in-Chief to make military appointments without consulting his Cabinet was also confirmed.

It remained for McClellan to beat Lee, or at the least to force him out of Maryland. By great good fortune McClellan captured a copy of one of Lee's orders, revealing that Lee and Stonewall Jackson had divided and could not immediately concentrate their armies. Napoleon, or even Lee himself, would have administered a shattering defeat, given such an opportunity—but these two generals were remarkable for the swiftness of their movements. McClellan, who was not, checked Lee at Antietam on September 17 in a battle in which neither side won real advantage. Lee, however, had not found Maryland ready to rise and was plagued by desertions of men who were willing enough to fight for Virginia but thought of Maryland as foreign soil. He retreated, though reluctantly and slowly—so slowly that Lincoln thought he could have been cut off north of the Potomac. When McClellan failed to cut off Lee, Lincoln vowed that he must and would get rid of his general if Lee once more placed himself between Richmond and the Army of the Potomac. It was a resolve which he must have pondered often, for no new appointment of a commander for the Army of the Potomac was going to be easy.

After his retreat from the Peninsula, McClellan had been bypassed by the creation of Pope's Army of Northern Virginia out of detachments originally trained under his orders. He had, however, not been officially superseded in his command of the Army of the Potomac. After Pope's defeat McClellan had simply taken over demoralized troops, who had cheered him wildly, believing that all went well under Little Mac, as in a sense it did. McClellan had been as useful to the government after Second Bull Run as after the First in restoring order, getting the army back into shape, replacing equipment. In the eyes of his adherents he had proved that he was indispensable. He had checked Lee at Antietam, where the army had given a good account of itself. If he had not the swiftness of Lee and Jackson, neither was he rash. The army, which had suffered ten thousand casualties at Antietam, was grateful for a chance to lick its wounds without much being demanded for a while. In fact, the bond between McClellan and his army was stronger than ever after Pope's fiasco. Lincoln had to ask himself whether he could replace Little Mac with another general who would be obeyed. Was there any such man?

A personal incident which occurred about this time illustrates the serious crisis which Lincoln was facing. He happened to hear that Major John J. Key had replied to the question of why Lee's army was not captured after Antietam with: "That is not the game . . . the object is that neither army shall get much advantage of the other; that both shall be kept in the field till they are exhausted, when we will make a compromise and save slavery." Lincoln asked Key personally whether this was true and—finding the officer defended his point of view instead of denying it—dismissed him from the army. To Key's appeal for reinstatement the President answered that he bore him no ill-will and had merely acted as a warning to others. He condoled with Key on the death of his sixteen-year-old son, killed fighting for the Union in Kentucky, but could not reinstate him without appearing to agree with what he had said. The episode illustrates the terrible danger of opposing a general like Lee with an army whose officers considered the war a game. It also helps to explain Lincoln's appointment of General Burnside to succeed Little Mac after Antietam, an action which has been universally condemned as a piece of bad judgment.

Burnside was the direct soldier who had told McClellan's staff that they were talking treason. He had made his reputation in command of an expedition against the South Carolina coast, an operation on no great scale, but of importance to the blockade of the South. He had proved himself a competent corps commander, was a personal friend of McClellan's, but had not been one of his regular subordinates, which meant that he could not be resented as a traitor to his commanding general. Even McClellan would be bound to help his friend through the early stages of taking over command. Militarily, Burnside proved the worst of Lincoln's generals for the Army of the Potomac, but it is difficult to see what more suitable man was available to take over McClellan's army.

In estimating Lincoln's military judgment it is only fair to remember that he had to consider his problems from a political point of view as well. He did not know his West-Point-trained commanders as they knew one another, and he found it hard to discover what precise combination of qualities was needed to make a first-class general. Neither Scott nor his incompetent nominee General Halleck was capable of giving Lincoln the advice he needed. It was only to be expected that he should make some costly errors.

# 9

## Emancipation

FOR MORE THAN A YEAR after the outbreak of war, Lincoln had cautiously refrained from meddling with Southern slavery. He did not believe that either President or Congress had authority to interfere with the institution in states where it existed. However, the power of the military to confiscate slaves was quite another thing, since by using them as teamsters, personal servants, or diggers of entrenchments, Confederates could free a larger proportion of their troops for actual fighting than was possible within the Union army. Nevertheless, Lincoln, who had to consider the border slave states remaining in the Union, was quick to force generals Frémont and Hunter to rescind orders which freed all slaves within their military districts. His objection was not that this could not be done, but that it was untimely and should not be done piecemeal. Such a decision must be the prerogative of the Commander-in-Chief. Nevertheless, by February, 1862, the Federal armies had about five thousand Negroes on their hands in Virginia and another nine thousand on the coast of South Carolina. Some of these were literally escaped slaves; others had been captured; and yet others were overrun as

Southern plantations, deserted by their owners, came under occupation. Destitute Negroes looked to the Union armies to sustain them and were willing to perform such tasks as they could for subsistence wages.

This drift of slaves toward the Union armies was unwelcome to such generals as McClellan, who wanted to put the country together again just as it had been. Some commanders were punctilious about returning slaves to rebel owners under the provisions of the Fugitive Slave Act. Private soldiers, on the other hand, even if not abolitionists, generally resented being used as slave catchers for the benefit of rebels. To make matters more complex, some Negroes seeking refuge with the Army of the Potomac were runaways from loyal Maryland. Still others were free Negroes seeking a chance to better their condition. In Washington, where the District Court judges favored slavery, a brisk trade grew up in kidnapped Negroes who were turned over to Maryland "owners" without much inquiry into their actual status.

These situations kept the question of slavery before Congress, which in March, 1862, forbade the use of soldiery to restore escaped slaves to rebel owners. In April it abolished slavery in the District of Columbia in a measure which Lincoln threatened to veto until it was amended to include compensation to owners and the promise of a scheme for colonization of free Negroes outside the United States. Congress likewise abolished slavery in the Territories. Early that same year a treaty with England had been ratified which committed the United States to more cooperation in eliminating the slave trade. A law of 1820 which imposed the death penalty for importing slaves into the country was put into effect for the first time in February, 1862.

The grimmer the war became, the stronger grew Northern feeling against the slave-labor system of the South, quite simply because it maintained the rebellion. On July 15, Lincoln returned from his visit to McClellan's army with the general's advice on the conduct of the war in his pocket, stating that the Army of the Potomac would not fight to extinguish slavery. The very next week Congress passed an act giving freedom to the slaves of those convicted of treason, those who joined in rebellion or aided rebel forces. Slaves captured, abandoned, or escaping from the enemy were also freed; and it was stated that the President might use these in any way to win the war, implying that they might become soldiers as well as servants. Startled at how far Congress was prepared to go, Lincoln hesitated over whether he ought to sign this bill. He consented in the end to accept the explanation that such slaves were war captives and therefore government "property." No mechanisms were devised to enforce this law, and no guidelines were worked out to define its provisions. Its presence on the statute books was merely a reminder that Congress was not prepared to let slavery win the war. It was an answer less to the arguments of McClellan than to his failure to take Richmond.

Lincoln's immediate reaction was to call together congressmen from the loyal border states and urge them to adopt a scheme for freeing their slaves with full compensation. If they wanted to proceed gradually, he was ready to accept 1900 as the final date for freedom. But the continuance of the war meant the doom of slavery, and all that remained was to offer the loyal states favorable terms. Border-state congressmen must have seen where the signs pointed, but their constituents still expected to be rewarded for their loyalty by retaining their slaves. Less than a third of those assembled supported Lincoln's plan.

This lack of consent from the border states made it impossible for Lincoln to free slaves within the Union. By July, 1862, however, the Union, which had started the year with important military movements, had lost the initiative. The failure of the Peninsular campaign was soon to be followed by the defeat of Pope at Second Bull Run which laid Maryland open to invasion. Halleck's western

campaign had been conducted so slowly and drawn together such vast forces that it had given his opponents
breathing space. Corinth was taken and New Orleans remained in Union hands, but the Mississippi, which had
been nearly won, was restored to the Confederates for a
hundred and fifty miles, protected by Vicksburg which,
though not originally a strong fort, was becoming nearly
impregnable. Confederate General Braxton Bragg in Chattanooga was gathering forces which would in less than two
weeks start an ambitious movement through Tennessee up
into Kentucky. In fact, the Confederacy had absorbed
heavy blows without destruction and was now ready to
move forward. The Union, despite its superior resources,
had so far proved unable to conquer the South.

The crisis of the summer of 1862 was especially perilous
because major European countries, in particular Britain,
were feeling the effects of a cotton famine. The huge towns
of the British Midlands were full of starving unemployed
workers, and from the start there had been a group in
Great Britain which had seen commercial advantage in the
dismemberment of the United States. The French Em-
peror, his head full of schemes for a French-controlled
Mexican empire, would be glad to weaken a future neigh-
bor and rival. Unless the Union could prove that it was
determined to conquer, there was danger that France and
England would come to terms with the South.

It was therefore for military reasons that Lincoln con-
templated freeing Southern slaves by virtue of his power
as Commander-in-Chief. On July 22, he broached the subject to his Cabinet, asking no advice except on details. The
decision, he said, was one which he had considered long
and earnestly. What he required was Cabinet support of
his military power to take such action, not advice as to its
wisdom or even about his constitutional position. Not unnaturally, his plan produced a mixed reaction. Smith and
Blair, the latter a border-state man, were strongly against
it. Stanton, who by virtue of his office knew best how

slavery helped the Southern war effort, was entirely in its favor, supported by Attorney General Bates, who though moderate about the slavery question, was greatly concerned about the course of the war. Chase, the strongest anti-slavery man in the Cabinet, merely mumbled that he thought it went too far, leaving the impression that he had rather the deed were done by President Chase two years later than by Lincoln at this moment. Welles, who had already discussed the matter with Lincoln, was silent, but Seward was full of fears about its effect abroad. He added that the proclamation should in any case wait for a Union victory, lest it be considered a desperate last threat before giving in.

This reception gave no great concern to Lincoln, though he did concede the force of Seward's argument that the announcement ought to wait for a victory. It was not his habit, however, to take a vote or to consider that Cabinet opinion must support him in matters on which he had made up his mind. He allowed his advisors great freedom of action within their departments, which tended to reconcile them to occasions on which their opinions were discounted in advance. It was not likely that Seward or Blair would wish to resign from positions which gave them both a great deal of power.

In deference to the suggestion of Seward, the emancipation document was pigeonholed for the time being, so that an awkward period followed during which Lincoln was urged by abolitionists to do what he had secretly made up his mind he would do at a suitable moment. His response to these ill-timed attacks included a letter to Greeley of the *Tribune* which summed up as well as anything could his unchanging position:

"My paramount object in this struggle is to save the Union, and is not either to save or destroy slavery. If I could save the Union without freeing any slave, I would do it; and if I could save it by freeing all the slaves, I would do it; and if I could save it by freeing some and leaving others alone, I would also do that. . . .

"I have here stated my purpose according to my view of my official duty; and I intend no modification of my oft-expressed personal wish that all men everywhere should be free."

It is not often that one reads so clear a definition of the difference between a man's wishes and his duty. In the heat of the racial struggle which has gone on for over a hundred years since these words were written, they may seem cold. It is therefore worth remarking that nothing in the course of the war seemed to give Lincoln more personal satisfaction than this proclamation which he made as part of his duty to achieve something else. Over and over again when Negroes cheered him, he seemed to remind himself that here at least were people to whom he had given something positive and lasting. As a realist, he understood that he had not given much, for which reason he spent energy on colonization schemes which were doomed to disappointment. He also took an interest in Negro education, which he might have assisted more had he lived longer. He did not, like some idealists, assume that freedom would solve all problems.

On September 22, five days after Antietam, Lincoln discussed with his Cabinet the final draft of the proclamation which he intended to publish the following day. As was often his practice in serious moments, he tried to lighten the atmosphere by reading a selection from the humorist Artemus Ward. Stanton and Chase, who had no sense of humor, were impatient at this waste of time. Bates joined them in contempt of a President who had a taste for such trivialities. The rest put up more or less tolerantly with Lincoln's little ways, but even Seward, whose appreciation of a joke was his strongest bond with Lincoln, would never have chosen a reading of this kind for such a moment. The President, laughing heartily at what he read, no more consulted his Cabinet on how to conduct a meeting than he did on the essentials of his proclamation, which took the form of a promise that he would free slaves on January 1, 1863, in all areas still in rebellion.

"I, Abraham Lincoln, President of the United States of America, and Commander-in-chief of the Army and Navy thereof, do hereby proclaim and declare. . . .

"That on the first day of January in the year of our Lord, one thousand eight hundred and sixty-three, all persons held as slaves within any state, or designated part of a state, the people whereof shall then be in rebellion against the United States shall be then, thenceforward, and forever free. . . .

"That the executive will, on the first day of January aforesaid, by proclamation, designate the States and parts of states, if any, in which the people thereof respectively, shall then be in rebellion against the United States; . . ."

Antietam was one of those battles which was rather a turning point than an outright victory. Lincoln's response to this half-success was a proclamation that he would free slaves in a few months, but only in those places where he lacked power to enforce his edict. It might, therefore, have appeared that this conditional announcement would have little force. On the contrary, it was recognized immediately as momentous. Seward had feared that it would be resented in Europe as a promise to destroy the cotton kingdom on which so many livelihoods depended. He was astonished to discover that the most benighted European aristocracies were ashamed to defend Southern slavery against a government which had vowed to destroy it. North and South were to be left to fight their quarrel out, now embittered by the knowledge that Northern victory would ruin the Southern slave system and encourage retaliations by Negroes for what they had suffered.

Strangely enough, the one thing the announcement did not do was to strengthen Lincoln, either inside his Cabinet, in Congress, or with the people. McClellan had been right in thinking many Northerners looked back nostalgically to the good old days and did not like to be told they were fighting for what amounted to a revolution. The 1862 elections in November returned Democratic majorities in New York, Pennsylvania, Indiana, Ohio, and Illinois—all key states which had played a very large part in Lincoln's election. At the same time, discontent with the way the war was going also brought to Congress an increased proportion of Republican extremists. Thus the last two years of Lincoln's term were marked by a growing division between those who thought he went too far and those who blamed him for timidity and compromise. Each side put pressures on him, which tended to force him to depend on the other—and then accused him of weakness of character because he did so. Naturally, the worse the war went, the greater his difficulties became. A serious crisis with constitutional implications arose in December after Burnside had sacrificed the flower of his army in a hopeless assault on Lee's fortified lines at Fredericksburg. In anger and dismay Republicans in Congress determined the time had come to force a change of administration.

The immediate object of their resentment was Seward, who had recently published a volume of his letters to diplomats abroad containing some remarks which would have been better deleted. Primed by Secretary of the Treasury Chase, their particular friend in the Cabinet, the radicals moved in to attack. A resolution was passed, supported by all Republicans in the Senate except Harris of New York, an old friend of Seward's, that a committee should protest to Lincoln about the way in which the government was being run and insist on a "partial reconstruction" of the Cabinet in accordance with radical wishes. This committee, representing a serious crisis for Lincoln within the ranks of his own party, demanded not only the dismissal of Seward and a more radical Secretary of State in his place, but more regular Cabinet meetings and greater powers for it as a body.

Lincoln, who already had Seward's resignation in his pocket, listened patiently for several hours and asked the

group to come back on the following day for more consultation. When they did so, they were somewhat dismayed
to find the whole Cabinet present, with the single exception of Seward. Lincoln told them that though he had not
always consulted his whole Cabinet before taking action,
he had at least kept them informed and listened to them.
In fact, he said, they had all supported him—a statement
which was only true in the sense that none of them had
been willing to resign when overridden. However, when
he called on Cabinet members one by one to confirm what
he said, it was hard for them to suggest that they had ever
been anything but a happy family. Moderates like Bates
were unwilling to have a radical replace Seward, foreseeing that such an appointment would insure their own
downfall. Stanton, though in many ways sympathetic with
the committee, perceived that his power would be seriously curtailed if radicals who aspired to manage the war
dominated the Cabinet.

Chase, on whose account of Cabinet meetings the committee had relied, was in a dilemma. He prized his own
reputation for integrity too highly to admit before his colleagues that he had complained secretly to Republicans in
Congress while still retaining his Cabinet office. Reluctantly Chase agreed with the rest of the group, leaving the
deputation from the Senate, as it were, with its head
chopped off. The committee retired in chagrin, angry with
Chase, who was both embarrassed and indignant at the
position into which he had been forced. Next morning he
reappeared in the President's office with a paper which he
said was his own resignation. It appears that he had intended to do no more than flourish it, but Lincoln hastily
whipped it out of his fingers, saying that the problem was
now solved. Accordingly, he announced that both Seward
and Chase had offered resignations which he had not accepted. It being now impossible to press for the resignation
of one without that of the other, the Republican committee
recognized a stalemate. It did not precisely forgive Chase,

whose prospects of the Presidency were thereafter dimmed. All the same, it needed him in the Cabinet and was forced to put up with Lincoln's coalition as the price of retaining him there. Thus ended a serious attempt by the Legislative Branch to dominate the Executive, appoint Lincoln's Cabinet, demand that he obey rather than consult it, and alter the balance of the Constitution. The radicals had been outmaneuvered by a politician whom it suited them to describe as weak and inept.

Lincoln did not dismiss Burnside from the Army of the Potomac after Fredericksburg, but shortly became aware that the general was a target of criticism by his senior officers, some of whom wanted McClellan recalled once more, while others were anxious to put forward their own claims. Prominent among the latter was Joseph Hooker, a handsome, dashing man, every inch the soldier, who was one of Burnside's corps commanders. As winter wore on, Burnside tried to retrieve his reputation by an advance which was derided by his subordinates, rained out, and bogged down in mud. A group of officers brought complaints officially to Lincoln. Burnside claimed that his orders were not carried out and demanded the dismissal of the malcontents.

Once more it was necessary to make a change in command, but Lincoln was unhappy at the way in which the decision had been forced on him. The Army of the Potomac had become a very complex institution, almost a state in miniature. On January 25, 1863, Lincoln transferred Burnside and two of his commanders to other duties. He then offered the command to Hooker, writing him at the same time a masterly letter to let him know that his intrigues had been observed:

"I think that during General Burnside's command of the army you have taken counsel of your ambition, and thwarted him as much as you could, in which you did a great wrong to the country and to a most meritorious and honorable brother officer. I have heard, in such a way as to believe it, of your recently saying that both the army and the Government needed a dictator. Of course it was not for this but in spite of it, that I have given you the command. Only those generals who gain successes can set up dictators. What I now ask of you is military success and I will risk the dictatorship. . . . I much fear that the spirit which you have aided to infuse into the army, of criticizing their commander and withholding confidence from him, will now turn upon you. I shall assist you as far as I can to put it down."

The real advantage of Hooker from Lincoln's point of view was that he was not a McClellan man, and that if ever the Army of the Potomac was to recover from the loss of its Little Napoleon, someone must command who was not associated with him. Lincoln was quite determined never to recall McClellan, whom he summed up in one terse sentence: "He has got the slows." No one with that particular fault could destroy Jackson and Lee. The only question was whether Hooker, chosen in part because he was not McClellan's man, could do so either.

At about the same time that the Army of the Potomac was undergoing this further change of commanders, Ulysses Grant, who had arrived at Memphis on the Mississippi, was about to set out downriver against Vicksburg. He had already made one attempt to reach it overland in December, had been halted in front of Granada a hundred miles off, and had been forced into retreat when cavalry raids destroyed his long supply line and his advanced base at Holly Springs. Indeed, since his dramatic seizure of Fort Donelson, Grant had not achieved a great deal, unless his near-defeat at Shiloh may be counted an achievement. Lincoln had been tempted to use a political general named McClernand, who had promised that he could raise an army and open the Mississippi. In the end, however, Halleck, little though he liked Grant, preferred the West Pointer to an amateur. Besides, Lincoln, who had run through many commanders in a vain search for certain qualities, had already considered Grant and delivered his verdict: "I can't spare this man. He fights."

# 10

## Let Us Die
## to Make Men Free

WHEN JULIA WARD HOWE WROTE the "Battle Hymn of the Republic," in November, 1862, she had ignored the indifference of many Union soldiers to the plight of the Negro. About two months earlier Abraham Lincoln, with fuller authority and greater understanding of consequences, had done a similar thing. His warning of the coming Emancipation Proclamation was published on September 23, 1862, and was followed the next day by the suspension of habeas corpus throughout the whole Union in cases of suspected treason. The effect was that civilian critics of the government might now be imprisoned without trial and sentenced by a military court. Furthermore, though a national conscription act was not made law until March, 1863, some states were already resorting to compulsion, which raised the question of how far a government had power to interfere with private lives. It is true that the South, in defiance of the very principles on which the Confederacy had been founded, had introduced conscription in the spring of 1862. Southerners, however, saw themselves as fighting for existence and had greeted Lincoln's promise of emancipation as a death warning of coming catastrophe either for the white race or the black. The North, on the other hand, still had the option—or at least some thought it had—of giving up the struggle.

The reaction of the country to Emancipation, though partly expressed in the large number of Democrats returned in the November elections, seemed muted for a time because Lincoln made no further reference to his promise, leaving room for some to hope that he would not carry it out. On January 1, 1863, however, Lincoln signed the Emancipation Proclamation, merely asking witnesses to note that if his hand trembled, it did so because he had just come from his official New Year reception, where he had been shaking hands for a solid three hours. The year 1863 was dawning with the Army of the Potomac nearly in mutiny against Burnside, and with Grant's advance on Vicksburg checked. Rosecrans and the Army of the Cumberland were desperately fighting to stave off defeat at Murfreesboro, where casualties were to reach a higher proportion of those engaged than in any previous battle. December and January together saw other Union setbacks, including the loss of Galveston, the exploits of Southern commerce raiders, and the stalling of a Union advance up the Mississippi from New Orleans. Accumulating disasters seem if anything to have reinforced Lincoln's determination to proclaim Emancipation—which was, it must be remembered, a new war weapon rather than an act of justice to the Negro. Not unnaturally, however, continuous bad news increased the influence of those who had lost faith in the aims of the war. Two weeks after Emancipation, they found a spokesman in Clement L. Vallandigham.

Vallandigham was a Congressman from Ohio who had lost his seat in the November elections, but shortly intended to campaign for the Democratic nomination for Governor of his state. He rose during the lame-duck session of Congress to propose an end to fighting. If the Union would only lay down its arms, leave slavery alone, restore communications, visit, trade, and intermarry with the South, all differences between the two would die away. This was an appealing prospect to many Northern Democrats, weary of a war not of their making which was taking a direction they abhorred. The black man had never been popular in the free North, where immigrants feared that he would drive down wages. In consequence, a revived opposition of anti-war Democrats, soon to be nicknamed Copperheads, began to flourish. Since a very thin line separated their position from treason, military commanders needed great discretion in using their powers under martial law.

That plain, blunt soldier Ambrose Burnside had been relieved of his command of the Army of the Potomac after his defeat at Fredericksburg had been followed by an unsuccessful midwinter campaign. He was now commanding the Department of Ohio because nothing of particular military importance was going on there. In May, 1863, Burnside arrested Vallandigham for an inflammatory speech against the war, tried him by a military commission, and sentenced him to imprisonment for the duration. Vallandigham immediately became a popular martyr; and the new Democratic Governor of New York State, Horatio Seymour, announced that the President's handling of this case would show whether war was really being waged to put down rebellion or to destroy the free institutions of the North. A meeting held at Albany under the auspices of Erastus Corning, a New York Democrat and member of Congress, passed a series of resolutions condemning the suspension of habeas corpus which it forwarded to Lincoln in defense of Vallandigham's right to speak his mind. Lincoln answered in a long and reasoned paper in which, as was so often the case in his political writings, he summed up the issue as he saw it in memorable words:

"Must I shoot a simple-minded soldier boy who deserts, while I must not touch a hair of the wiley agitator who induces him to desert? This is none the less injurious when

Lincoln's first inauguration in front of the east portico of the Capitol. The wooden dome of the Capitol has been taken down and a crane set up to build the present marble one. It is impossible to see the figures clearly because precautions against assassination kept everyone at a distance. *(Library of Congress)*

Mary Todd Lincoln as photographed in 1861 in full ball dress. Note the enormous crinoline, expensive material, and low-necked style which displays her sloping shoulders. Mary was proud of her arms and shoulders which, she felt, were as smooth and well shaped as those of many a younger woman. The plainly dressed hair surmounted by an elaborate headdress usually adorned with flowers was also typical of her ballroom style. *(Lloyd Ostendorf Collection)*

ABOVE LEFT Robert Todd Lincoln who, at his mother's wish, spent the major part of the war at Harvard. (Harvard University Archives)

ABOVE RIGHT William Wallace Lincoln (Willie) was considered to be in temperament and intellect most like his father. He died on February 20, 1862, at the age of eleven. Neither parent ever got over his loss. (Chicago Historical Society)

RIGHT Thomas Lincoln (Tad) was the youngest of Lincoln's children. He was temperamental, naughty, and spoiled, but had an affectionate nature. The photograph was taken by Mathew Brady in 1861. (Chicago Historical Society)

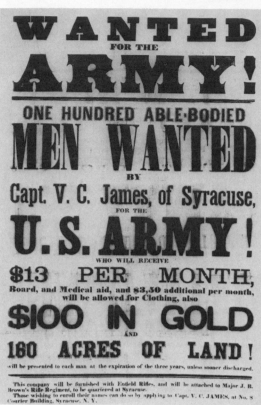

ABOVE LEFT Jefferson Davis, President of the Confederate States. This photograph was taken by Mathew Brady in Washington a year or so before secession. Davis was perhaps the most obstinate man on either side, and he looks it.

ABOVE RIGHT 1861 recruiting poster from Syracuse, New York, asking for three-year volunteers.

BELOW Newspaper cartoon showing Rebellion held by Jefferson Davis and attacked by the skill of Halleck, the strategy of McClellan, the Draft Law of Stanton, and the Emancipation Proclamation of Lincoln.

ABOVE Lincoln pays a visit to the Army of the Potomac after Antietam in 1863. "Little Mac," the commanding general, is the man with the moustache who stands directly facing Lincoln.

BELOW LEFT Robert E. Lee at his house in Richmond a few days after his surrender at Appomattox. He is in uniform, but without insignia.

BELOW RIGHT Lt. General Ulysses S. Grant, commander of the Union armies, standing outside his tent.

ABOVE Burned-out waterfront of Richmond after evacuation of the town by Lee's army.

RIGHT The last photograph taken of Lincoln, April 1865. In this famous portrait, Lincoln looks utterly tired and yet relieved of strain. The lips are almost smiling, with an expression particularly hard to capture at a time when people being photographed had to remain motionless for several minutes. His tie is crooked, as usual.

effected by getting a father, or brother, or friend, into a
public meeting, and there working upon his feelings, till
he is persuaded to write the soldier boy, that he is fighting
for a bad cause, for a wicked administration of a contempti-
ble government too weak to arrest and punish him if he
shall desert. I think that in such a case, to silence the
agitator, and save the boy, is not only constitutional, but,
withal, a great mercy."

Despite these stout words, Lincoln did not actually consider Burnside's action judicious. As it was necessary to
back him, however, the President turned the situation into
a farce by decreeing that Vallandigham, since he loved the
South so well, should be deported thither. This was done,
and the angry man was forced to get home by a long,
roundabout journey through Canada, made all the more
difficult by the tight Northern blockade. The President,
when informed of his return to Ohio, blandly refused to
believe it, trusting that Vallandigham had been sufficiently
inconvenienced and would not again make himself conspicuous. The result, however, of this and other incidents
was the formation of secret anti-war societies whose size
and effectiveness were often exaggerated, but whose intentions were to aid the South. During the last two years of
the war, the President was reluctant to act against these
groups despite recommendations from generals on the
spot. In somewhat similar fashion, he continued to resist
protection of his own person, claiming that he must associate freely with the people.

During the summer of 1862, the Lincolns had taken refuge from the heat of Washington in a cottage three miles
outside the city on the grounds of a pleasant wooded estate
which had been developed by General Scott as a home for
disabled soldiers. Lincoln's friends had soon been disturbed by his habit of riding unaccompanied and in the
dark from his office in the White House to spend the night
with his family. Once he was fired at—and told the story
to his friend Ward Lamon, now District Marshal, as a good

joke, lamenting the loss of an eight-dollar plug hat. On a later occasion, Lamon had a report from a detective which so disturbed him that he drove out to the Soldiers' Home in person, where he met a suspicious carriage which proved to contain Edwin M. Stanton, who had been attracted by the same rumor. Lincoln was eventually persuaded to accept a cavalry escort, which he frequently sent away on the grounds that, since he was known to be protected, it would not much matter if he and his wife went for an occasional drive without being deafened by the clatter of hooves and the clank of cavalry sabers. The same reasoning allowed him to ride fairly often to the Soldiers' Home alone, though he did reluctantly accept an infantry guard outside the cottage and, in the fall of 1862, at the White House itself. Since, however, the sentries were not allowed to screen the people who entered the White House, it is difficult to say what protection they offered to Lincoln. At one time Mary persuaded him to carry a heavy stick when he walked over to the War Department after dark—but the value of this weapon was also dubious.

In 1863, Horatio Seymour, the Governor of New York, presented an even more difficult political problem than did Vallandigham. Lincoln had sent him a note expressing goodwill when he took office, but the two were essentially at loggerheads. Seymour was not an anti-war Democrat, but the product of a revived Democratic Party, conscious that before its disastrous split in 1860 it had dominated American politics for many years. It aspired to lead again, perhaps with the prospect of electing a Democratic President in 1864—which would initiate another vast turnover of patronage and jobs. The Democrats made their appeal to moderate men who were disgusted by the increasing vindictiveness of radicals in Congress and their support by profiteers whose object quite plainly was to exploit a conquered South. Moderate Republicans of Lincoln's own sort were often either tempted by the Democratic view or embittered enough to affiliate with the radical Republican wing. Thus the President found himself increasingly iso-lated, as radicals tried to control him and Democrats to pull the rug from under him.

In 1863 the three policies which Seymour and the Demo-crats chiefly opposed were the purge of the government's Democratic critics, the Emancipation Proclamation, and the draft. The objectionable thing about this last, which was finally passed by Congress in early March, 1863, was that it transferred authority for raising troops to the Fed-eral government, giving it a direct control over individuals which was unprecedented. Regional quotas were fixed by the War Department, and state governments were wel-come to fill these if they could do so. If not, Federal mar-shals, after conducting a census of the able-bodied, held a lottery in each electoral district, drawing names out of a revolving drum. A man so selected might buy a substitute or pay the fixed sum of three hundred dollars to get out of service. The draft, thus was a heavy burden on the laboring classes and was particularly felt in New York, where the poor were usually Irish, Democratic, anti-Negro, and lack-ing in the devotion to the Union common among those who had left Europe for political rather than economic reasons. Seymour protested the size of New York quotas; and his opposition to the system encouraged criticism in Democratic newspapers, while inflammatory speakers raised their voices against the draft in saloons or at street-corners.

Once more Lincoln defended his position in a well-rea-soned paper, but his audience was in general not a literate one. Feeling came to a head in July with a tremendous three-day riot in New York, commencing at an office in an Irish quarter where names were being drawn for the draft. Soon the mob went on to lynch Negroes, battle police, attack the house of the Mayor, and rage unchecked through the streets, looting and burning. City authorities had no troops to draw on in this emergency because the local militia had been hustled off to Pennsylvania, where

Lee's invasion was threatening Harrisburg and Philadelphia. Detachments of the Army of the Potomac had to be
sent to New York before the operation of the draft could
be resumed. In other parts of the country, shots were fired
against soldiers taking the census, and systematic efforts
were made to hide men from the draft.

Thus beset by enemies within and outside his party,
Lincoln in 1863 looked more like a target than a leader in
a great war. Democrats blamed him for giving in to Republican extremists and thought him tyrannous when he employed strong measures. Radicals felt he had to be dragged
or pushed into actions essential to the Union. Both parties
criticized the conduct of the war. Indeed, only one group
took him more seriously than perhaps he took himself.
News of the Emancipation Proclamation passed down the
Negro grapevine with a speed which astonished both
North and South alike. Wherever the Federal armies came,
what had been a trickle of runaway slaves became a flood,
impossible to cope with, denuding fertile plantations of
labor, crowding refugees into camps which had a higher
death rate than the notorious Confederate prison at Ander-
sonville. General Grant wrote from Mississippi in August,
1863: "Slavery is already dead and cannot be resurrected. It
would take a standing army to maintain slavery in the
South, if we were to make peace today, guaranteeing to the
South all their former privileges."

Not unnaturally, Lincoln was soon encouraging the recruitment of Negro regiments, if only as a method of em-
ploying black manpower without depriving poor whites of
their jobs. Negro troops were not as well-paid as whites,
who generally held them in contempt until they proved
that they could fight. Outraged Southerners declared they
would enslave black prisoners and kill their officers, so that
Lincoln against his will was forced to threaten to execute
Southern prisoners in reprisal. Fortunately both sides perceived the serious danger to which this sort of competition
would expose them. One or two incidents occurred, but

Southerners mostly confined themselves to burying slain white Union officers in the same pit as their men. Lincoln, even when confronted with a massacre of black troops at Fort Pillow, refused to make good his threat against Southern prisoners, pointing out that it would only lead to counter-reprisals, and these in turn to others. One thing had been made clear: by entering the army, Negroes had established a claim to be American citizens in the fullest sense.

Considering the defeats and political crises which disturbed the Union during December, 1862, and the early months of 1863, it is hardly surprising that the President's friends thought he looked drawn and haggard. In his camp across the Rappahannock, Lee—whose physique had never yet failed him—caught bronchitis, from which he seemed unable to recover. Lee's problems, which chiefly concerned supply, were more direct than Lincoln's, but no easier to solve. There was no respite, in fact, for either of them. During the political crisis of December, Seward had handed in his resignation, saying that he was tired of the cares of office. "Ah yes, Governor," Lincoln had retorted, "that will do very well for you, but I am like the starling in Sterne's story. 'I can't get out.'" To a closer friend he had admitted that the Republican Senators wished to get rid of him, adding, "I am sometimes half disposed to gratify them." Nevertheless he did outmaneuver his opponents, retain his Cabinet, survive the disaster of Fredericksburg, and proclaim Emancipation—distressing all who knew him with the change for the worse in his appearance, but going through his daily program just as usual.

It was still surprisingly easy for anyone to see the President by simply joining the queue outside his office. It is true that he had been forced to cut down the hours which he devoted to interviews and that the secretaries, Nicolay, Hay, and Stoddard, made a good number of enemies by trying to protect the President's time. On the other hand, there were definite sorts of people other than politicians whom the President insisted on seeing. Among these, for instance, were inventors of new weapons. The war had broken out at a period when the rifle, though known and possessed by Lincoln's own grandfather, had not superseded the smoothbore musket as the standard military arm. In similar fashion, though the breechloader existed and was easier to use and more rapid in firing, it still had a tendency to clog in battle conditions, owing to the quality of gunpowder and the use of paper cartridges. Lincoln was indefatigable in his interest in mechanical devices such as mortars, primitive machine guns, repeating carbines, submarines of an experimental sort, and rifled cannon. More than once he went out with a companion to fire some new model weapon at a target set up in the Treasury Park, a fenced but untended stretch of ground which bordered on the White House lawn and the open sewer of the Washington Canal.

In John A. Dahlgren, Commandant of the Navy Yard and virtual chief of Navy Ordnance, Lincoln found a kindred spirit with an equal interest in improving the quality of weapons. On the other hand, the far more important General Ripley, head of Army Ordnance, was sixty-five when the war broke out; and his attitude toward new weapons was succinctly expressed to a Vermonter who was trying to get volunteers from his state armed with rifles. Brandishing an old flintlock musket which had been altered to use percussion caps, Ripley shook it in the face of his petitioner, exclaiming: "There is the best arm that was ever put into the hands of a raw volunteer! When he throws that away, as they generally do, he does not throw away twenty-five dollars' worth of government property."

In fairness to Ripley it must be said that he had serious problems of standardization. The consignments of outdated arms imported from Europe—including cannon of varying sizes—presented extreme difficulties of ammunition supply under battle conditions. Ripley wanted no new weapons to cause further complications and either refused to test those the President recommended or gave adverse reports on their performance. At the outbreak of war there had been less than sixty professional ordnance officers in the entire army, a fair proportion of whom had joined the South. In consequence it proved impossible to replace General Ripley until nearly the end of the war.

Lincoln soon turned to private companies formed by inventors of this or that weapon and personally gave them substantial orders in the hopes that their products would be proved in battle. It became Ripley's aim to keep these unwelcome objects out of use. His task was the easier, since only too often the financing of such companies was unsound, or else the inventor was a perfectionist who would not standardize his model or keep expenses within his estimate. Early in 1862 there was a tremendous row about mortar boats which Lincoln had ordered for Ulysses Grant in Cairo, Illinois, at the vital junction of the Ohio with the Mississippi. Both Stanton and the President had made efforts to get these boats to Grant, but they were not present for the attack on Fort Donelson, which resulted in a costly naval repulse. Their first success was at the taking of Island Number Ten in May.

The Spencer repeating rifle and its companion, the Spencer carbine, were patented by their inventor only a few weeks before the war broke out. Lincoln first saw the rifle in June, 1861, at the Navy Yard, where it had been tested. Seven hundred had immediately been ordered. Lincoln took it out to his private rifle range and even whittled what he thought was an improvement on its gunsight. Not until December, and then only at Lincoln's express order, did Ripley give an order for ten thousand. The Spencer rifle ran into production troubles and was not in the hands of soldiers until the Battle of Chickamauga in September, 1863, where its murderous effect so shocked the colonel commanding that he very nearly ordered his men to stop shooting altogether. The Spencer carbine, considered even more effective, especially as a cavalry weapon, was not in the hands of Union soldiers in quantity until the middle of 1864.

Stanton at the War Office battled furiously with Ripley

for better armaments, but even his bullying ways did not make an enduring impression. Meanwhile, by the end of 1862, Lincoln had begun to be wary of new weapons on the grounds that they would not come in time to win the war. By then he had ordered samples of a primitive machine gun and of various breechloading or rifled cannon. He had talked with a variety of obvious madmen with models of everything from death rays to flying machines. Nicolay and Hay were eventually allowed to send most inventors to Stanton, to the Navy Yard, or even to Ripley, who could be trusted to turn down their products. This did not, however, mean that Lincoln's nonpolitical visitors decreased in number. Rather they changed in character as people brought personal tragedies caused by the war to his attention.

The bigger the armies grew, for instance, and the more professional they became, the longer grew the list of death sentences for desertion, for sleeping on picket duty, and for other military sins committed in an age when nervous breakdowns were not understood or when backwoods soldiers went home without permission to deal with emergencies there. To the irritation of Stanton and even of the generals in the field, Lincoln was notoriously soft-hearted in the matter of pardons. They objected that army discipline must be maintained. Lincoln agreed, but soon committed the same offense again as distressed relatives or even the simple record brought to his attention the plight of the individual, not of the army.

Despite his frequent personal kindness, there was an ambivalence in Lincoln which made him push for the murderous Spencer carbine and insist a general's business was to destroy the opposing army at any cost. Southerners thought him ruthless. They also noted that he had promised at his inauguration not to interfere with their slaves —but had found a way to do so by his Emancipation Proclamation of 1863. Worse still, in 1864, when the Thirteenth Amendment banning slavery was debated by Congress,

Lincoln, who had long insisted that Congress had no power to interfere with slavery inside the individual states, used his personal influence to get the amendment passed. Southerners told one another that his promises were only kept as long as they proved useful.

However that may be, one thing was certain: by early in 1863 the load that Lincoln was bearing would have been intolerable for a man of less physical stamina, and was nearly so to him. He could not take a holiday, but he could at least get away from Washington to visit the Army of the Potomac, which Hooker in less than three months had re-formed and restored. The general had turned his attention to reducing the number of men on the sick list, and had kept the soldiers busy drilling, while stressing good equipment and physical fitness. By uniting his cavalry under a corps commander of its own, he had given it a chance to face Lee's on equal terms, something which was going to be of great importance during that summer. Best of all, he had weeded out his corps commanders, promoting men well tried in battle and encouraging the transfer of those too devoted to his predecessors. In early April when forsythia blooms in Washington and grass is freshly green, army commanders could make plans to move as soon as roads dried out. It was a good moment for Lincoln to make his visit to the army in northern Virginia, have a talk with Hooker, and remain for several days. Little Tad was wild to go with the party, while Mary Lincoln, recovered to some extent from Willie's death, was eager to play her part as the President's wife in public.

Disappointingly, their start was delayed by bad weather; and when they did embark at the Washington Navy Yard to cross the Potomac, it started to snow so heavily that their little steamer was forced to anchor in the nearest inlet instead of making straight for Aquia Creek, the army depot. It was snowy and gusty when they docked next morning, but their reception left nothing to be desired. A gaily decorated freight car took them about five miles inland, where they transferred to a couple of ambulances escorted by an honor guard of cavalry. Arrived at Hooker's headquarters, they found three comfortable tents fitted up with camp-beds and blankets where the delighted Tad could live like a real soldier. An impressive review of the cavalry followed, though held in melting snow and mud. Mary Lincoln watched it from a six-horse carriage, but Tad was allowed to ride behind his father, who was accompanied by Hooker, looking spectacularly handsome on his great white horse. The rest of the official cavalcade included generals, staff officers, and a mounted guard of honor, at the head of whom the President in his usual black and stovepipe hat rode efficiently but without dash on an ugly horse. After the review, Lincoln insisted on visiting the hospital tents which were nearest headquarters and speaking personally to every patient.

There were infantry reviews on the following days. The weather brightened and Lincoln, who liked brass bands and was delighted to see the army fit and well, began to look more cheerful and even to crack jokes. They had to drive about eight miles to review the First Corps and were taken over the muddy roads in an army ambulance drawn by six mules, whose driver let fly with volleys of oaths at awkward moments. Presently Lincoln leaned forward and touched him on the shoulder.

"Excuse me, my friend," he asked mildly. "Are you an Episcopalian?"

"No, Mr. President," replied the driver, startled. "I am a Methodist."

"Well," Lincoln remarked, "I thought you must be an Episcopalian because you swear just like Governor Seward, who is a churchwarden."

The driver took the hint and kept his mouth shut, while Lincoln enlivened the trip by pointing out which trees cut down for firewood had been felled by experienced axemen.

Tad wanted to see the enemy, so they went down to the bank of the Rappahannock, across which a couple of

Southern pickets, one clad in a Union army coat, could be seen standing by a fire which they had kindled in the chimney of a burnt-out house. Presently an officer came out to examine Lincoln's party through a field glass and made a low bow before retiring. This being a period when neither army was ready to move, there was conversation between outposts and swapping of newspapers, tobacco, food, or liquor. But the ruins of Fredericksburg lay visible below Marye's Heights, where Burnside had thrown away the flower of his army.

For the President no complete holiday was possible. On arrival at Hooker's headquarters he had been suffering from painful anxiety about a Federal attack on Charleston, which was just taking place. All the news so far was bad, destroying his pleasure in the sights and scenes around him. Hooker was tight-mouthed about his plans but aggressive in spirit. "When I take Richmond," was so constantly on Hooker's lips that Lincoln remarked to Noah Brooks, a newspaperman who had become one of his intimates, "That is the most depressing thing about Hooker. It seems to me that he is overconfident."

Nothing occurred to reverse this impression. After many disappointments, Lincoln was not resilient. When Brooks congratulated him on his improved looks, he admitted the relief of being out of Washington, but added, "Nothing touches the tired spot." Perhaps it was this inner fatigue which made him say earnestly to Hooker as they parted, "In the next fight, *put in all your men!*"

Noah Brooks called at the White House on May 6, a little less than four weeks later, to find the President anxious about the battle that Hooker was fighting around Chancellorsville. Things were not going well, but all was yet uncertain. At Lincoln's suggestion Brooks went to sit with Dr. Henry, an old Springfield friend who was visiting the White House. About three o'clock in the afternoon, the door opened, and Lincoln came into the room with a telegram in his hand. Brooks noted that his usually sallow face was almost precisely the color of the gray paper on the wall. "Read it," the President said in trembling tones as he thrust out his hand. "News from the Army." Clasping his hands behind his back, he walked up and down the room repeating, "My God! My God! What will the country say? What will the country say?" He might well ask. Would a new defeat exhaust the endurance of a nation which was losing unity? Beset by Republicans and Democrats alike, Lincoln had needed success. Instead of it he heard that General Hooker had failed to put in all his men and had been defeated by a ragged, starving army, half the size of that which had paraded before him a few weeks earlier. Lee had won his most brilliant victory, even though at the cost of the life of Stonewall Jackson.

# 11

# Gettysburg Summer

LINCOLN'S CAPACITY to act was never shown more clearly than on the day he received news of the defeat of Chancellorsville. Even before expressing his despair to Brooks and Henry, he had sent a message to summon Halleck, the General-in-Chief. No sooner did a carriage containing the general draw up before the White House than Lincoln darted inside and drove off to visit the army, leaving Dr. Henry in tears and Brooks trying to console him.

Arriving to take his post as General-in-Chief the preceding summer, Halleck had found the courage to order McClellan's retreat from Richmond, but had not been forceful enough to make him hurry. The consequence had been Pope's defeat at Second Bull Run, which appears to have killed Halleck's desire to make any further decisions. On January 1, 1863, Lincoln had been forced to give time in his busy day to a difficult interview with Burnside, who wished to redeem his defeat at Fredericksburg by another attack across the Rappahannock. None of his corps commanders believed in his plan, and Burnside was ready to resign unless some were relieved or at the least sharply recalled to their duty. Lincoln sent a note over to Halleck, instructing him to go out to the army, assess the situation, and give definite orders. "If in such a difficulty . . . you do not help," he told his General-in-Chief, "you fail me precisely in the point for which I sought your assist-ance. . . ." The immediate result of Lincoln's note was that Halleck, too, sent in his resignation.

At this disastrous moment of the war, Lincoln could hardly rid himself of two generals on the same day. He withdrew his letter to Halleck; and Burnside was allowed to go through with his operation, which bogged down hopelessly in winter rains and led to his dismissal. After this, Halleck would give Lincoln advice or relay his orders, provided that he did not have to make decisions. He had, however, his uses, both as figurehead and as military aide. Lincoln could not send him out alone to interview Hooker after Chancellorsville; but by taking Halleck with him, Lincoln had the benefit of a military view of the disaster.

Hooker's defeat, as it turned out, was no more than a serious setback. His army was still larger than Lee's, and a goodly part of it had not been engaged in the fighting. Hooker even had an excuse for losing control of the battle because he had been stunned when a shell hit a pillar against which he was leaning and seems to have been in a dazed condition for the rest of the afternoon. Nevertheless his corps commanders, meting out to him the kind of treat-ment he had given Burnside, accused him of a failure of nerve. Halleck and Lincoln were not ready to dismiss him on the spot because this would lower army morale and encourage subordinate generals to criticize their command-er. It would also offend the Congressional Committee on the Conduct of the War, which liked Hooker because he was earnest about pursuit of the war. Lincoln and Halleck returned without doing anything, while news of the defeat was mitigated by the electrifying tidings that Grant had crossed the Mississippi and that the fall of Vicksburg was, barring accidents or blunders, a matter of time.

Back in his camp on the Rappahannock, Hooker worked

to restore his army, weakened not only by his Chancellorsville losses, but by the imminent departure of thousands
whose enlistment time was up. He was talking confidently
about another attack when Lee began to slip out of his
entrenchments in the general direction of the Shenandoah
Valley and the fords of the Potomac. Covering his movements by cavalry so skillfully placed that Hooker was for
some days unable to discover where he was going, Lee had
started on his second invasion of the North. It did not
matter that he left Richmond uncovered, because Hooker
must move to protect Washington. In Pennsylvania,
whither he was bound, Lee would be campaigning in an
unravaged land where it would be easy to feed his men and
horses. If he won a battle, took Philadelphia, set fire to
Harrisburg, or moved on Pittsburgh, he was certain to
increase the dissensions in the North, of which he was well
aware. He might even force Grant to give up his hold on
Vicksburg and send troops to the rescue. It was barely
possible that foreign recognition, so often denied, might
follow a success. Against all these hoped-for gains, Lee had
to weigh great risks. Yet he would achieve nothing by
continuing to starve inside his encampments until Hooker
felt strong enough to attack again with an army twice his
size and better equipped.

Whether Hooker would have been allowed to fight a
second battle, had Lee remained where he was on the Rappahannock, we shall never know. But once Lee moved, it
became hard to change generals in the middle of a crisis.
Though Hooker's troop dispositions were sensible, lack of
confidence caused him to ask Lincoln about moves which
he ought to have seen for himself would not be wise.
Should he, for instance, fall with his full strength on Lee's
rear guard, still strongly entrenched in the lines which had
defeated Burnside? Should he let Washington go and
march on Richmond? Lincoln patiently recommended he
do neither, but his opinion of the general's judgment must
have been lowered.

It became apparent very soon that Hooker felt himself
distrusted, if not by Lincoln, certainly by Halleck, who
was trying to direct fresh troops to him and send on information which might not yet be known at Hooker's headquarters. Halleck's telegrams were frequent, and many of
them appeared to lay restrictions on the movements of the
general in the field. Hooker complained to Lincoln, who
answered patiently that Halleck by no means wished to
withhold support though he did resent Hooker's direct
communications with the White House. If the generals
would deal frankly with one another as the President did
with them both, the situation would be resolved.

Tactful as this reply was, it was not precisely candid.
Though anxious to give his support, Halleck did distrust
Hooker, as did Lincoln—which was only natural after
Chancellorsville. If Halleck was hovering over the scene
like an anxious mother, Hooker had only himself to blame.
Yet in fairness to Hooker, he was not the first general to
find that in operations near Washington he did not get a
free hand. Instead of taking Lincoln's advice about frank-
ness with Halleck, Hooker involved himself in a quarrel
over Harpers Ferry. Halleck wished the town defended
and felt that its garrison, well dug-in on the heights, could
protect the Baltimore and Ohio's railroad bridge, a huge
iron structure which had already twice been destroyed and
over which supplies were going out to Grant's army before
Vicksburg. On the other hand, Hooker took the view that
his task was to defeat Lee and that to impose on him responsibility for garrisons which he was not allowed to
evacuate was an unfair restriction on his movements, the
more so as he already had orders that he should on no
account expose Washington. On June 27, he wired to the
General-in-Chief that he was unable to fulfill all these separate tasks, and in consequence he requested to be relieved
of his command.

Neither Hooker's actions after sending this wire, nor the
situation, which was obviously leading up to a major bat-

tle, gave reason to suppose that his outburst of anger was meant to be taken literally. But Lincoln and Halleck had had enough of Hooker, while Stanton had always been against his appointment. Moreover, the corps commanders of the Army of the Potomac had been carefully reviewed in January when a successor to Burnside had been sought. George Gordon Meade, commander of the Fifth Corps, had been the runner-up on that occasion and was now available as a replacement. But if a change of command was to be made so soon before a battle, with Lee already in Pennsylvania, militia called to arms, widespread panic, and a financial crisis in the North, then it must at least be done with perfect smoothness. Colonel Hardie, an adjutant in Halleck's office who was personally known to Meade and Hooker, was sent out with instructions to go first to Meade's headquarters. When he got there late at night and aroused the general from sleep, Meade's astonishment caused him to imagine that he was going to be put under arrest. When he heard what Hardie's errand was, he protested that General Reynolds was senior to him and better qualified. Since, however, his orders admitted no refusal, he hastily threw on a working uniform which happened to lie handy and rode across with Hardie to Hooker's headquarters. Everybody behaved very well. Hooker, though immensely chagrined by his dismissal on the eve of battle, did his best to initiate Meade, a task the more difficult because insecurity had led Hooker to withhold news from his corps commanders.

Meade took over on the twenty-eighth and allowed himself a single, hectic day to learn his duties, relying heavily on Hooker's excellent staff who, though as much distressed as their master, gave loyal support. On the twenty-ninth, Meade set the army once more upon the march. It stumbled upon Lee's before either of them expected at Gettysburg on July 1.

Unquestionably Lee was the most brilliant general on either side in the Civil War, but like every commander who has ever fought a battle, he had some weaknesses. It happened, far more by chance than any generalship of Meade's, that a combination of Lee's faults weighed heavily against him in the Gettysburg battle. When it was over, and the flower of Lee's Army of Northern Virginia lay strewn across the valley, by the fence along the Emmetsburg Road, and up the slopes of Cemetery Ridge, Lee went riding among his beaten troops, telling everyone: "It's all my fault . . . the blame is mine . . . you must help me." By sheer hard fighting, the Army of the Potomac had its victory at last.

Congratulations came pouring in on Meade, but one voice was missing. Abraham Lincoln was waiting for the pursuit and capture of Lee's damaged army. His expectations were high because the crossings of the Potomac were too swollen with recent rains for Lee to get back into Virginia. Lee was forced to wait with his trains of wounded and his depleted army, his back to the river and nowhere to go till the waters went down.

Meade was a defensive general who had won at Gettysburg because Lee had attacked him. He had had almost no time for sleep since taking over command, and his army had suffered enormous casualties. He was content to let Lee recross the Potomac—while the general public, rejoicing in the simultaneous fall of Vicksburg, which had surrendered to Grant on July 4, was not disposed to be critical. All the more did Meade resent the silence of Lincoln and the continuous goading of Halleck, who urged pursuit. When the chance was irrevocably lost, Halleck wired that the President was exceedingly disappointed at the opportunity let slip. This was too much for Meade, who offered his resignation and received a half-apology from the General-in-Chief. He never got the letter which Lincoln had drafted, mentioning his gratitude, to be sure, but dwelling heavily on his disappointment and containing such phrases as: "I do not believe you appreciate the magnitude of the misfortune involved in Lee's escape. . . . Your golden opportunity is gone, and I am distressed immeasureably because of it." Had the general received this, Lincoln would have had to look around for another commander for the Army of the Potomac. As things were, by August 4, a month after Gettysburg, the armies were back in their old encampments on either side of the Rappahannock. Much blood was yet to be shed before Lee and his army surrendered.

Very different from his letter to Meade were Lincoln's words to Grant: "I write this now as a grateful acknowledgment for the almost inestimable service you have done the country." He went on to say that on many occasions he had been distrustful of Grant's strategy, especially when he crossed the river and turned northward east of the Big Black in the daring maneuver which ultimately brought success. "I feared it was a mistake," Lincoln wrote. "I now wish to make the personal acknowledgment that you were right, and I was wrong."

Lincoln set aside August 6 as a day of national thanksgiving for the victories of the summer, but there had been one conspicuous exception to the successes of Northern generals. For the six months since the battle of Murfreesboro, Rosecrans had remained in camp, demanding reinforcements, supplies, and horses, but finding excellent reasons why he should not advance. The victories to east and west of him at Gettysburg and Vicksburg now exercised an irresistible pressure, so that in late July he began a movement which was far more dangerous than it would have been when the pressure of Grant on Vicksburg and the campaign of Lee in Pennsylvania had dried up Confederate reinforcements. With considerable skill he maneuvered his opponent Bragg out of Chattanooga, the gateway to Georgia, while General Burnside, moving into East Tennessee, captured Knoxville. In fact, the Confederacy, split in two by the Federal control of the Mississippi, which soon followed Vicksburg, was threatened in its inner core by Rosecrans. Longstreet with twenty thousand men was rushed out to Bragg, while in response Burnside was ordered to join Rosecrans at once.

On Sunday, September 20, while Lincoln was sleeping in the cottage at the Soldiers' Home, John Hay rode out with a summons from Stanton to an urgent conference. A battle had taken place at Chickamauga and the entire Union left wing had broken up in scenes reminiscent of the panic at First Bull Run. Luckily by next day the news was better. General Thomas in command of the right wing had not only repulsed the enemy on his own front, but had protected the rout of the rest. Rosecrans fell back to Chattanooga without being pressed by Bragg, but the Confederates advanced to occupy the overlooking hills, so that their artillery commanded all roads except a few tracks of bottomless mud. It was possible Rosecrans could not retreat; but if he did not do so, he was bound after a time to be starved into surrender.

Even after two and a half years of war, Lincoln was incredulous to discover that Burnside, repeatedly ordered to reinforce Rosecrans without delay, had not made an effort to do so. "It makes me doubt whether I am awake or dreaming," he wrote. "I have been struggling for ten days . . . to get you to go to assist Gen. Rosecrans in an extremity, and yet you steadily move the contrary way." But the Commander-in-Chief, however furious, cannot express his feelings if he does not want to lose a general whom it would take time to replace. Lincoln put the note aside and simply wired, "Go to Rosecrans without a moment's delay." In addition Hooker, now a corps commander again, was rushed out from the Army of the Potomac with thirty thousand men who, by a miracle of Union logistics, in twelve days were thirty miles from Chattanooga. Sherman, sent by Grant with seventeen thousand men, took longer because he had to repair the railroad as he went.

At Chattanooga the situation had deteriorated. Rosecrans's men were on half-rations. A single wagon of supplies took eight days to arrive by a roundabout route—

half-empty because it had to carry forage for its horses. The War Department, which had somewhat earlier sent Charles A. Dana, Assistant Secretary of War, to report on Rosecrans, was getting from him a far more depressing picture than the general presumably would have sent himself. Rosecrans, who had all too clearly lost control of the battle, seemed dazed by his present position and was not, at least in Dana's view, taking serious measures to avert a surrender which he continued to say he would never make. By good fortune Bragg had lost so heavily in the course of his victory that he did not attack. He did not need to, however, unless something was done beyond sending reinforcements—since they in their turn would need to be fed. By this time the administration knew the name of its best general. They sent Grant.

Grant had spent a good deal of the summer in New Orleans, bored and disgusted with General Banks, to whose assistance he had been ordered. In such a mood, he was liable to one of his bouts of drinking. Whether for this reason or by sheer accident, Grant—who rode like a centaur—had a serious fall and badly crushed his leg. Back in Cairo, he was still on crutches, though he was able to ride if strapped into his seat. On October 17 he was summoned to Louisville, Kentucky, and was on his way by train within an hour. As he happened, however, to pass through Indianapolis, he met Lincoln's messenger there, none other than Stanton himself. Grant was given his choice between two orders, both creating the military district of the Mississippi, including all the area between the Alleghenies and the river, except for the southwest command, reserved for Banks. Both orders put Grant in general charge, but the second gave Rosecrans's command in Chattanooga to General Thomas, who had saved the recent battle. Unhesitatingly, Grant chose this alternative, and his judgment was affirmed by news which Stanton got from Dana at Louisville, revealing that Rosecrans was planning a retreat. Immediately Grant wired to Thomas to assume command and to hold on. He answered, "We will hold Chattanooga till we starve." Grant proceeded to Bridgeport, fifty-five miles from Chattanooga, whence he had to travel on horseback, actually lifted down and carried in the many places where roads had been washed out. On the twenty-third, imperturbable and unimpressive, Grant and his crutches entered Chattanooga, where he began with his accustomed efficiency to put together plans which had been worked out earlier but never applied with any zeal. Within a week he had opened the Bridgeport road. Within another, his supply lines were secure and his men on full rations.

While all this was going on, the states which had elections in the off-year of 1863 were playing politics as usual. Springfield, Illinois, though it had rejected Lincoln's party in 1862, still occupied a political position halfway between radical Chicago and the Copperheads "down Egypt" near Kentucky and the Ohio River. In early September, the National Union Party, as Republicans were now calling themselves, planned a mass meeting in Springfield and invited Lincoln to speak. It must surely have been a temptation to see his home again, but a holiday so far from Washington was not to be considered. Instead Lincoln wrote one of his able state papers in the form of a letter to James C. Conkling, the committee chairman and an old personal friend. Simple, eloquent, cautiously optimistic, it answered criticisms about the continuance of the war and the future of the Negro with that inspired common sense which was so characteristic. The nation, Lincoln pointed out, had needed the help of the Negro. "Why should they do anything for us, if we will do nothing for them? If they stake their lives for us, they must be prompted by the strongest motive—even the promise of freedom. And the promise being made, must be kept." Turning to his hopes for the future, he said: "Peace does not appear so distant as it did. I hope it will come soon and come to stay; and so come as to be worth the keeping in all future time. It will then have been proved that, among free men, there can be no successful appeal from the ballot to the bullet. .... Still, let us not be over-sanguine of a speedy final triumph. Let us be quite sober. Let us diligently apply the means, never doubting that a just God, in his own good time, will give us the rightful result."

These are the sober words of a thoughtful man who had done much pondering over what he was struggling for and how to attain it. They were well received in Springfield and throughout the Union, except among those whose political business it was to decry them. The elections that November showed that Gettysburg and Vicksburg, and some said the President's words, had profoundly affected the general state of mind. The Union ticket carried every free state except New Jersey, while miraculously several men who favored emancipation were elected in the slave states within the Union. Men commented, moreover, that the President had at last become a party asset, standing almost above party in the affections of many Union-loving people.

Very shortly after the battle of Gettysburg, the governors of eighteen states had appointed trustees to establish a cemetery for the men who had died there. Its dedication was scheduled for November 19; and Edward Everett, a celebrated orator from Massachusetts, had been chosen to deliver a eulogy on the occasion. Formal invitations were sent to the President, his Cabinet, members of Congress, the diplomatic corps, and important state politicians. Not many of these were expected to come, and it was only as an afterthought that Lincoln was asked to follow Everett with some brief remarks, declaring, as it were, the cemetery open, and giving it the blessing of the Federal government.

It was not in fact likely that Lincoln would accept, since he generally confined himself to his official public functions, being too busy to do otherwise. However, a prominent Boston man had written to him suggesting that, as he had put Emancipation into its proper perspective in the letter to Conkling, it would be helpful if he also defined the central issue of the war. Whether in response or because his mind was working on similar lines, Lincoln surprised his Cabinet by deciding to go. When it was casually arranged that he arrive by the morning train, say his few words, and get back, he insisted on going to Gettysburg for the night—lest the train be late and people disappointed. It was not easy for Lincoln to take time to prepare what he wanted to say—and in fact he boarded the train with a scribbled draft which he worked over and then again changed slightly after the speech was delivered. On November 18, he left Tad with a fever and Mary Lincoln fearing lest he die like Willie. No doubt Lincoln was anxious too and was relieved to get a reassuring telegram about Tad that evening.

The dedication of Gettysburg Cemetery attracted about fifteen thousand people, including souvenir hunters combing the fields for buttons, bullets, and little bits of shells. The cemetery was not by any means finished, and coffins waiting for their tenants were piled around. Still, Everett made a fine speech for those days, when speechmaking was the most highly skilled form of popular entertainment. His words were lofty, his gestures emphatic, his voice famous; and he gave full value to the occasion by speaking for two solid hours. When he sat down, the President was introduced. Rising to his ungainly height and putting on a pair of steel-rimmed spectacles for reading, Lincoln unfolded two small sheets of paper before delivering, in that queer, high voice which had always carried in the open air, a speech of two hundred and sixty-eight words. He sat down again before his audience knew he had well begun. There was an astonished silence and then some rather scattered applause. Not till the papers published his words the next morning did many comprehend what he had said.

The Gettysburg Address was much more than a speech put together in odds and ends of time and revised on a

train. This is not how great writings are created. The truth
is, Lincoln had lived with this war and his purpose in
waging it ever since he first heard of the bombardment of
Sumter. Being a man of reflection, he had thought much.
Being also under the necessity of explaining himself, not
once but thousands of times, he had hammered his ideas
into words. The phrases of the Gettysburg Address can be
found in embryo in his earlier writings, not all put together, but a sentence here and there—often less polished,
but now linked in his memory with other words he had
said on other occasions. The request for brevity forced him
to combine the expressions which had given him most
satisfaction and to deliver them unmixed with anything
else except a tribute to the men who had died for the cause
he was defining. Many poets have written lines which we
feel would be made worse by the omission or addition of
a phrase, but it is seldom that an orator achieves this perfect effect.

"Four score and seven years ago, our fathers brought
forth upon this continent, a new nation, conceived in Liberty, and dedicated to the proposition that all men are
created equal.

"Now we are engaged in a great civil war, testing
whether that nation, or any nation so conceived, and so
dedicated, can long endure. We are met on a great battlefield of that war. We have come to dedicate a portion of it,
as a final resting place for those who here gave their lives
that that nation might live. It is altogether fitting and
proper that we should do this.

"But in a larger sense we cannot dedicate—we cannot
consecrate—we cannot hallow this ground. The brave
men, living and dead, who struggled here, have conse-
crated it far above our poor power to add or detract. The
world will little note, nor long remember, what we say
here, but it can never forget what they did here. It is for
us, the living, rather to be dedicated here to the unfinished
work which they have, thus far, so nobly advanced. It is

rather for us to be here dedicated to the great task remaining before us—that from these honored dead we take increased devotion to that cause to which they gave the last full measure of devotion—that we here highly resolve that these dead shall not have died in vain; that this nation under God shall have a new birth of freedom; and that government of the people, by the people, for the people, shall not perish from the earth."

It is never safe to leave Lincoln at a high point because his dignity, though natural to him, still surprised his audience. His awkwardness, his natural manner, and his humor made for sudden transitions from the lofty to the prosaic. He did not lay claim to greatness or wish to behave as though he had it. It is entirely in keeping with his character that he should come back from Gettysburg feeling ill and be shortly in bed with a disease diagnosed as varioloid, a mild form of smallpox. A few intrepid persons penetrated to his bedside, but the lines on the stairs of the White House dwindled away. The President, evidently enjoying the only kind of respite granted him, was heard to murmur that now at last he had something which he could give to everyone! What was more, during his illness he received the best kind of present—good news from Chattanooga, where Grant had made his attack on Bragg's besieging army. The troops under Hooker had performed a marvelous feat of arms on Lookout Mountain, storming a position which had seemed impregnable. For the first time since the war began, a major Confederate army had fled the field of battle in confusion.

# 12

## Victory Delayed

BY THE BEGINNING of 1864, Union prospects looked far brighter than they had in early 1863. Arkansas and Texas had been permanently split from the Confederacy by the conquest of the Mississippi River; Louisiana, Tennessee, and Mississippi were under Union occupation. The route to Georgia through the mountains had been opened. Supplies to Lee's army were no longer sufficient for him to make a major offensive. Throughout the Union President Lincoln had become not merely respected, but beloved. His countless acts of kindness, his determination, his ability to express convictions in words which common people could remember, were appreciated because men saw light at the end of the tunnel. But while trust in the President had grown among the people, it had withered among politicians. In a few months Democrats and Republicans, the latter rechristened the Union League Party, would be choosing delegates to their 1864 conventions. No President since Andrew Jackson had received a second term, and it was widely felt that a one-term arrangement had been hallowed by time. Lincoln let it be known that he was available because there was work to be done and he did not think it wise, in his own words, to "swap horses in midstream." Many, however, doubted whether they could win with a candidate who let the war drag on. Still more objected that Lincoln would interfere with their views on Reconstruction. Radicals looked around for other candidates.

It was an open secret that Ulysses Grant was shortly going to become General-in-Chief and would direct the winning of the war. Discovering that in 1856 he had voted for Buchanan, Democrats made approaches to him, only to learn that the general considered himself the servant of the administration and was not interested in overthrowing it. Moreover, his letter about the death of slavery in the South made him unacceptable to many Democrats. On the other hand, Union Leaguers had a radical candidate ready to their hand.

Of the various men whom Lincoln had beaten in 1860 and then incorporated in his Cabinet, Bates was too old to be considered and Seward, whose lively sense of humor had finally given him a good deal of intimacy with Lincoln, was resigned to being Secretary of State. Qualities which had made him possible in 1860 were unacceptable in the grimmer days of 1864. There remained Salmon P. Chase, Secretary of the Treasury, who represented the radicals in the Cabinet and had long made it his business to cultivate their leaders in Congress. Chase was a handsome, humorless, religious man who prided himself on freedom from any taint of moral laxity. As a politician, however, he did not consider intrigue a disgrace unless it was discovered. His inside information had emboldened the Republican Senators to demand control of the Cabinet in December, 1862. Chase had let his supporters down on that occasion because his reputation was more important to him than backing up his fellow conspirators. This had been clear to all concerned, and Chase had lost ground. He devoted 1863 to regaining it.

The patronage of the Treasury was enormous. Not only

did Chase control over twelve thousand jobs throughout the country, but the advertisement of Treasury bonds for sale was part of the income of many newspapers. Directly and through agents, Chase spent 1863 in putting men in office who were prepared to work actively for him and to contribute money. Lincoln, though urged to dismiss a man who was intriguing against the administration from within, merely replied that Chase was a good Secretary of the Treasury. It was not easy for the President to upset the delicate balance of Cabinet opinion and offend the radicals in Congress for a personal reason. The unity of the Republican Party might be at stake—and this in an election year. Lincoln waited for Chase to overreach himself, while the two men, never congenial, confined their intercourse to official matters.

In February, 1864, Senator Pomeroy of Kansas, who was Chase's unofficial manager, issued a circular to state conventions, some of which came early in the year. It stated that the cause of liberty and the honor of the nation would suffer by Lincoln's re-election, and that Chase possessed more qualifications for office than any other man in politics. The President, it was asserted, was organizing official patronage to buy himself supporters, and it was up to state conventions to foil this corrupt plot by nominating Salmon P. Chase.

The Pomeroy circular, though marked strictly private, was published at once. Its attacks on Lincoln, which did not lack force, aroused great criticism of Chase, since it seemed impossible that the letter could have been issued without his knowledge. Touched in his vanity, Chase disclaimed responsibility and offered Lincoln his resignation. Lincoln answered calmly that he had not read the circular and did not mean to do so. He had not been surprised because he had known a good deal about Mr. Pomeroy's committee, though he had remained as ignorant as his friends would allow. Having thus implied that Chase through his closer radical connections must have known

far more, the President concluded that the Treasury ought
to be headed in the interest of the public service and that
he did not "perceive occasion for a change." After this
masterly letter, Lincoln's relations with Chase became
more difficult than ever. Furthermore, since everyone believed that the remarks about Lincoln in the Pomeroy letter had indeed been inspired by Chase, they aroused great
indignation against him, inducing many state conventions
to nominate Lincoln, whose position was virtually assured
before the National Convention opened.

The man who did most to get rid of Chase was Frank
Blair, brother of the Postmaster General and the Missouri
member of that clannish and ambitious family. Frank had
gone into the army and done much better than most political appointees. He was at this time a brigadier general, but
he had also won a seat in Congress which he could not take
without resigning his commission. Lincoln, who wanted
him as Speaker of the House, suggested he should take his
seat. If he failed to get the job, Lincoln would reappoint
him to the army. Blair did not become Speaker, but lin-
gered in the House for several weeks with the intention of
speaking his mind. Both of the brothers Blair were forceful
men, but Frank, tall, wiry, and red-bearded, had his reputation as a soldier to give weight to what he said. In two
devastating speeches, he attacked the Treasury Department for corruption, fraudulent deals with the enemy in
cotton, and all kinds of unsavory scandals. A good deal of
this, inherent in the situation, was not precisely Chase's
fault. But a minister who chooses his agents because they
will vote for him as President has his eye on the wrong
ball. Frank Blair spoke from detailed knowledge of what
was going on in the West. Having destroyed Chase as a
political force and made the Blairs a number of active
enemies, he went back to the army.

Still Chase hung on to his office. The Union League
Convention was to be held on June 7, and his conviction
that he was the right man was as strong as it had been in

1860. Once more he was disappointed. Except for twenty two favorite-son votes from Missouri (which went to Grant, who was not even a candidate), every state, including Chase's own Ohio, voted for Lincoln on the first ballot.

After this it was possible for Lincoln to rid himself of Chase for other than personal reasons. An opportunity soon arose. It was Lincoln's practice to leave appointments in the various departments to those who headed them, provided always that the congressional delegation from the state involved gave its approval. Without this, he foresaw, the party could not hold together. Thus when Chase nominated an assistant treasurer in New York, Lincoln refused to confirm him on the grounds that Senator Morgan of that state was strongly opposed and had suggested three other candidates. Stiffly Chase asked for a private interview on the subject. Lincoln refused, saying that the difficulty did not lie "within the range of a conversation between you and me." Chase resigned again on June 30, and Lincoln, with what must have been a sigh of relief, let him go. Chase was hurt and astonished that Lincoln's letter accepting his resignation had made no response to "the sentiments of respect and esteem that mine contained." As may be seen afterwards, the President reserved these for a later occasion.

It need not be supposed that Chase was the only radical candidate to be considered. Frémont, for instance, was backed by a section of the Party, but his military reputation was by now so bad that he did not appeal to Republicans as a whole. It was a period when politicians seemed less important than soldiers—and the best of the latter were busy. All the same, Lincoln's attitude toward Reconstruction had made him thoroughly unwelcome to radicals in Congress and to the state organizations which had elected them.

Lincoln's concept of the peace he wanted was moderate and reasonable. The Union must be restored. Slaves who had been promised freedom must get it. But he hoped for a peace that would endure and a solution to the racial problem of the South which would make sense. He did not, for instance, think that Negro field hands with a vocabulary of about two hundred words were capable of voting —yet. He was prepared to move gradually, let bygones be bygones, and concentrate on reuniting the country. Accordingly he added to his regular message to Congress in December, 1863, a proclamation guaranteeing full pardon to all rebels except a few leading ones, provided they would take an oath of allegiance to the Union and swear to support the Emancipation Proclamation and all acts of Congress dealing with slaves. When in any rebel state one-tenth of the number voting in 1860 should wish to establish a loyal government, they should be permitted to do so, be protected by Federal power, and would be considered members of the United States under the Constitution.

Lincoln based the proclamation on his power of granting pardons, but he was well aware that Congress had the right to exclude representatives of restored Southern states if it pleased. Furthermore, though for the moment all seemed to approve his plan, it was only a question of time before President and Congress would be at odds about where power lay and what terms were to be granted to those who surrendered. Only a few weeks after Lincoln's proclamation, the Wade-Davis bill began to take shape in House and Senate, not merely with the intention of imposing stiffer terms on Southern states, but also of asserting the right of Congress to decide them. The Wade-Davis bill required a loyalty oath from a majority of the 1860 voting population before a state could be recognized. No one who had held state or Confederate office or who had borne arms against the United States could vote for or serve as delegate to a state constitutional convention. No Confederate officer was eligible for elected office. Congress, in other words, did not desire complete reconstruction of the Southern states for years, perhaps for a generation. Delay would give the majority a chance to pass other laws and to take policy out of the hands of the President into its own. Lincoln gave the Wade-Davis bill a pocket veto and published an explanation of why he had done so. Free-state governments were already established by a tenth of the 1860 voters in Louisiana and Arkansas. He did not wish to tear them down. Congress had incorporated in the bill a provision prohibiting slavery in reconstructed states. Lincoln had never thought Congress had power to interfere with slavery within the states. He did not now—except by their passing a constitutional amendment.

The leaders of Congress, radicals, but members of Lincoln's own party, were as angry with him as they had ever been. They published an answer in the New York *Tribune* which took the form of a savage, personal attack on Lincoln for usurping authority which did not belong to him and creating governments expressly to vote for him in the forthcoming election. Lincoln would not even read it. Its authors, after all, were his "supporters," men of the party who had elected him to office and sustained him—more or less—through a terrible war. "To be wounded in the house of one's friends," he said, "is perhaps the most grievous affliction that can befall a man." He had indicated that if the voters really wanted a different form of Reconstruction from the one he had already put in motion, he might be forced to change his policy. He did not think they would when they understood the issues.

The Wade-Davis bill was passed by Congress on July 3, 1864, and the angry response of the radicals to Lincoln's veto was published on August 5. The previous March a slightly built man with dark hair and inexpressive features overgrown by a thick, reddish beard and moustache stepped off a train onto the Washington platform, leading a small boy by the hand. Father and son made their way to Willard's hotel, where they were received without enthusiasm. Willard's was used to every sort of distinguished guest, so that the stooped shoulders and shabby uniform of the latest arrival made little impression on the clerk at the desk until the stranger signed his name as U. S. Grant. There was a flurry among the servants, but none of the passersby (and everybody did pass at some time or another through Willard's) noticed the man who was about to be created Lieutenant General—the first since Washington, unless one counts the purely temporary rank of Winfield Scott. Grant made his way to his room and presently came down to dinner. At this point he was recognized; the dining room was soon buzzing, and someone, mounting on a chair, called for three cheers. Grant looked embarrassed, astonished, even annoyed; but he rubbed his moustache with his napkin, got to his feet, and made a clumsy bow. He was allowed to finish his dinner with such aplomb as he could muster, but was mobbed as he tried to make his way out of the dining room. Exposed in this fashion, he could do no more than call on President Lincoln that very evening, where he found himself at the usual weekly reception, more crowded than ever because a rumor was already going around that he would be present. Once more he managed to arrive inconspicuously; but as soon as he was announced to the President and was seen shaking hands, everyone made a wild rush to have a look at him. Crinolines were mashed and people got on sofas, chairs, or tables to be out of harm's way. Grant, who was forced to take refuge on a crimson-covered sofa, looked scared. Presently he was smuggled out and, after a private interview with Lincoln and the formal presentation of his new commission, left Washington for the Army of the Potomac.

The significance of Grant's commission was that he outranked everybody, including the General-in-Chief. He had, in fact, been brought east to win the war, and it was entirely up to him to decide how to do it. His plan was very like that of Lincoln, a concerted move forward by all the Federal armies at once. "Those who can't skin can hold a leg," agreed the delighted President, well knowing that the Confederacy did not have the manpower to reinforce every theater of war at the same time. The Army of the Potomac was to attack Lee; and while it did so, Benjamin Butler, in command at Norfolk, was to put together about thirty-three thousand men from the occupation troops around Norfolk and in South Carolina, and move up the James River toward Richmond. Sherman, striking out from Chattanooga, was to consider his objective the army which had lately been Bragg's and had been transferred after his defeat to Joseph Johnston, one of the Confederacy's most skillful generals but not in favor with President Jefferson Davis, who considered him lacking in aggressive spirit. Atlanta, grown during the war into a big Confederate arsenal, would be Sherman's secondary objective. It was somewhat more than a hundred miles away over hilly country, right in the heart of Georgia. As soon as he could disentangle himself from his operations on the Red River, Banks should move from New Orleans toward Mobile, while Sigel, now covering the Shenandoah Valley, should advance toward its head. The Confederacy, attacked from five points at once, was bound to yield somewhere.

Unfortunately for Grant, Generals Banks, Sigel, and Butler, all political appointees, were not equal to the jobs assigned to them. This left the main attacks to Sherman and to the Army of the Potomac, whose command situation was now a fearful and wonderful thing with Meade its general and Grant its super-general. Since Meade and Grant were dedicated soldiers, free from the ambitions which had led other generals to ally themselves with congressional factions, the system managed to work, but not perfectly. Halleck, left in Washington in charge of a central office, had a job which he did adequately since responsibility was no longer his, even in name.

Unhappily Grant did not win the war in the summer of 1864. He failed partly because the threat to Lee's rear up the James River by Butler was easily countered, and partly because the superiority of the defensive over the offensive had become greater throughout the war as men learned techniques of entrenchment. Victories, including those of

Lee, had been possible because the land was big enough to maneuver in. This was far less true when Lee stood on the defensive before Richmond, because the Southerners held interior lines and knew the point that Grant was driving for. Lee's weakness was that though he might inflict twice the losses that he suffered, he could not in the end survive the exchange. Lincoln already understood this, saying after Chancellorsville that great though Union losses had been, they could be afforded, whereas the Confederate losses could not. But true though this was, Grant's battles were fought near Washington, where their cost was made very visible by the long trains of wounded evacuated from field hospitals.

Meanwhile Joseph Johnston and Sherman were fighting things out across Georgia. Atlanta being a good way from Chattanooga, Sherman had more room to maneuver than Grant—and he persistently tried to put himself across his enemy's supply line—at which point Johnston would retreat, and the whole movement would have to be repeated. Progress was slow, and Sherman's army constantly diminished because he had to leave garrisons to guard the rickety railroad which brought his supplies from Chattanooga, while Johnston, whose lines of supply were shortened as he retreated, picked up strength.

The honeymoon era of Grant's control of the army lasted just long enough to insure Lincoln's renomination as his party's candidate for President. Little over a week later the Army of the Potomac, which had by now moved from the Rapidan to Petersburg, sustained about ten thousand casualties in four days and settled down to a siege which showed no sign of ending. About four weeks later, on July 19, Lincoln issued a call for another half-million recruits, effective as of September 5. The proclamation reinforced the almost universal impression that Grant was feeding men into a gigantic meat-grinder.

This might not have been so bad if it had been obvious that Lee was in effect pinned down south of Richmond and would never be able to take the offensive again. But late in June he detached General Early with seventeen thousand men to get in the rear of General Hunter, who had replaced Sigel and was advancing down the Shenandoah Valley. Early did so and drove Hunter back upon the Kanawha River, which left the way open to Washington and Baltimore. Grant hastily sent a division to Baltimore, but it was insufficient to deter Early. Advancing through Hagerstown and Frederick, which he forced to pay ransom to avoid being burned to the ground, Early reached Silver Spring, where he set fire to the home of Montgomery P. Blair, part of the Blair estate where the President had played with the children on the lawn with his coattails flying. Refugees came pouring into Washington, where the Quartermaster-General hastily organized the military clerks of his office into fighting troops. On July 11, Early's guns could be heard from the White House, but luckily more troops from Grant arrived. On the twelfth, the President went out to Fort Stevens on Seventh Street, which had been hurriedly strengthened and was engaging a scattering of Early's forward troops. Standing up to get a good view with the innocent courage of a lifelong civilian, Lincoln is said to have been told "Get down, you damn fool!" by young Captain Oliver Wendell Holmes, later a distinguished Associate Justice of the Supreme Court. Lincoln was no more concerned about the safety of Washington than he was about his own. What he wanted was the capture of Early and his men. They slipped away, however, on the night of July 12, leaving Grant and Lincoln damaged in reputation and the country crying out for a peace which had seemed just around the corner months ago.

Horace Greeley of the New York *Tribune* started a clamor that Confederate emissaries were at Niagara, just across the Canadian border, waiting to negotiate. Lincoln insisted that Greeley go himself to talk with them, accompanied by his own secretary, young Hay. Not surprisingly the Confederates turned out to have no official authority and were in Canada in the hope of helping the anti-Lincoln forces in the coming election. News of Greeley's mission got about, however, and it was rumored that Lincoln was responsible for the negotiations coming to nothing. Since Greeley refused to allow his letters to be published without including some discouraging expressions about the bankrupt state of the country, Lincoln shouldered the blame instead of explaining.

In mid-July, Grant's next costly effort to break through into Petersburg was bungled by Burnside, whose troops were to have led the assault. To the Shenandoah Valley Grant sent tough little Philip Sheridan with orders to follow Early to the death. Sheridan's force proved not strong enough, and Grant considered leading reinforcements in person. But he disliked every demand which might weaken his hold on Lee. Lincoln wired him: "I have seen your despatch expressing your unwillingness to break your hold where you are. Neither am I willing. Hold on with a bull-dog grip and chew & choke as much as possible." The advantage of Grant from Lincoln's viewpoint was that when he suffered a repulse, no matter how costly, he did not retreat, but started planning another attack. Eventually, as the President calculated, he would break through Lee's weakened lines; but his failure to do so in July and August threatened to be catastrophic. There was a movement to call another convention for the end of September and force Lincoln to resign. Even friends told him that he could not be re-elected. In his study Lincoln wrote out the following promise: "This morning, as for some days past, it seems exceedingly probable that this administration will not be re-elected. Then it will be my duty to so co-operate with the President elect, as to save the Union between the election and the inaugeration; as he will have secured his election on such ground that he cannot possibly save it afterwards." He sealed the paper and asked his Cabinet members to sign it on the back. Then he put it in his desk without telling anyone what it contained.

At this low ebb in Lincoln's fortunes the Democrats held their convention in Chicago, having postponed it as long as they could to take advantage of the universal longing for peace. They were still divided into those who under Vallandigham demanded peace at once without victory, and those under men like Seymour who thought that the desperate position of the South would make it possible to restore the Union by offering favorable terms. When it came to drawing up a platform, Vallandigham was the dominating figure—the Democrats going on record in favor of immediately stopping the war. But the only candidate likely to win was General McClellan, who could be presented as the victim of Republican persecution and a man who would have won the war if the government had backed him. Unfortunately for the look of things McClellan, though readily accepting the nomination, announced that in the names of his slain and wounded comrades he could not support immediate peace without restoration of the Union. Thus platform and candidate were at variance, but the Democrats remained hopeful of drawing votes from both types of opposition to the Lincoln government.

They had hardly broken up before news came over the telegraph from Sherman: "Atlanta is ours and fairly won." It had after all not been true that the siege of Atlanta would be a stalemate as long and desperate as that of Richmond. With the Union forces established in the heart of Georgia, the war again looked nearly won, and Lincoln's prospects immediately soared. On September 12, Sheridan, who had recently been reinforced at Lincoln's suggestion, launched a smashing blow at Early and used his victory to devastate the Shenandoah Valley. All mills and barns, every straw and wheat stack were burned, cattle carried off. The once-fertile land was turned into a desert which could never again support an advancing army. Grant's generals were waging war to win and apparently would soon do so.

It now looked probable that Lincoln would be re-elected after all. Even the extreme radicals, who had put up Fré-

mont in opposition, could do no better with their candidate than use him as a bargaining counter. The resignation
of Chase had upset the balance in the Cabinet and the
radicals were determined to have their revenge by getting
rid of Montgomery Blair, whose brother Frank had played
such a notable part in Chase's fall. Montgomery himself
saw that he would have to go, and Lincoln had his resignation in his pocket. Frémont was persuaded to withdraw in
the interest of party unity, and Lincoln allowed Blair to
leave the Cabinet, appointing William Dennison of Ohio,
a man of high character and great charm, to take his place.

These victories and political maneuvers unified the Republican Party in support of the administration. With the
future of the country at stake, Lincoln did not hesitate to
fight under the old cutthroat political rules. Ohio, Pennsylvania, and Indiana held state elections in October—and the
results in these important states would be an informal
national poll which was expected to have great effect on
the presidential election. Ohio and Pennsylvania allowed
soldiers to cast absentee ballots. Indiana did not, and Indiana had twenty-nine regiments and a couple of batteries
serving with Sherman. Lincoln asked Sherman to grant
wholesale furloughs to these men, and Sherman did so,
though his military plans were affected thereby and his
position at the end of a long supply line from Tennessee
was uneasy. All three states with the help of the soldier
vote recorded Republican victories.

During these months of anxiety and preoccupation, it
cannot have been easy for Lincoln to give much thought
to his personal affairs. But in the preceding April he had
received a letter from his cousin Dennis Hanks about his
stepmother Sally Bush Lincoln who, when he left for
Washington, had been seventy-two and getting too feeble
to live alone in the shack which Thomas Lincoln had built
in Coles County, Illinois. Dennis's letter, which was more
or less an appeal for funds, was disquieting:

"I Received your Little check for 50.00 I shoed it to

Mother. She cried like a Child. Abe she is mity childish heep of trouble to us. Betsy is very feble and has to wait on her which ort to have sum person to wait on her we are getting old. We have a great many to wait on of our Connections they will come to see us while we Live. . . ."

Dennis either wanted money for a servant to look after Sally and his wife, or he wanted to get rid of the old lady who called the President of the United States her "best boy in the world" and loved him as much, if not more, than she did her own three children. When Lincoln had lived in Springfield and had gone twice yearly on circuit with the court, it had been fairly easy for him to keep an eye on his relatives. It was impossible now. Infrequent letters from illiterate people offered no solution, while his legal and political friends in Illinois had no standing and little acquaintance with Sally Bush Lincoln and her kin.

No doubt Lincoln did what he could, but six months later, in the midst of his troubles about the coming election, he got another letter about Sally, this time from his cousin John Hall. "Grand Mother she is quite poor. I write to inform you that Grand Mother has not and does not receive one cent of the money you send her Dennis & Chapman [Dennis's son-in-law] keep all the money you send her, she now needs clothes and shoes, they have all the money in their Pockett, & Uncle Dennis is cussing you all the time and abusing me & your best Friends for supporten you they make you believe they are taking Care of her which is not the case. I & Mother are now takeing care of her and have for the past four years—If you wish her to have any thing send it by check here to the bank at Charleston or send some her I tell you by the honor of a Man she does not get it & he and Dennis has threatened to put her on the county. . . ."

We do not know what Lincoln did about this letter, but we know he loved his old "Mama" and can only wonder how he straightened out the tangled affair. Old Sally was still living in her own old shack on Goose Nest Prairie with one of her grandsons when Lincoln died. "I knowed they'd kill him," she said. "I ben awaitin' fur it." Mary Lincoln, who had never in her life been out to see her, was too prostrated to do more than write her a note and send some clothes, which the family indignantly described as perfectly useless.

While the state elections were going on in October, the administration was fighting for re-election with every resource at its disposal. Cabinet members were assessed for contributions to the cause and in most cases saw that appointees in their vast departments gave financial and practical help. Lincoln promised to make James Gordon Bennett, editor of the New York *Herald*, minister to France in return for his paper's support. Officially the President did not make election speeches, but he was careful to meet groups of soldiers as they passed through Washington and in informal talks explain the issues at stake. There were some lengths, however, to which he would not go. When a deputation pleaded with him to gain popularity by modifying the draft, he merely answered: "What is the Presidency to me if I have no country?"

Election Day in Washington was wet, and the streets looked empty, but returns were favorable to Lincoln from the start. Lincoln, who had felt grave and anxious, showed no exultation as he sent the early telegrams over from Party headquarters to the White House, saying that Mrs. Lincoln was more worried than he.

Mary Lincoln was not merely worried—she was desperate. To her favorite dressmaker she confessed that she owed over twenty-seven thousand dollars to New York stores, adding, "If he is re-elected, I can keep him in ignorance of my affairs; but if he is defeated, then the bills will be sent in, and he will know all." Since early in 1864, she had been making appeals, sometimes accompanied with tears, to men whom she regarded as owing political debts for favors done them. If they would only help with her bills and avoid scandal, she would change her ways. She did get some assistance from those who feared her influence with her husband or her knowledge of petty graft—yet as the election neared, her frenzy mounted. If Lincoln's enemies found out how much she owed, they would be able to cast doubts on her husband's integrity and might throw him out of office.

Unaware of the source of his wife's anxieties, Lincoln presided over an oyster supper at midnight on Election Day and told his friends how after the election of 1860 he had gone home and thrown himself down on a sofa facing a large mirror which hung on the opposite wall. In it he saw his own face with two images, one not quite covering the other. One face was his own natural color, the other paler. Mrs. Lincoln had taken it as a sign that her husband would be twice elected, but would not live through his second term. Lincoln had a mild interest in such superstitions, but Mary, though her fears were easily aroused, generally forgot one source of alarm upon discovering another. In any case, Lincoln was once again President.

# 13

## The End in Sight

SHERMAN'S CAPTURE OF ATLANTA at the end of August, 1864, had virtually insured Lincoln's re-election by giving proof that the Union was winning the war. Neither the defensive skill of Johnston nor the daring of Hood, who had replaced him, nor even the long and vulnerable railroad which brought Sherman's supplies from Tennessee had prevented the Union army from establishing itself in the heart of Georgia. Flushed with hope, many ceased to blame Lincoln for the blunders which had prolonged the war and hailed him as the leader whose persistence was being vindicated. Nevertheless, both Lincoln's re-election and the caliber of Republicans returned to Congress indicated that the Union which was coming out of the struggle would be different from that which over six hundred thousand men had died to preserve.

For one thing, the office of the Presidency had changed. During the war Lincoln had exercised wider powers than his predecessors—freeing slaves by proclamation, suspending habeas corpus, granting amnesty to rebels, recognizing new state governments founded by a tenth of the voting population. Taken all together, such acts formed a body of precedent which enormously strengthened the Executive Branch. Lincoln had justified them as necessary in war. But would not the need for an enduring peace soon become as vital to him as winning the war in the first place? It was possible that after fighting to preserve government *of* the people, Lincoln might find himself defending government *for* the people. Even supposing, however, that he settled his differences with Congress over Reconstruction, would future Presidents not learn from his example that many degrees of urgency calling for special measures could be handled by the Chief Executive?

If the Presidency was stronger than it had ever been, the same thing was true of the Federal government. The most important sign of this was the conscription act, allowing the central government to draft citizens inside their own states. The suspension of habeas corpus permitted other citizens to be arrested by Federal officials, tried by court-martial for treason, or held indefinitely without trial. Emancipation of slaves, though proclaimed by the President at a time when he had no power to impose it, was becoming a fact in Georgia and wherever else the Union armies came. It had dawned at last on slaveholders of the loyal border states that they were not powerful enough by themselves to maintain the institution. These states had always been largely slave breeders and found slavery unprofitable when deprived of Southern markets. Some border-state men had not protested when a constitutional amendment banning slavery in the United States passed the Senate in April, 1864, and only just failed to win its two-thirds of the House. Once safely re-elected, Lincoln threw his own weight behind this amendment, pointing out to House members in the lame-duck session that they might as well pass it, since the new Congress when sworn in would certainly do so. He bought what votes he could by promise of favors and the amendment passed in January, 1865.

Appropriately, in the middle of October, 1864, when the

old order was noticeably dead and the new one had not taken definite shape, Chief Justice Taney of the Supreme Court died at the age of eighty-seven. Taney, associated in men's minds with the Dred Scott decision, was in his own person a reminder of that half-slave, southern-dominated Union which had vanished forever.

Lincoln's attitude toward the Supreme Court had been determined as much as anything by the Dred Scott decision. Refusing to accept its general implications, such as admitting slavery into the Territories, Lincoln had merely considered it a decision on the status of Dred Scott. On more general points he had hoped for a gradual reversal as a change in administration altered the personnel of the Court. Accordingly, when the split between North and South produced vacancies, he did not fill them with distinguished jurists, but with men who shared his point of view. Typical of these was David Davis, whom Lincoln had known as judge in the Eighth Judicial Circuit of Illinois. Davis had headed the delegation whose shrewd bargaining had won Lincoln the nomination in the 1860 Republican Convention. He was no profound lawyer and lent the Court little distinction, but his opinions on slavery matched Lincoln's, while party solidarity was reinforced by this signal reward for political favors.

Taney's death, which had not unnaturally been expected ever since Lincoln's first inauguration, gave opportunity for a more distinguished appointment. Over the years, Lincoln had gotten used to the notion that Salmon P. Chase was the man for this position. A distinguished lawyer with anti-slavery convictions, a former Governor and Cabinet member, acceptable to the radical Republicans in Congress, Chase was well qualified in every way, provided that the post would satisfy his almost insane ambition. By the time Taney actually died, Chase's intrigues against Lincoln from inside the Cabinet had led to an estrangement between the two men. For a long time they had hardly spoken save on official matters. Since Chase's resignation their contacts had been rare.

In these circumstances, Chase and his friends felt uncertain whether Lincoln would give him the position of Chief Justice. Other able lawyers were suggested as days stretched into weeks while Lincoln did nothing. Unable to bear the suspense, Chase wrote the President a personal letter, which Lincoln tossed to his secretary, saying: "File it with his other recommendations."

The fact was that Lincoln still felt that for the good of the Party and the satisfaction of its leaders in Congress, Chase should be created Chief Justice. In the past, however, though it had always been his practice to appoint men to office for political reasons, he had carefully considered how well the man he preferred would do the job. Experience had caused him to have doubts about Chase. Would he act in the Supreme Court as he had done in the Treasury—with an eye to the advantage of men who would support him for President in 1868? Lincoln even took advice as to whether he could make it a condition that Chase renounce the Presidency altogether. It was pointed out to him, however, that a President had no right to prevent the party or the people from choosing whom they pleased as his successor. Either he must trust Chase to do the duties of his high office, or not appoint him. In early December, Lincoln did at last recommend Chase to the Senate. It is notable that no personal grudge had caused his hesitation. The Presidency had become more powerful, but the man who held it was still the same shrewd, kindly person.

No anecdote of Lincoln's life shows more clearly his readiness to overlook every form of personal injury than his famous advice to Captain Cutts, brother-in-law of Stephen A. Douglas and a soldier of conspicuous bravery, whose uncontrollable temper had caused him to receive an official reprimand from the Commander-in-Chief. Disclaiming all intention of a reprimand, save in form, Lincoln spoke to Cutts with great kindness, while giving him advice which formed the basis of his own principles of action. "The advice of a father to a son 'Beware of entrance

to a quarrel, but being in, bear it that the opposed may
beware of thee' is good, yet not the best. Quarrel not at all.
No man resolved to make the most of himself can spare
time for personal contention." Lincoln practiced what he
preached. When a friend exulted over the news that Senator Davis, a consistent radical critic of Lincoln, had not
been re-elected in November, 1864, the President answered: "You have more of that feeling of personal resentment than I. Perhaps I have too little of it, but I never
thought it paid. A man has no time to spend half his life
in quarrels. If any man ceases to attack me I never remember the past against him."

Intellectually and practically, Lincoln had grown with
his greater burdens. It was no longer necessary for him to
appeal to one of his generals: "The bottom is out of the tub.
What shall I do?" He had learned to deal with generals and
had exercised considerable influence on Grant's strategy,
while leaving him complete control of its execution. He
had shown himself capable of managing not merely Seward, whom he liked, but Stanton, whom nobody seemed
to like and who still regarded his chief at times with something like contempt. Yet Lincoln's shingle was still hang-
ing out in Springfield, and he thought nostalgically of going home again to practice law.

His eloquence had greatly developed since 1858, when
Douglas had called him the best stump speaker in the West.
Dry jokes and personal allusions had been pruned away.
Lincoln the President did not like impromptu speeches.
Instead he labored over letters which were in fact public
statements of his position. His messages to Congress, just
as carefully worked out, were not personally delivered. His
First and Second Inaugurals and the Gettysburg Address
were read from texts and not spoken from notes. He had
shifted from a provincial to a national audience and had
stripped off everything that might obscure his meaning,
achieving forms of expression which were memorable to
the country at large and in many cases are remembered
still.

In November, Sherman cut his communications with
Tennessee and set out from Atlanta through the heart of
Georgia for Savannah, blazing a trail of devastation sixty
miles wide along the course of his three-hundred-mile
march. His opponent Hood sought to emulate Lee by in-
vading Tennessee in Sherman's absence; but Sherman had
left Thomas behind to guard against this maneuver. By
abandoning his strung-out lines, Sherman was able to leave
Thomas a force larger than Hood's while still retaining
over sixty thousand men in his own army. On December
15, Thomas won a great victory which he followed up in
such style that Hood's army ceased to exist as an effective
fighting force. On Christmas Eve, Lincoln received a telegram from Sherman: "I beg to present you as a Christmas
gift the city of Savannah." In the middle of January the
port of Wilmington, long a haven for blockade runners,
was finally closed.

All these events had their effects on Lee's defense of
Richmond. Supplies dried up, so that there was a terrible
shortage of overcoats, blankets, and even shoes inside his
lines that winter. Desertions rose when men from Georgia
and (as Sherman started north) from the Carolinas heard
terrible news from home. Nevertheless, the Confederate
capital still held out. Peace movements might arise in
North Carolina and Governor Brown of Georgia might
refuse to send soldiers outside his own beleaguered state,
but President Jefferson Davis and General Robert E. Lee
seemed still of one mind. It was possible to be captured and
—in Lee's view at least—to be conquered. To negotiate a
peace could only be considered if the United and the Confederate States remained two countries.

The position of the effective leaders of the Confederacy
was clear to Lincoln because his own was equally unyield-
ing. Other men felt that inexorable logic must lead to a
peace offer from the South. It was surely wiser to let the
Confederacy realize its position than to drive it into unconditional surrender. Prominent among would-be negotiators was Francis P. Blair, a personal friend of Lincoln's,

who had perhaps the longest political record of anyone on the Washington scene. In the middle of December, the old statesman asked if he could go south to see Jefferson Davis and persuade him to accept terms.

"Come to me after Savannah falls," Lincoln told him.

Accordingly, as soon as Christmas was over, Blair asked for and received a pass to travel south. He had, however, misjudged his old friend Jefferson Davis and brought back nothing with him but a promise that Davis would send commissioners to treat if Lincoln wished it, "with a view to secure peace between the two countries."

This blatant refusal to treat on Lincoln's terms could not be acceptable. "You may say," Lincoln replied to Blair, ". . . that I . . . am . . . ready to receive any agent whom he . . . may informally send me with the view of securing peace to our one common country."

It might be supposed that after this exchange there was nothing more to say; but events were too strong for both Presidents. Davis could not refuse to appoint three peace commissioners: Alexander H. Stephens of Georgia, Confederate Vice President; Judge John A. Campbell of Alabama, former Justice of the U.S. Supreme Court; and R. M. T. Hunter of Virginia. His instructions still ran that they should hold informal conferences "for the purpose of securing peace to our two countries." They duly arrived at Grant's headquarters, and were met by an envoy from Lincoln who reported their unacceptable position. By this time, however, Grant had joined the ranks of those people who felt necessity would force the Confederate envoys— no matter what they said—to listen to reason.

Lincoln now perceived that he could not refuse to listen if the Confederates would offer surrender. Accordingly, he and Seward met the envoys aboard the *River Queen* in Hampton Roads. A rather strange conference followed between people who had been once acquaintances or even personal friends, but could no longer find any common ground. Lincoln would make no bargains until the Confederates laid down their arms. Hunter pointed out that King Charles I of England, who had a very high idea of his kingly office, had stooped to negotiate with men in arms against him. Lincoln replied drily that he was not "posted" on history. All that he distinctly remembered about Charles I was that he lost his head. Hunter supposed that Lincoln looked on the leaders of the Confederacy as traitors. That was "about the size of it," Lincoln grimly agreed. There was a short silence. "Well, Mr. Lincoln," retorted Hunter with a smile, "we have about concluded that we shall not be hanged as long as you are President— if we behave ourselves."

That was indeed about the size of it. The only positive thing that came out of the conference was Lincoln's admission that North and South were equally responsible for slavery. He thought that the United States government should compensate slave owners if the institution were voluntarily abolished. Two days after the conference he proposed to his Cabinet that the country appropriate four hundred million dollars as compensation to owners, provided that hostilities should stop by April 1. Rarely was a more magnanimous gesture made by a victor, but the Cabinet unanimously disapproved. Congress was not in a forgiving mood and would see no reason to fight for victory and pay for it as well. Lincoln agreed sadly that it would be best to say nothing of his proposal outside the Cabinet.

The commissioners returned to Richmond, but Jefferson Davis could not let the Confederacy fall to pieces without making a further effort. He instructed General Lee to approach Grant with suggestions for a military convention. Grant had the reputation of knowing little about politics and might sign an agreement which Lincoln would feel himself obliged to honor. Grant, however, had at least a clear conception of where military affairs began and ended. He wired to Lincoln, who replied at once that he was not to negotiate for anything but the surrender of Lee's army. All other decisions were reserved for the President. Nothing now remained for President Davis but to let matters take their inevitable course. To Lee, nations or armies had been conquered before and might be again, but Jefferson Davis shut his eyes to this fact, not even admitting that the Confederacy might be destroyed so long as its people, of whom he was the representative, still believed in it.

Lincoln's second inauguration on March 4, 1865, occurring only a few weeks before the inevitable end of the war, was a more hopeful occasion than his first one. It was a raw March day, and the procession passed up Pennsylvania Avenue through mud. In 1861, Republicans new to power had flocked to Washington to seek appointments. Four years later, the throng of applicants was necessarily smaller because the Republican Party had settled in. A couple of jarring personal details marred the occasion. Mary Lincoln, who a few months earlier had been promising in tears to reduce her expenses, spent two thousand dollars on her gown for the inaugural ball. Andrew Johnson, who had been ill, primed himself with whiskey to get through the ceremony of being sworn in as Vice President —and so overdid it that he was scandalously and loudly drunk. Lincoln's Second Inaugural Address was short and not as popular as it might have been, had he exulted in the prospect of victory instead of admitting that the guilt of slavery lay on North and South alike. "If God will that [war] continue, until all the wealth piled by the bondman's two hundred and fifty years of unrequited toil shall be sunk, and until every drop of blood drawn by the lash, shall be paid by another drawn by the sword, as was said three thousand years ago, so still it must be said: 'The judgments of the Lord are true and righteous altogether.' " This is not rhetoric that victors often use, nor do they plead for malice toward none and charity for all, regard for the widow and orphan, and for a just and lasting peace. Not all the victors who heard Lincoln held the opinion that the United States was still one nation, to which the states that had seceded still belonged.

# *14*

## Victory

BY THE MIDDLE OF MARCH, 1865, Sherman was moving north from Savannah and had reached North Carolina, where General Johnston, restored to command after the annihilation of Hood's army, had collected a scratch force of thirty-five thousand, hardly sufficient to delay the victors for a day. Lee's army starved in front of Richmond, while inside the town a barrel of flour fetched fifteen hundred dollars.

In Washington, even Lincoln's iron physique was failing under the strain of months of increased work. The Thirteenth Amendment, peace negotiations, a call for new troops, the need to raise more money, work on his Second Inaugural Address, an influx of visitors for the occasion, the last days of the old Congress, his own plans for peace and those of people who thrust advice upon him—all these had made additions to the demands of his working day. On January 14, he had not had the strength to get out of bed and had held a Cabinet meeting in his bedroom while the doctors said there was nothing wrong with him but fatigue. He struggled up on the next day to conduct business as usual.

In the middle of March Grant sent a most timely invita-

tion to the President and Mrs. Lincoln to visit his headquarters. Sheridan was about to join him, and thus
strengthened, he planned a move around Lee's right
against the two railroads which still connected Richmond
with the South. Lee would have to protect these, yet his
lines were already stretched so thin that he could not do
so without leaving gaps elsewhere. The end was actually
in sight, and Grant wanted to talk over surrender terms,
the occupation of Richmond, perhaps even the cancella-
tion of army supplies which would no longer be needed.

During his years of office Lincoln occasionally visited
Francis P. Blair in Silver Spring, took a trip with his wife
and sister-in-law to Mount Vernon, or made some other
day-long excursion. Other than this, his chief recreations
had been carriage drives with Mary and visits to the theater, opera, or concerts, out of which he got a few enjoyable
hours. His only real holidays had been visits to the army,
which refreshed him, even though they combined business
with pleasure. Not unnaturally, this particular occasion
promised to be more relaxed than any previous one. Mrs.
Lincoln took her favorite milliner as maid. Noah Brooks,
who was replacing Nicolay as private secretary, came
along, as did Lincoln's personal bodyguard, a recent acqui-
sition. Tad, celebrating his twelfth birthday during the
holiday, expected to have more fun than anyone else. Robert Lincoln, now serving as an aide on Grant's staff, was
detailed to meet the *River Queen* at Harrison's Landing on
the James and bring his family to Grant's headquarters.

Robert Lincoln was by now twenty-two and, at the insistence of his mother, had remained quietly at Harvard,
where he had graduated the preceding summer. Like any
young man of spirit he had felt that he ought to be in the
army, but Lincoln had feared lest Mary go out of her mind
with anxiety for Robert after the loss of Willie. He had
therefore asked Grant to find a place for the young man on
his staff, an act of weakness which did not bring great
criticism upon him because so many other men in public

office had found safe employment for their sons, including
Seward, whose eldest son was Assistant Secretary of State.

Lincoln was not the only one on this little expedition
who was very near the edge of a complete breakdown.
Mary Lincoln had taken a number of holidays as the war
went on its weary way, sometimes with Tad and Robert.
She was, however, always sensitive to her husband's
moods, so that the last weeks had been hard for her. It was
also noticeable that the government (in the persons of
Stanton, District Marshal Ward Lamon, and a few others)
was becoming ever more anxious about the chance of Lincoln's assassination. Doorways had been cut to let him get
from his bedroom to his office without going through the
upper hall, where people still hung around trying to see
him. Four bodyguards had been detailed to continuous
duty, two from eight to four, and the others filling out the
twenty-four hours. Even at that, Ward Lamon, armed with
pistols and bowie knife, would sometimes sleep in the corridor outside Lincoln's room. Lamon had heated words
with the President about attending the theater with a couple of friends, neither of whom, snorted Lamon, was a
match for any able-bodied woman. The Lincolns' weekly
receptions went on as usual, but people were now required
to take off their wraps before they joined the line filing past
the President. Though this was represented as a courtesy,
its real purpose was to prevent anyone smuggling in a
knife or pistol.

None of these precautions made a visible impression on
Lincoln, except that it annoyed him to have people in
attendance. In a pigeonhole in his office were eighty
threats on his life, and his secretaries had very likely destroyed more. It was obvious to him that an assassin who
did not care about his own escape could certainly kill him.
In his waking hours at least, he thought little about this.
But the mysterious hints about conspiracies unearthed by
spies of Stanton, the presence of bodyguards, and the tense
attitude of Lamon were the worst of all things for a de-

voted wife who suffered from nerves. If Mary Lincoln was on edge, it was understandable. Unfortunately, however, her temper tantrums, which had generally been confined to the White House, broke forth on a public occasion.

On the second day of their visit, Robert E. Lee directed an assault on Grant's lines which was, though nobody yet knew it, the last attack which Lee's army would make on its own initiative. So easily was Lee's attack beaten off that a big review staged for the President was only delayed three hours, while Grant thought it safe for Lincoln to go up and see the battlefield. Meanwhile, Mary Lincoln and Grant's wife, Julia, were escorted to the scene of the review in an army ambulance which jolted horribly over roads deep in mud and roughly corduroyed. Mrs. Grant was a plain, shy woman, whose conversation appeared to consist of "Yes" and "No." Colonel Badeau, Grant's military aide, who was in attendance on the ladies, attempted to fill in the blanks with chatter, in the course of which he remarked that Grant had ordered all wives out of the lines of the Army of the Potomac, proof positive that he was going to move in for the kill. Very insistent, General Grant had been, allowing no exceptions except Mrs. Grant and Mrs. Charles Griffin, who had a special permit from the President.

A special permit from the President! "Do you mean to say," exclaimed Mary Lincoln sharply, "that she saw the President alone?" Her voice rose to the screech which had made young Hay christen her "the Hell-cat." "Do you know that I never allow the President to see any woman alone?"

Mrs. Grant appeared appalled, while Badeau tried to smooth the matter over. Mary Lincoln demanded to be let out. She would speak to the President herself and discover whether he had dared to see that woman alone! She reached forward and tried to yank at the reins to stop the ambulance. When it dawned on her that there was no way of seeing Lincoln until she arrived, she sat back in quivering silence, with Mrs. Grant beside her nearly in tears and Colonel Badeau profuse in apologies which died away into silent despair. When the ambulance reached its destination, General Meade came forward to help Mrs. Lincoln down. She immediately tackled him about Mrs. Griffin. Although he was not naturally tactful, Meade was a quick-thinking man and at once assured Mary Lincoln that Mrs. Griffin's permit had been issued by the Secretary of War, and not by the President.

On the following day there was another review, this time of the Army of the James. Mary Lincoln and Julia Grant found themselves being jolted in another ambulance over another long, corduroyed road. The President had left earlier with Major General Ord, who had succeeded General Butler as commander of this army. Behind him, Mary fretted and fumed about being late. She was indeed late and learned from some tactless informant that Mrs. Ord, a handsome woman with an excellent seat on a horse, had ridden beside the President to the parade ground. As Mrs. Ord, unconscious of having given offense, came up to greet the President's wife, Mary let fly. Mrs. Ord burst into tears, and everyone else stood by in horrified silence, trying not to catch the President's eye.

Even this was not the worst of it. That evening Lincoln gave a dinner on the *River Queen* for the Grants and various other officers. Mary delivered a tirade to Grant, who sat at her right hand, about the unfitness of General Ord for command, and, evidently unsatisfied by his response, raised her voice to tackle her husband at the other end of the table, commenting freely on Mrs. Ord and Mrs. Griffin. After dinner, when she was able to move around, she attacked Lincoln more than once, refusing to listen to his appeals that she calm down or to his explanations that no one had deliberately offended her.

In any rational woman such public scenes would be unforgivable, the more so because Mary's jealousy, which had been manifest for some time, had no foundation. It is true that women flattered the President, but Mary's own manner was coquettish when she was introduced to strangers. In her it meant nothing except that she thought a woman should always remember her sex when conversing with a man. Yet she was so suspicious of others that Lincoln used to ask her before a reception what ladies he might talk to. About those who came to see him in his office, he naturally kept his own counsel. In fact, things had been bad before, but scenes in public on such a scale were new.

Mary spent the next three days "indisposed" in her cabin, presumably because she did not want to face the officers who had seen her lose control. On the third day Lincoln rather neatly solved the situation by having a dream that the White House was on fire. He was always superstitious about dreams, so his insistence that Mary should go and see that all was well may not have been assumed. Still, none could blame him if he drew an exaggerated picture in order to excuse her return. At all events, she went; but the President, with his usual delight at being away from Washington routine, did not accompany her. No doubt he knew more than she about what was shortly to happen.

While Mary kept to her cabin, Sherman had come up from the coast of South Carolina to join with Grant and Lincoln in discussing plans to end the war. Sherman, who had only met the President once before, and that four years ago, wanted to be certain that Lincoln actually meant that the important thing was to end the bloodshed and send everyone back home. Did he really mean everyone, including leaders of the rebellion? What about, for instance, the most obvious case of all—what about the President of the Confederacy, Jefferson Davis? Could he simply be sent home?

He was not at liberty to speak his mind, replied Lincoln, after a pause, but he would tell a story. A man who had sworn off liquor went to stay with a friend and accepted after a bit of persuasion a glass of lemonade. The friend produced some for him, but suggested it would taste better if he poured in a little brandy. Very well, the guest agreed —provided that the brandy were poured in "unbeknown to him." Lincoln left the subject at that, clearly implying that Sherman could let Davis get out of the country if it could be done "unbeknown."

It was on the following day that Grant began the last of his sideways movements, using Sheridan's cavalry together with two infantry corps to strike at the railroads which still connected Richmond with the South. Lee, who had already foreseen that sooner or later such a movement would stretch his forces too thin, had warned Jefferson Davis that the Confederate government would very soon have to leave Richmond. He had said, however, on Wednesday, March 29, when Sheridan began his movement that he expected to give Davis ten or twelve days' notice. The following Sunday, while Davis was in his pew at church, a note was brought to him which turned his complexion a pale gray. He left without taking communion. There had been a breakthrough. Lee could hold his lines no longer and would pull out that night. The government should make what preparations it could for leaving also.

Richmond was to be abandoned at last, though not undamaged. Demolition squads of the retreating army set fire to ammunition dumps, tobacco warehouses, a couple of vast flour mills, railroad bridges, and three ironclad vessels in the river. Naturally these fires spread, so that the whole waterfront and most of the business district of the town were destroyed in the conflagration. Not till the following morning, however, did the besieging forces discover that Petersburg, which had held them off from Richmond for many months, had been abandoned. Lee's lines were empty of defenders, and Richmond presumably was theirs for the taking.

After Mary had left for the White House, Lincoln had

transferred himself from the *River Queen* to Admiral Porter's flagship, the *Malvern,* where he received the news on
Monday that Union forces were in Petersburg. Nothing
would do for him but to go to Petersburg in company with
Tad and Admiral Porter. They found Grant in the town,
which was almost deserted. Grant naturally was moving
men in pursuit of Lee's army, which he hoped to cut off
before it reached the Carolinas and made a junction with
General Johnston. Lincoln got back to the *Malvern* and
read a telegram from Stanton pointing out that he had no
business exposing himself in Petersburg. But Lincoln was
in a state of bliss which was beyond caution. He answered,
"It is certain now that Richmond is in our hands, and I
think I will go there tomorrow. I will take care of myself."

He went to Richmond the next day with Admiral Porter
—who was unable to refuse the Commander-in-Chief—
and he took Tad along to look about him. For the last four
years the enemy had maintained his capital not many miles
from Washington. For its possession two great armies had
contended since First Bull Run. Now at last it was in
Federal hands, and this one triumph seems to have symbol-
ized victory to Lincoln. He did not want revenge, the
capture of Jefferson Davis, the humiliation of the South.
He only wanted to walk for one day through the streets of
Richmond.

It was an act of the sheerest folly. There was so much
wreckage in the river that neither the *Malvern* herself nor
a tug sent in by Porter with thirty marines for the protection of Lincoln could cross it. The President was eventually landed by a large rowboat two miles from the center
of town, accompanied by Tad, Admiral Porter, and a
guard of ten marines. There were no Union soldiers to be
seen, and Lincoln walked all the way into Richmond, conspicuous as ever, his tall hat standing about a foot above the
rest of the crowd. He was followed by a cheering flock of
Negro ex-slaves and watched from every window by silent, hostile people, many of whom must have possessed

firearms but lacked the resolution of the innkeeper who
had shot Ellsworth on the first day of war in Virginia.
Arriving at Jefferson Davis's official mansion, "the Southern White House," which had been taken over as army
headquarters, he sat down at his rival's desk and asked if
he could have a glass of water.

General Weitzel, in command of occupying forces, was
as unable as Porter to control his Commander-in-Chief.
The best he could do was to find a carriage and mounted
escort and accompany the President personally around the
burned-out section of the town. "Jeff Davis ought to be
hanged!" commented one of the escort when they passed
the infamous Libby Prison. Lincoln looked around and
leaned over to say with calm distinctness, "Judge not, that
you be not judged." Weitzel asked him if he had any
suggestions about the treatment of the inhabitants of Richmond. "If I were in your place," replied Lincoln, "I'd let
'em up easy; let 'em up easy."

About this time, to the relief of the general and admiral,
the *Malvern* banged off a gun to tell the world that she had
managed to drop anchor on the Richmond side of the river.
Admiral Porter was able to insist that the party get back
aboard. Tired by a satisfactory day, Lincoln turned in
early, while the admiral posted a now superfluous sentry
outside the presidential cabin.

Lincoln was in no hurry to get back to Washington,
except that he was anxious about Secretary Seward, who
had been seriously injured in a carriage accident during his
absence. However, though Seward had dislocated his
shoulder, broken his jaw in two places, and was in terrible
pain, the doctors were sure that he would recover. For the
moment he was in no condition to see anyone, so Lincoln
was able to stay where he was. Mary Lincoln, disappointed
at having missed the visit to Richmond, had gathered a
party of friends and was returning expressly to tour the
town. It would be only polite to remain until she arrived,
while in the meantime dispatches from Grant's army were

most encouraging. Stanton forwarded a note from Sheridan, saying, "If the thing is pressed, I think Lee will surrender."

"Let the *thing* be pressed," said Lincoln to his wife, to Grant, to everybody. Away from Washington for two full weeks and fed daily with encouraging news, he was a man transfigured. Yet even then the Comte de Chambrun, who was one of Mary's party, noted how over and over again "all his features would bespeak a kind of sadness as indescribable as it was deep. After a while, as though it were by an effort of his will, he would shake off this mysterious weight under which he seemed bowed; his generous and open disposition would again reappear."

On April 9, Palm Sunday, on a rainy evening, he landed at the foot of Sixth Street and, dropping Mary and Tad off at the White House, took his carriage on to visit Seward. Lincoln found him with his jaw in an iron frame, his face swathed in bandages, and his slight person on the far side of the bed, which had been pulled out from the wall so that his weight need not rest on his bruised shoulder socket. He was able to mumble a greeting and listened while Lincoln sprawled over the bed, supported on one elbow, so that he could bring his face close to Seward's and tell him all the good news of the last weeks. But presently the exhausted Seward fell asleep, and Lincoln tiptoed out and down the stairs to his waiting carriage. That very evening, as he was undressing for bed, the President heard a knock and opened his door to a War Department messenger. The man brought him a telegram which had just been received by Stanton.

"General Lee surrendered the Army of Northern Virginia this afternoon upon terms proposed by myself. The accompanying additional correspondence will show the conditions fully.

U. S. GRANT
*Lieutenant General.*"

Except for the mopping-up, the war was over.

# 15

## The Last Days

WHILE LINCOLN WAS VISITING Petersburg on Monday, the news of the capture of Richmond arrived in Washington. Church bells started to peal; fire engines clanged through the streets; locomotives and steamboats whistled. Army batteries began an eight-hundred-round salute, and the navy fired its biggest Dahlgren guns, which rattled all the windows in town. Children rushed out of school and clerks out of government offices. Men fell on each other's necks, made up quarrels, linked arms, and marched around town singing. Flags appeared everywhere, as did liquor flasks. Stanton and Seward made impromptu speeches and were cheered to the echo. An even bigger celebration was planned for Tuesday night, by which time the public buildings had put up vast transparencies lit by candles, or had outlined mottoes across their façades in gas jets. Every window of every building, including the insane asylum and the prisons on First Street, blazed with light.

In front of the Patent Office a speakers' platform had been erected for a great Republican rally. The principal speaker was Andrew Johnson, the new Vice President, a politician who had risen from obscure beginnings with the aid of a natural gift for fiery oratory. Johnson was from Tennessee and had better reason for hating the Confederacy than many, since East Tennessee, though loyal to the Union, had remained in Confederate hands for most of the war and had suffered severely. When the crowd roared, "Hang him!" at the name of Jefferson Davis, Andy Johnson was quick to respond, "Yes, I say hang him a hundred times!" He called amid cheers for the confiscation of the property of traitors, repeating, "I would arrest them; I would try them; I would convict them; and I would hang them." When Lincoln read a report next day, he was so indignant that he refused to see Johnson when the latter came down to visit Richmond. Lincoln had not spoken to the Vice President since his drunken performance at the inauguration.

When the guns began their salutes again for Lee's surrender at Appomattox, there was somewhat less excitement, partly because Washington had already had its spree, and partly because it was raining. This time, however, since Lincoln was in town, crowds arrived to serenade the White House. Inside, Lincoln, light-hearted as a clerk on holiday, was writing to ask if Tad could have a navy sword and if Stanton would send the boy a captured Confederate flag from the bundles which had lately arrived at the War Department. The crowd on the White House lawn clamored for a speech, but Lincoln said that he would speak that night or possibly the next one. He would have nothing to say "if you dribble it all out of me before." He called instead for the musicians to play "Dixie," which he claimed was a tune now belonging to the whole nation by right of capture. The suggestion was well received, and people dispersed, only to regather several times during the day. But Lincoln insisted he would not speak until the following evening.

Accordingly, in the gathering dark on April 12, crowds assembled in front of the White House, despite a slight drizzle. Lincoln came to the window with a candle in his left hand and a roll of papers in his right containing the speech over which he had been laboring most of the day. Unable to manage both at once, he gestured to Noah Brooks, who stood behind the curtain, to hold the candle while he read, dropping each sheet on the floor as he finished it. They were gathered up by Tad, who could be heard plainly by the hushed crowd outside calling, "Another! Another!" In this somewhat peculiar manner, Lincoln delivered his last and possibly least popular speech.

His audience had come to celebrate. They were thinking of victory, peace, even revenge, in one glorious jumble, while Lincoln chose to talk about Reconstruction. But the Southern states had seceded, hadn't they? They ought to comply with some pretty strict requirements before they could be readmitted as equal partners to the Union! Yet Lincoln was saying that it would be wiser not to discuss whether they had ever been out. And what about the Negro vote? Lincoln was defending the government set up in Louisiana based on a tenth of the white voters and excluding Negroes. He was saying that it was better than no arrangement at all and that we should have the fowl sooner by hatching the egg than by smashing it. Plenty of people thought he was going to get the same old unreconstructed fowl they had known before the war. He was not even setting up a clear plan for discussion. He merely stated that the problem was different in the separate regions of the South, adding that it might be his duty to make some new announcement to Southerners. As few cared to listen to hints that he might further extend his pardoning powers, this eloquence produced no rousing cheers. The drizzle had turned to rain, but even the weather had not so dampened spirits as had the President.

Lincoln himself did not seem disappointed at the half-hearted applause as he sat quietly with a few friends in the Red Room, where he told them about a dream he had had a short while earlier. Ward Lamon recorded it in the following version of Lincoln's own words.

"There seemed to be a deathlike stillness about me. Then I heard subdued sobs, as if a number of people were weeping. I thought I left my bed and wandered downstairs.

"There the silence was broken by the same pitiful sobbing, but the mourners were invisible. I went from room to room. No living person was in sight, but the same mournful sounds of distress met me as I passed along. It was light in all the rooms; every object was familiar to me, but where were all the people who were grieving as though their hearts would break?

"I was puzzled and alarmed. What could be the meaning of all this? Determined to find the cause of a state of things so mysterious and shocking, I kept on until I arrived at the East Room, where I entered. There I met with a sickening surprise. Before me was a catafalque, on which rested a corpse in funeral vestments. Around it were stationed soldiers who were acting as guards; and there was a throng of people, some gazing mournfully upon the corpse, whose face was covered, others weeping pitifully.

" 'Who is dead in the White House?' I demanded of one of the soldiers.

" 'The President,' was his answer. 'He was killed by an assassin.'

"Then came a loud burst of grief from the crowd, which awoke me from my dream. I slept no more that night and, although it was only a dream, I have been strangely annoyed by it ever since."

This story, so mysteriously prophetic, was followed by a brief silence. The dream was not, so far as we can tell, a subconscious reaction to Lincoln's imprudence in Richmond, but had occurred a few weeks earlier, most likely as a result of alarms which had attended the inauguration. When other friends said good-night, Ward Lamon, still Marshal of the District, stayed behind with John P. Usher, now Secretary of the Interior, to beg Lincoln to take better care of himself. Lincoln laughed and called Lamon a monomaniac on the subject of his assassination. Lamon, due to leave for Richmond next day on a special assignment, asked Lincoln to promise not to go out after dark until he returned.

"I promise to do the best I can towards it," Lincoln told him.

Next morning, Thursday, April 13, the Grants arrived in Washington. Grant had left Sherman and Meade to deal with what was left of Johnston's army and was on his way to New Jersey to see his children, stopping over for a couple of days to confer with Stanton on demobilization problems. The moment the general set foot in the street, he was mobbed, an experience as distasteful to him as ever. He took refuge at the War Department, where he received a note from Mary Lincoln inviting him to join herself and her husband for a carriage drive around the city that very afternoon. Uncertain whether it would be proper to refuse, Grant consulted Stanton, who assured him that he could plead pressure of work. When he did so, however, Mary Lincoln replied with another invitation to General and Mrs. Grant to accompany the Lincolns to a performance of *Our American Cousin* at Ford's Theatre on Friday evening. Grant accepted because he lacked courage to turn down the President's wife for the second time. Julia Grant, however, who had seen enough of Mary Lincoln to last a lifetime, insisted that they must leave for New Jersey that very evening. In consequence the Grants first officially accepted and then withdrew, once more encouraged by Stanton, who told the general that Washington was dangerously full of Southern fanatics and that he invariably refused to accompany the President on his imprudent visits to the theater. Lincoln, though he did not particularly want to see *Our American Cousin*, knew that many would have bought tickets on purpose to see Grant, and resolved to satisfy them as far as he could by going himself. Besides, Mary had initiated the scheme, and Lincoln may have been afraid of a scene if he refused.

About the time of Lincoln's re-election in November, 1864, John Wilkes Booth had made up his mind to kidnap the President and carry him south. His original idea had been that Lincoln could be exchanged for Confederate prisoners of war. The shortage of manpower which was destroying the South had been accentuated by Northern refusal to continue an exchange of prisoners which profited their enemies more than themselves. Booth, the son and younger brother of famous actors, had inherited, together with much of their talent, an extraordinary power of self-dramatization. About twenty-three years old when the war broke out, he was one of those Marylanders whose sympathies were with the South. He did not, however, interrupt his theatrical career to enlist, telling friends that he had promised his mother not to do so, though some supposed he had a morbid fear of being scarred or crippled. It was entirely in character that the young man may have decided to purge himself of guilt by performing a spectacular feat which would cause his name to be written in letters of gold in the annals of the Confederacy.

The most difficult thing about a conspiracy is often the enlistment of fellow members. Booth was a loner, belonging to no underground Southern group and unpopular even with his fellow actors because he was a notorious scene stealer. He had, however, powers of fascination which attracted hangers-on, a few of whom he was able to recruit as assistants. Though extravagance generally left him poor, he spent about four thousand dollars for horses and feed, and even for the living expenses of one or two of his prospective helpers. By January 18, he had worked out an elaborate scheme to kidnap Lincoln during a visit to Ford's Theatre. One of his friends, a secret Southern courier named John Surratt, was to turn off the master gas valve under the stage, plunging the theater in darkness. Booth would force the President at gunpoint to submit to being tied and gagged. He would then lower him to the stage, where Surratt would be waiting, and the pair would hustle him out to a covered wagon standing in the alley outside the rear door. Other conspirators would be in charge of relays of horses at strategic points on the route south. At the last moment, Lincoln changed his mind and did not go to the theater.

The conspirators scattered in alarm, only to reassemble when they found that they were not suspected. Mrs. Surratt, John's mother, who kept a boardinghouse in Washington and had an elder son in the Confederate army, was pleased enough to fill her rooms with Southern sympathizers and probably stupid enough to ask no questions about mysterious comings and goings. There was a good deal of buying pistols, oiling them, arriving on strange horses, and conferring in upstairs rooms; but the widow Surratt accepted John's assurance that all was well. In February, a different scheme was planned for which Booth enlisted Lewis Powell, who had changed his name to Paine, presumably because he was from the Northern point of view an escaped prisoner, and from the Confederate one more or less a deserter. Paine was a big, good-looking man, immensely strong and stupid, who had met Booth on one of his pre-war southern tours and had been seemingly bewitched by him. Now that he met his hero again, Paine expressed willingness even to kill at Booth's command. It was arranged that Paine should hide in the bushes bordering the path down which Lincoln walked to the War Department and shoot him as he came home late at night. When the time came, Paine lost his nerve, apparently because Lincoln was accompanied by Major Thomas Eckert.

Booth reverted to his original scheme and, calling together all six of his co-conspirators for the first time, outlined it to them. They did not like it. What if the President refused to be tied up? How could they abduct him from the middle of Washington and from a crowded theater? On March 20, the President was going out to the Soldiers' Home, where he usually spent the summer, to see a theatrical performance. How much simpler it would be to inter-

cept his carriage at a quiet spot along the road! They drew
up plans and stationed themselves in their chosen position,
but the President was detained at the last moment.

In Mrs. Surratt's boardinghouse, Louis J. Wiechman
shared a bedroom with John Surratt. Wiechman worked
for the Federal government at the office of the Commissary
General of Prisoners. He was a sly, inquisitive man, and
the odd behavior of some of his fellow boarders was not so
easily explained to him as to Mrs. Surratt. He retailed as
a piece of gossip in the office that a "secesh" group in his
own boardinghouse was plotting to do away with the President. A certain Captain Gleason took alarm and questioned him. Wiechman apparently did not have much to
say, but a sense of self-preservation sent him hurrying to
another officer with the names of the habitués of the Surratt boardinghouse. Considering that Stanton had many
spies investigating plots and never hesitated to arrest men
on suspicion, it is astonishing that nothing was done about
the matter. Perhaps Stanton was not really looking for one
actor and a half-dozen seedy followers. His imagination
embraced bigger conspiracies. Ward Lamon, who might
have shown more interest, was at the end of an entirely
different chain of command and did not get reports from
the Commissariat General, which dealt with prisoners.

After the failure of the Soldiers' Home attempt, Booth's
conspiracy almost broke up. He could not reassemble his
men when it was supposed that Lincoln would attend the
theater on March 27. Some of the band, including John
Surratt, deserted. Booth was left with Paine, his stupid but
muscular killer; Atzerodt, a boastful drunkard; and Herold, little more than a boy. Booth was out of funds, and
time was running out, too. In fact, by the end of March it
might already be said that for practical purposes Booth no
longer had a country to which he could take a kidnapped
President. It would be easier to murder him.

By April 9, when Lincoln returned from his visit to
Grant's army, there was no longer even any point in mur-

der. Richmond was taken. Lee had surrendered. The war was over, and Lincoln's death would not revive it. On the other hand, the collapse of the Confederacy and the Washington victory celebrations had a maddening effect on Booth. He determined to kill not only Lincoln, but his designated successors, the Vice President and Secretary of State, leaving the country literally without leadership. If the South could not be saved, it should be avenged.

The arrival of the Grants in Washington presented Booth with his chance. The Lincolns were bound to do something in their honor. A ball could hardly be arranged at such short notice, and Mrs. Lincoln was economizing on public entertainments. A state dinner, though formal enough, would not satisfy the people, who wanted a glimpse of their hero. What could be more suitable than a theater party, inexpensive and yet public? Booth went over to Ford's and was lucky enough to hear almost as soon as the management that the President was coming.

It was not surprising that Booth's plans had generally centered on Ford's Theatre, since he knew the place as well as the back of his hand. He had played there on various occasions; was familiar with the Ford brothers, who owned and managed it; had his mail addressed there when he was in Washington; and caused no comment if he appeared at any hour of the day or were found wandering about the building. It was simple for him to slip into the presidential box for a look at a rehearsal of *Our American Cousin* and to pick out a moment in the third act when only one character was left on the stage, so that it would be easy for himself to jump down from the box, run across the stage, and escape through the back door into an alley behind the theater. He noted that the door to the President's box could not be locked because the catch was broken. Nobody bothered him while he bored a spyhole through the door so that he could see clearly the position of the high-backed rocking chair which the management put in for the President. There was a dark little passage which led to this box from the "dress circle," or lowest balcony. This was closed off by a door opening inward. Booth found a length of wood to wedge between the door and the opposite wall and, because it was a little too long, carved a piece out of the plaster so that when it was jammed in place the door could not be opened. Lincoln's bodyguard would of course be sitting outside that door, but Booth planned to knife the guard and be inside before anyone could stop him. Having made these preparations while the youngest of the Fords was collecting flags to drape the front of the box, Booth took his leave.

On the preceding day he had planted Atzerodt in a room in the boardinghouse occupied by Vice President Johnson, with instructions to murder him on Friday night. Johnson was in fairly tough physical shape and had a black attendant who stood behind him at meals. Atzerodt spent a good deal of time asking pointed questions which would surely have seemed suspicious had he not been so clearly drunk and ineffective.

There was not much to be done with Atzerodt, but Paine was quite another matter. The only trouble was that Paine, though he had by this time been in Washington for several weeks, could not find his way about. Someone had to direct him to Seward's house and devise a plan to get him inside, up the stairs, and into the bedroom where the Secretary of State lay with his jaw encased in iron and his head bandaged. Paine could be counted on to do what he was told, but Herold was going to have to show him Seward's front door, hold the horses, and direct the escape. Herold also should have been used to infuse courage into Atzerodt but could not be spared. Booth was perfectly confident about his own role. He had a derringer with a single shot, which would be enough for the President. He would carry a knife to take care of the bodyguard and of Grant or anyone else the President might invite to share his box.

While Booth's plans were taking shape, Lincoln was having a three-hour Cabinet meeting of great importance.

It was now mid-April, and he had until December, when Congress would reassemble, to get the country running. He did not want to waste a day, and it was essential that the Cabinet agree, at least in outline, on practical measures. The mails, for instance, must be re-established throughout the South, which would mean taking over post offices and appointing postmasters. Communications by road or ship would have to be restored. Federal judges would have to be appointed and courts opened. New Indian agents, pension agents, surveyors, and other employees of the Department of the Interior would be required. The War Department and the Navy must take possession of Southern forts, arsenals, shipyards, and ordnance. Some sort of skeleton government must be constructed for the Southern states, and where a military occupation was necessary, the President was anxious that states should not be lumped together in one district but treated from the first as separate entities. The Treasury should take charge of customs houses and begin to collect revenues. In short, the business of the government must be resumed, and there was plenty for every member of the Cabinet to busy himself with. Some general planning was also discussed; and though Stanton, for instance, showed a more revengeful spirit than Lincoln, it did not seem as though their positions were very far apart. It was a good Cabinet meeting, perhaps the most constructive that Lincoln could remember. After it, he had an interview with Andrew Johnson, omitting reference to Inauguration Day or to the Vice President's offensive speech of April 3, and probably filling him in on Reconstruction details. In fact, Lincoln had a good day, rounding off his office hours by seeing Mrs. Nancy Bushrod, an escaped slave, whose husband had enlisted in the Union army, but whose pay allotment had mysteriously stopped coming. He told her the proper papers would be ready next day and that she could come and fetch them. He added that she yet might see days when all the food in the house was one loaf of bread. When that happened, "give every child a slice and send your children to school."

The President went for a drive after four o'clock with Mary Lincoln. What with the victory still so new and the Cabinet meeting which had gone so well, he was feeling in a rare cheerful mood. Mrs. Lincoln remarked on it, and he patted her hand. "Mother, I consider that this day the war has come to a close," he said. "We must both be cheerful in the future. Between the war and the loss of our darling Willie, we have both been very miserable." Mary had nothing to say. The mention of Willie left her silent, but Lincoln went on talking about Reconstruction, the end of his term, a trip to Europe, a quiet law practice in Springfield. "I never felt so happy in my life," he exclaimed.

They got back to a pleasant surprise. Two old friends from Illinois were calling at the White House. Lincoln brought them in and read them a newspaper column by the humorist Petroleum V. Nasby, and they all told jokes and roared with laughter. Since the Illinoisans had dinner engagements, the Lincolns ate alone with their two sons. Robert was going out, while Tad, who generally adored the theater, was not included on this occasion. Mary Lincoln had asked the daughter of Senator Ira Harris and her fiancé, Major Henry R. Rathbone, to take the place of the Grants. A little after eight, when Lincoln had postponed until the next day a couple of interviews, the Lincolns got into their carriage and set out. John F. Parker, the four-to-twelve bodyguard, had already strolled over to Ford's and taken a look around the box before coming down again to wait at the entrance for the President.

# *16*

## The Last Hours

THE LINCOLNS ARRIVED at the theater a little
before half past eight and were ushered into a box that had
been created by taking out the partition between the two
upper boxes on the righthand side as seen by the patrons
in the first balcony. The double box gave plenty of room
for the President's comfortable rocker, armless chairs for
the ladies' crinolines, and a couch for Major Rathbone and
his dress sword. The two boxes below and the four on the
opposite side of the stage were left empty as a courtesy to
the President. As the party entered, the actors onstage
froze in their positions while the band played "Hail to the
Chief." The box faced slightly toward the audience, and
afforded its inmates an excellent view of the backs of the
actors' heads, or at best their profiles. Major Rathbone and
his fiancée were visible to most of the audience, while
Mary Lincoln could be glimpsed by a good many. The
President, relaxed in his favorite chair, was concealed by
the box curtains and the bunting draped outside it in his
honor. During the performance of the third-rate comedy,
whose only merit was its leading lady, people continued to
whisper that Grant might arrive later.

Outside the white door leading to the box from the first balcony sat the bodyguard, Parker. Though by turning his head he could see the stage, he found the performance dull. Parker, who had arrived three hours late to take up his duties on that very day, was unreliable. His record in the police department had been poor, and there seems no reason why he should have been appointed to guard the President except that he had volunteered, quite probably to escape the draft. More ambitious police officers did not wish to be sidetracked to duty which might cost them chances of promotion. What was involved in guarding the President, moreover, was so little understood that there seems to have been a feeling that anyone would suffice for so simple a job. Parker left his post and went downstairs to ask Lincoln's coachman to join him in a glass of ale at a nearby tavern, where he remained for some time, ordering several glasses.

In the presidential box Clara Harris and Major Rathbone were holding hands. Lincoln saw them and, relaxed by his happy day, put his own big hand around Mary's. "What will the young people think?" she protested in a whisper.

"They won't think anything," her husband assured her.

Booth rode up to the back door of Ford's about half past nine, booted and spurred for a quick getaway, and found a boy to hold his horse. He came up into the wings, was told that he could not at that particular moment cross behind the stage, and made his way to the President's side of the theater through the basement. He had plenty of time before the moment he had chosen in the third act, so he went out the front door and bought himself a whiskey in the very tavern where Parker was drinking his ale.

Just after ten Booth walked back to the theater, passing the ticket seller—who knew better than to charge him— with the remark that he wanted a quick look at the leading lady on stage. He ran upstairs to the first balcony, his gun in his pocket and his sheath knife stuck into his trousers with the handle concealed by his coat. To his surprise the bodyguard was not outside the door to the passage, which meant that he could slip through it, wedge it with the bar he had concealed behind it, and choose his time. Inside, he crouched beside the box door to put his eye to the hole he had bored in it that morning. By the light from the stage he could plainly see where the President was sitting, while he heard the action rising to the climax which would lead to the sweeping exit of mother and daughter, leaving "Our American Cousin" alone on the stage. It came. Booth opened the door in one swift movement, raised his pistol to the back of the President's head, and fired.

Muffled by the box, the shot sounded like a paper bag exploding, while blue smoke eddied out onto the stage. Mary Lincoln and her guests glanced around more startled than alarmed. The President, who appeared to be asleep, did not stir. Booth looked at the others, quoting quite calmly the state motto of Virginia, "Sic Semper Tyrannis," which may be rendered, "Treat all tyrants this way." He pushed his way between the Lincolns toward the front of the box. Major Rathbone, who had presumably recognized the smell of gunpowder, jumped up to grapple with him. Booth pulled out his knife and slashed down so hard that the major, throwing up his left arm, was cut to the bone. Rathbone staggered, but tried to snatch Booth with his right hand. The actor pushed him back violently, calling out, "Revenge for the South." Reaching the rail of the box, which was eleven feet above the stage, he gripped it with both hands as he vaulted over. Letting go, he pushed himself away from the wall with his right hand, twisting so that his right spur caught in one of the flags which decorated the box. The stuff tore free, but the murderer landed hard on his left foot and broke it just above the instep.

Booth fell forward on his hands, pushed himself upright, managed to rush past "Our American Cousin," who was standing frozen in the middle of a gesture, and fell again as he headed for the wings. Once more he got up and, hobbling clumsily on his broken foot, disappeared from sight as Mrs. Lincoln screamed and Clara Harris, leaning out of the front of the box, called loudly for water.

Brandishing his knife, which he still retained, Booth shoved his way past actors in the wings, reached the alley, kicked aside the boy who was holding his horse, struggled onto it, and was off at a gallop, outstripping the news of what he had done as he made for a rendezvous south of the Potomac with Atzerodt, Paine, and Herold, who were to have committed the other two murders at approximately the same minute.

Mrs. Lincoln shrieked again, and all over the theater people got to their feet. Men from the first balcony headed a rush for the white door, which proved to be securely jammed. "He has shot the President!" yelled somebody. Major Rathbone, soaked in blood, staggered out of the box and shouted to those pushing at the door to stand back while he took down the bar which held it shut. After several appeals he was able to open the door and plead that none but doctors be admitted. Dr. Charles Leale, twenty-three years old and a military surgeon, pushed forward. Taking no more than a brief glance at Rathbone, who said he was bleeding to death, he hurried into the box. Lifting up Mary Lincoln, who had flung herself across her husband, he turned his attention to the President, who looked as if he were dead.

Young though he was, Leale was competent. He ordered someone to get a lamp, someone else to lock the door against any but doctors, and other men to hold matches while he found the President's wound. He had supposed, after seeing Major Rathbone, that the deed had been done with a knife. It was not until he had got men to help lay Lincoln on the floor and had himself gently lifted his head that he felt blood under his hands. Booth's shot had entered low behind the left ear and had moved up and across the brain to lodge behind the right eye. Leale made two discoveries, Lincoln was not, as he had imagined, dead; but his wound was undoubtedly mortal.

Despite this certainty, Leale started to give artificial respiration, later handing over this task to two other doctors while he tried to stimulate heart action. Under this treatment the President's breathing became stronger, sounding like a gentle snore. Somebody brought a lamp and someone else offered brandy. Leale dribbled a little into Lincoln's mouth and saw that he swallowed.

"Can he be removed to somewhere nearby?" he asked. It was impossible to do more on the floor of that box, ill-lit and crowded with people.

"Wouldn't it be possible to carry him to the White House?" someone queried.

Leale shook his head decisively. It was too far and, besides, the road was cobbled. "He will be dead before we reach there."

A man was sent out to find a lodging across Tenth Street, where some houses which had seen better days stood facing Ford's Theatre. Very slowly indeed they bore Lincoln down the little passage, up the aisle, down the stairs from the balcony, with Leale going first holding the President's head and stopping every few paces to be sure no lethal clot was forming in the wound. Two soldiers supported Lincoln's torso by a sling passed underneath it, while two more grasped him by the thighs. The cortège came painfully out of Ford's and headed across the street—but the house opposite was locked and empty. Next door at 453 Tenth Street, a tailor named William Peterson held a candle to light their way in. Peterson had a downstairs bedroom which he usually rented out for the night. A soldier picked up his gear and departed so that they could bring in the President. It was a shabby room, about fifteen feet by nine and containing a bed much too short for a six-foot-four man. They laid him diagonally across it, his head in one corner and his feet sticking helplessly out past the edge of the footboard.

At last doctors could undress the patient, get sheets and a comforter, hot water, and heated blankets. They covered him from head to foot with mustard plasters to stimulate the circulation. Still he breathed heavily. His eyes were open—the left contracted and the right dilated—but he was unconscious and blind. People began to arrive: Robert Lincoln in tears, the Surgeon General, the President's physician, and his pastor. Outside a crowd waited as Cabinet members, summoned from their beds by the tidings, gathered also.

Secretary of War Stanton, most industrious of men, had earned an early bedtime, but at half past eight or thereabouts he paid a brief courtesy call on Secretary Seward. Though it was now ten days since his accident, the Secretary of State was still in such pain that he could hardly understand what his visitor said. Seward's two sons, his wife, and his daughter Fanny had arranged watches so that one of them could be constantly with him. Stanton himself had sent over two convalescent soldiers who were well enough to act as male nurses. Shortly after Stanton took his leave, the doctor called and gave his patient a sedative, with the aid of which he sank into exhausted slumber. Fanny Seward, supported by one of the male nurses, took over in the darkened room at nine o'clock.

Partly in consequence of this visit, when a soldier came pounding on Stanton's door while he was undressing to tell him that not only had the President been shot but that Seward had been brutally attacked in his own house, Stanton simply said, "Humbug," and went up to bed. Yet the soldier, as it happened, was right. Booth's fellow conspirators had not performed their tasks as efficiently as he, but enough had been accomplished to excite the wildest rumors.

Andrew Johnson, lonely and overtired, had gone early to bed. Atzerodt's instructions had been to knock on his door at a quarter past ten, shoot him if he opened in person, push past or if necessary shoot anyone else, and then mur-

der the Vice President. Atzerodt had no stomach for the
business and had only agreed when Booth pointed out that
his membership in the conspiracy would damn him
whether he struck his blow for the South or not. But even
after a number of drinks in the course of the evening,
Atzerodt could not get up his nerve. Aimlessly he mounted
his getaway horse and rode past Ford's Theatre, where
nothing had yet happened. He did not dare keep his rendezvous with the rest if he had not done his job. At the
same time, it was madness to wait at home until he was
arrested, especially as Booth had written a boastful letter
containing the names of all four conspirators. In the end,
Atzerodt thought of friends among whom he might hide
and went to ground.

Paine and Herold halted outside Seward's house. Herold
was to hold the horses and guide Paine out of town. Paine
had been provided with a package which looked as though
it came from a drugstore. He was to knock on the door,
saying that he came from the doctor and was ordered to
deliver his package to Seward in person.

Seward's door was opened by a black servant, William
Bell, who naturally protested that Paine could not go upstairs. The visitor resorted to roughness: "You're talking to
a white man . . . out of my way, nigger, I'm going up." He
pushed past Bell and started upstairs with the Negro behind him imploring him gently to see reason.

Frederick Seward, the eldest son, heard the commotion,
flung on a dressing gown, and came out of his bedroom to
quiet the noise which might awaken his father. He gestured for silence, demanding in a whisper what was the
matter. Paine replied in the same low tone that this "fresh
nigger" was trying to stop him from delivering the package which had been sent around expressly by the doctor.
Seward said he would take it in himself, but Paine refused,
giving young Seward the impression that he was a half-wit
who did not know any better than to carry out his instructions literally. Frederick replied that his father was proba-

bly sleeping, but he would see. Walking to the end of the
hall, he identified Seward's room for Paine by going inside.
He came back insisting that his father was asleep and that
Paine could not be allowed in the sickroom. "I will take the
responsibility of refusing," said the young Assistant Secretary of State with the assurance of a man who has been
brought up to give orders.

"Very well, sir," said Paine, as if impressed. "I will go."
He turned as though to descend the stairs, using the opportunity to pull out his pistol. Then, whirling, he leveled it
at young Seward's middle and pulled the trigger. It
misfired. Before the astonished young man could so much
as lift a hand, Paine leaped forward and brought the gun
butt smashing down upon his head. Frederick Seward
dropped in his tracks, while Paine, leaning over him,
struck several more savage blows with such force that he
broke the weapon.

"Murder! Murder!" screamed William Bell, running
downstairs and into the street, where his cries so frightened Herold that he tied Paine's horse to a tree and set off
without him.

Upstairs, Paine drew his knife and ran down the passage
to the door of Seward's room, only to find that someone on
the other side was trying to hold it shut against him. He
took a run, burst in, and was aware in the darkness—which
was only lighted by a glow from the hall—of somebody
moving. He slashed out and heard a scream of pain. His
business, however, was not with Seward's attendants, but
the Secretary himself. He flung himself across the bed,
reaching over it to stab again and again at the small figure
lying on its inner edge.

Two things saved Seward from dying. The first was the
iron brace encasing his jaw which incidentally protected
his neck. The second was that Seward had the presence of
mind to roll off the bed—onto his injured arm—and to gain
the partial protection of the bed, the wall, and a tangle of
bedclothes. Uncertain whether his victim was dead, Paine

lifted his arm for a final stab, but as he did so, two people
fell on him from behind. The male nurse whom he had
wounded and gentle Miss Fanny were trying to pull him
off the bed. Had either of them had a weapon, Paine might
have been in an awkward position, half-sprawled across
the bed and hemmed in by tables and chairs which he
could not see except along the narrow beam of light coming from the hall. After a furious struggle Paine burst free,
leaving Fanny Seward unconscious and the male nurse
seriously wounded. Paine rushed out into the passage, yell-
ing, "I'm mad. I'm mad."

In the hall he ran into Major Augustus Seward, the
Secretary's younger son, together with a perfectly innocent messenger from the State Department who apparently had walked in to deliver a message. Before the latter had time to assimilate the confusion, Paine plunged
his knife into his chest right up to the hilt and rushed
past him.

William Bell, still out in the street and calling for help,
brought soldiers running for the house, too late to catch
the assassin who, finding himself deserted by Herold, un-
tied his horse, mounted, and moved off at a walk, presumably uncertain where to go. Bell, with considerable courage,
pursued him for a block and a half until Paine was goaded
into making off at a trot.

The soldiers, rushing into Seward's house to see what
was the matter, found the messenger on the floor, choking
in his own blood. Frederick Seward was lying at the top
of the stairs in a coma, injured worse than his father. In
Seward's room Fanny lay unconscious, while the male
nurse, who had been badly slashed, was bleeding pro-
fusely. The Secretary, rescued from behind the bed, was
found to have one cheek laid open clear through into the
mouth and several other stab wounds, none fortunately
lethal. Major Augustus, badly bruised, but unwounded,
had fetched his pistols and was standing guard at the door,
too late to be of service. It was small wonder that Stanton,

regaled by fragments of this dramatic tale as well as by the story that the President had been shot, dismissed it as "Humbug!"

Andrew Johnson, sleeping peacefully without any idea of his own narrow escape, was roused by former Governor Leonard J. Farwell of Wisconsin, an old friend who had been with him earlier that evening but who had left because he had a ticket for Ford's Theatre. Farwell was thumping on the door and trying to look over the transom when Johnson lit the gas jet and flung the door open. "Someone," Farwell said, his voice lowered to a whisper, "has shot and murdered the President." Andrew Johnson, the tailor's son who had gone into politics and risen by the accident of having been "our Union man from Tennessee," had been selected as Vice President purely to facilitate the election of Lincoln, had been drunk at his own inauguration, and had hardly been noticed by the President since. He flung his arms despairingly around Farwell, clinging to him as though he would collapse without his friend's support. In a surprisingly short time guards were posted, while a crowd of people had poured into the lobby of the boardinghouse or were waiting on the street. Andrew Johnson got dressed and decided to go down to Ford's Theatre.

Gideon Welles, Secretary of the Navy and, apart from Seward, the only member of Lincoln's original Cabinet still in office, was awakened by his wife to hear that Seward was dead. He rushed over to the scene of carnage, arriving almost at the same moment as Stanton, who had finally been convinced. He had not been able to believe it, exclaimed Welles, till he saw it with his own eyes. He had also heard a rumor that the President was shot, but this was too much to credit on top of the massacre at Seward's.

"It is true," Stanton told him. "I had a talk with a man who had just left Ford's Theatre."

"Then I will go at once to the White House."

"The President is still at the theater," Stanton replied.

By this time the Peterson house on Tenth Street was drawing all kinds of people like a magnet. The great ones went inside, and the rest stood in the street. Beside the dingy bedroom where the doctors labored over Lincoln, marveling at the strength of the man who would not die, there was a dark little parlor in which a coal fire had been lit to warm Mrs. Lincoln, on either side of whom sat Clara Harris and Laura Keene, the charming leading lady who was the star attraction of *Our American Cousin*. Part of the time Mary was quiet, but when insensitive people condoled with her as though her husband were already dead, she would give way to fits of grief and demand repeatedly to be taken in to see him. Lincoln's features were growing distorted as a result of internal bleeding and the pressure of the bullet behind the right eye. The doctors, warned of Mary's coming, would replace the bloodstained napkins behind his head and try to make him more presentable for her —but she would scream or faint and have to be removed. Sometimes Robert would spend a while with her; then he would go back to the bedroom. They ought to bring Tad, Mary cried. His father would be bound to speak to Tad. "He loves him so." But Lincoln was beyond the reach of love. Dr. Leale, superseded in the case by the Surgeon General, sat down beside the bed and took Lincoln's hand. Sometimes when a man is in a coma, he becomes conscious in the very instant of death. Should this happen to Lincoln, blinded and unable to speak or see his friends, would he not be less frightened if he felt a hand in his? The concept was more fanciful than real—yet with a physique like Lincoln's who could tell?

Stanton had far more to do. Establishing himself in a back parlor with all the powers of the War Department in his hands, Stanton determined to crush the conspiracy, which he characteristically supposed was larger than it was. There was no doubt about the identity of Booth, who had been recognized by many people as he ran across the well-lit stage after the attack. But the attack on Seward broadened the issue. Stanton had guards placed around the homes of important people. He took over Ford's Theatre and arrested all its employees. He ordered the fire department to stand in readiness in case murder were followed by mass arson. He set up a special court of inquiry before which witnesses passed in a steady stream, convincing him that the assassins had been hired by the Confederate government, that hundreds of terrorists were in Washington at that moment. Policemen, military policemen, various networks of spies, and soldiers in nearby encampments were drafted to search for such men—inevitably encouraged by the prospect of earning rewards or rapid promotion.

By 1:30 A.M. Stanton had an official announcement of Lincoln's death signed and lying ready to have the time filled in. There must not be the slightest delay in swearing in the new Head of State. Everything was prepared except the man on the bed, whose hoarse breathing could still be heard over the murmurs of the doctors.

By five Lincoln was clearly dying. His breathing stopped for a few seconds at a time, and began again. His heartbeats were irregular, his lips blue, his feet cold as stone. Robert Lincoln stood in the doorway by the head of the bed, and Gideon Welles sat at the foot. In the parlor Mary Lincoln waited in exhausted silence. Feet tramped through the corridor to the room where Stanton was by now organizing pursuit of Booth, Herold, Paine, and Atzerodt, and sending men to examine Mrs. Surratt's boardinghouse. Examination of witnesses was bringing to light the facts.

The death struggle began about seven. The President had been moaning, but now at times he did not seem to breathe at all. They brought Mrs. Lincoln in to have a last sight of him, but she screamed hysterically and had to be removed. One final time Lincoln's chest heaved—and then relaxed. The Surgeon General listened for a heartbeat and found none. Stanton, who had been watching hat in hand, put it back on his head. "Now he belongs to the ages," he said, at least according to one tradition. The useless night was over. Abraham Lincoln, dead ever since Booth's shot, had ceased to breathe.

# 17

## Epilogue

MEN CARRIED LINCOLN to the East Room of the White House, where they laid him under a tall black canopy, such as he had seen in his dream. Word went out to churches across the north that funeral ceremonies should be held in each that Sunday. The body was then conveyed in a great procession to the Rotunda of the Capitol, where it lay in state. On April 21, Lincoln left Washington forever, deliberately sent home by the exact route along which he had passed in 1861 to take up office. But in Baltimore, through which he had sped so secretly in the early hours of the morning, the cortège stopped at the Exchange building, where his body lay surrounded by evergreens and lilies, while the scuffling feet of mourners passed him for hours.

In Pennsylvania, New Jersey, and New York he was received with similar honors. His train went up the Hudson by night, but every town and railroad crossing was thronged with people waiting amid the flare of torches to see the funeral car. When he reached Albany it was after midnight, but the crowds pressed forward to file by the dead man as though it were daylight. In Cleveland no

public building could house the concourse, and a canopy
was put up in the public square, lit all night long by gas
jets. Men poured in from all over the Northwest to Chicago to pay their last respects. Every train brought more
into Springfield for the interment. At the funeral his Second Inaugural was read, the words of a man who directed
a four-year war, yet never learned to bear malice.

This last was a lesson which Stanton had no desire to
learn. Booth had been killed resisting arrest before Lincoln
was laid in his grave in Springfield on May 4. Eight prisoners, including the possibly ignorant Mrs. Surratt and a
certain Dr. Mudd who had committed the offense of setting Booth's broken foot, awaited trial in prison, heavily
manacled and with heads and shoulders covered by stifling
sacks padded with cotton in which two small slits had been
cut, one at eye level, and the other by the mouth so that—
as well as they could manage with handcuffs on—they
could eat. After the trial, Herold, Atzerodt, Paine, and
Mrs. Surratt were hanged. Dr. Mudd and three others
were sentenced to imprisonment for life—but were
released after four years. John Surratt, who had escaped to
Canada, did not return to help his mother, for whom he
could have done little. His employment, however, as a
Confederate courier gave rise to a suspicion that the leaders of the Richmond government had been concerned in
the plot. Jefferson Davis, confined in circumstances of
great barbarity, awaited trial when the Federal government had marshaled its proofs. There were, however, none
to be found; and it became obvious that there never would
be any. Davis, insisting to the last that the Confederacy had
a right to secede and that he was its lawful President, was
paroled after two years without a trial.

Mary Lincoln, meanwhile, crippled by debts which she
dared not reveal and could not even add up, was not even
granted a small pension for several years, in part because
her husband had to all appearances left her enough to live
on. Eventually the murder of James Garfield, who left a

wife and young family, made it necessary to provide more adequately for the widows of slain Presidents, Lincoln's included. Meanwhile, however, Mary Lincoln—helpless, indiscreet, psychotic—had one difficulty after another and eventually went to Europe where it was cheaper to live.

With her went Tad. It is said that when he was awakened with the news that his father had been murdered, Tad dressed himself unassisted for the first time in his life. If so, he had recognized a fact apparent to everyone concerned with his future. Something had to be done about Tad, who could not speak intelligibly, who had not bothered to learn to read or in fact to do anything which involved discipline. Since he had inherited a third of his father's estate, Mary could hire him tutors or send him to European schools. Too much of his time was spent in cramming, and far too much in a darkened room laying cold compresses on his mother's forehead. Tad was affectionate, and his mother's sorrows made unreasonable demands upon him.

Mary brought him back to America when he was nineteen, a quiet studious young man, speaking clearly but with a slight German accent. But he proved too delicate to face an Illinois winter. In the first year of his return, he caught pneumonia and died. Thereafter Mary's wild ways and insane spending habits led Robert, now married and quite unable to manage his mother, to have her committed as a lunatic. She was rescued by her sister, Elizabeth Edwards, who kept her in her own house until she was well enough to go back to Europe, far from the people who had known her in her proud or happy days. In 1881, old, ailing, and obscure, she returned to Elizabeth, in whose house she lived in a bedroom, blinds drawn and lighted with candles, shunning even her relatives and the old friends of her dead husband. She died in 1882 and was buried beside Abraham Lincoln, since whose death she had never passed a happy moment.

Before any of these people died, before Lincoln was even

laid in his grave, his reputation had grown to heroic dimensions. Men extolled him as the second founder of his country, speaking of him as a President of all-seeing wisdom, unspotted virtue, unmatchable greatness. Yet this was the very man who had been warned some six months earlier that he could not even expect to be re-elected. What had Abraham Lincoln done to deserve this explosion of love and grief, such as has been given to only a few men in history? When William of Orange died in 1584, it is said that the little children cried in the streets. William of Orange had been the leader of his people for a generation, Abraham Lincoln for four years. The Dutch Republic and the American, the circumstances and the men were totally different; but there were reasons, some of them admirable, some merely human, which gave Lincoln a place in the hearts of his countrymen comparable to that of William in those of the Dutch.

In the first place he had just won the war and restored the Union. This achievement was so recent that, except in very cynical political circles, there was a temporary fusion between the people and the man who had led them. Many had complained of his conduct of the war, had feared for its outcome, or had demanded an early cessation of fighting. Victory had satisfied them all, with the result that there was no time or manner in which Lincoln could have died that would have made him more instantly popular. Secondly, it became fashionable to exalt Lincoln after his death in a way which would not have been universal while he was living. The central core of the radical faction of Congress, for instance, were not privately displeased to find the moderate Lincoln, who had been too wily for them, replaced by Andrew Johnson, Vice President for only a few weeks, more radical and with far less experience. But it suited the radicals to mourn Lincoln publicly, since the more they denounced the Confederates for murder, the easier it was to revenge themselves on the South. On the other hand, those who had hoped for a true reunion of the nation blamed disappointments on the death of the great statesman whose concern to heal all wounds had been so evident.

Many southerners, it is true, did rejoice at Lincoln's death, including the entourage of Jefferson Davis. With more honesty than tact, Davis defended them. Lincoln would never have accepted the Confederacy while breath remained in his body. Why should good Southerners care how he had died? They were not rejoicing over a plot they had hatched themselves, but over a stroke of good fortune. Yet even irreconcilables came to realize that they would have been better off if Lincoln had lived.

All these were reasons why criticisms, once so freely expressed, had perished with Lincoln. They are not, however, the whole story. At the time that Lincoln died he was very widely and personally beloved.

The people who loved him most were the Negroes. Everybody noticed how even their pathetic rags managed somehow to include a scrap of black in mourning for Lincoln. It was not merely that they looked on him as their liberator. One of the most attractive things about Lincoln was that though realist enough to understand how white people neither could nor would accept racial equality in his generation, he was able to greet Africans like everyone else. Frederick Douglass, escaped slave and champion of Negro rights, met Lincoln on several occasions and remarked that he was the only white man who gave no impression that he noticed what color skin he saw in front of him. One of the last acts of Lincoln's life was to see Nancy Bushrod and promise that her husband's pay allotment should be straightened out.

Black people felt that Lincoln cared about them, but the number of other individuals who were personally grateful to him was enormous also. He had, for instance, commuted countless death sentences. The verdicts of courts-martial came across his desk, and he could not persuade himself that a man should be shot because he went to sleep on pickct duty, deserted to look after his ailing wife, or even ran away. Some men were cowards, just as other men were imbeciles, or even heroes. Why shoot them for what they could not help? Many a family blessed the name of Lincoln because he had spared the life of someone dear, had listened to some trouble, had cut through red tape, had remarked that a twelve-year-old rebel could not do much harm and might as well be sent home. To other people he had written moving letters. Hearing, though untruly as it turned out, that a certain mother had lost five sons in the service of their country, he had written her a letter which ranks as a classic today. To Hooker, when he took over the Army of the Potomac, he wrote a letter containing criticism, but expressed in such a way that Hooker carried the letter about with him, showing it with affectionate pride as the sort of letter a father might have written to his son. Perhaps nowhere did thoughtfulness for the individual spread faster than it did in the army, where news of a single kindness ran quickly through a whole regiment. Lincoln had been frequently seen by the Army of the Potomac, which acquired a special devotion to him. Even troops from Sherman's Midwestern army, who had not known Lincoln personally but were furloughed to help swing the Indiana primary to him in 1864, shared their affection.

Another set of people who loved Lincoln included many who worked with or for him. The devotion of Brooks, Nicolay, Hay, and Lamon breathes through their writings. Lincoln came to Washington with a host of Illinoisan, Midwestern, and Northwestern personal friends. In Washington he added more, even including such unlikely admirers as Seward and Stanton. To Stanton, for instance, Lincoln's humor was a time-wasting nuisance. He was aware that he possessed far greater administrative ability than Lincoln and quicker, more merciless powers of decision. He was not a man in the least apt to look up to others. Yet Stanton often showed a deference, even an affection,

for Lincoln which was never really obscured by his irritation at too many pardons being given or what he considered indiscretions to congressmen about military plans.
"Now he belongs to the ages," may well be rejected as an
uncharacteristic thing for Stanton to say, but there is no
doubt he had learned to respect and care for for the man
whom he had once called "the original gorilla." His concern for Lincoln on his deathbed may be contrasted with
his unfeeling remark on Mary Lincoln, whose shrieks had
brought him running to the bedside from his inquiries in
the back parlor: "Take that woman out, and do not let her
in again."

One way and another there was a more widely diffused
love of Lincoln than either he or the nation had realized.
The immense black funeral car, the flowers, the gas illumi-
nations were not entirely the exuberance of a sentimental
nation in an age of sentiment. They were not all a political
parade with the object of making capital out of what had
happened. Something genuine had welled up which
turned vulgarity into mourning and sentimental feelings
into love.

It was not, however, Lincoln's acts of kindness or his
humor or even his lack of personal malice which endured
—it was his words. Quotable, memorable, and free from
flourishes, his sayings gave his reputation a solid quality
which still distinguished it when personal acts of kindness
were forgotten. It was the Union's good fortune at this
time to be led by a man who could pick out essentials and
make other people appreciate them. Within the limits of
his day and of its political issues, Lincoln's oratory was
matchless. It is not generally praise to say of a politician
that oratory is among his greatest gifts. But Lincoln was
not a windbag, or even just a remarkable analyst. He was
above all a practical statesman; and his greatest achievement is that he won a war to preserve democracy without
permanently weakening democratic principles. He understood also that civil wars are not like others and must end

in true reconciliation. Had he tried but failed to make an enduring peace during the years of his second term, we might have thought less of him. As things are, the nobility of his conception contrasts with some of the ignoble things that were done after his death.

# Chronology

*Preliminaries, 1860–1861*

November 6, 1860: *Abraham Lincoln* elected President of the United States.

December 20, 1860–February 1, 1861: Secession of South Carolina, Mississippi, Florida, Alabama, Georgia, Louisiana, Texas.

February 17, 1861: Inauguration of *Jefferson Davis* as Provisional President of the Confederate States.

March 4, 1861: Inauguration of *Abraham Lincoln* as President of the United States.

April 12, 1861: War opened by bombardment of FORT SUMTER by Confederates.

April 15, 1861: Lincoln calls out militia of loyal states, which results in secession of Virginia, Tennessee, Arkansas, North Carolina.

*War Events, 1861*

July 21, 1861: Confederate army under *P. G. T. Beauregard* defeats Union army under *Irvin McDowell* at BULL RUN (MANASSAS) in northern Virginia.

July 22, 1861: Lincoln summons *George McClellan* to command Union armies defending Washington.

September 3, 1861: Confederates invade hitherto neutral Kentucky. *Ulysses Grant,* stationed at Cairo, Illinois, responds by seizing Paducah on the Ohio.

November 8, 1861: *James Mason* and *John Slidell,* Confederate envoys to England and France are seized aboard a British vessel. War between the United States and England is averted by efforts of Lincoln; Charles Francis Adams, United States Ambassador to Great Britain; and Albert the Prince Consort, husband of Queen Victoria.

## War Events, 1862

January 13, 1862: Lincoln nominates *Edwin M. Stanton* for Secretary of War.

February 6, 1862: *Grant* takes FORT HENRY on Tennessee River.

February 16, 1862: *Grant* takes FORT DONELSON on Cumberland River.

February 20, 1862: Willie Lincoln dies in the White House.

March 17, 1862: *McClellan* starts to move Union Army of Potomac to the Yorktown Peninsula, in order to attack Richmond from the southeast.

April 6–7, 1862: *Albert Sidney Johnston* and *P. G. T. Beauregard* halt southward advance of *Grant* along Tennessee River by bloody battle at SHILOH in Tennessee.

April 24, 1862: *Admiral Farragut,* after several battles at the mouth of the Mississippi, captures NEW ORLEANS for Federals. In early May he advances upriver to BATON ROUGE and NATCHEZ, but fails to take VICKSBURG.

May 23–June 17, 1862: *Stonewall Jackson,* after marching up SHENANDOAH VALLEY, outflanks Federal General *Nathaniel Banks,* threatens Washington, and retreats, eluding pursuit.

June 26–July 1, 1862: *McClellan,* a few miles from Richmond, is attacked by *Robert E. Lee* in the BATTLE OF THE

SEVEN DAYS, during which both sides suffer great casualties. McClellan transfers his base to the James River and falls back from Richmond. He is shortly ordered to give up the Peninsular attack and return his army to northern Virginia.

July 21, 1862: Confederate general *Braxton Bragg* starts to transfer his army from Tupelo, Mississippi, to Chattanooga in eastern Tennessee in preparation for a two-month invasion of Kentucky. Though he fails to penetrate Ohio or even hold Kentucky, he inflicts great damage, halts Federal advance in Alabama, and his actions result in replacement of Union General *Don Carlos Buell* by Major General *William S. Rosecrans.*

August 30–31, 1862: General *John Pope,* commanding a new Union Army of Northern Virginia, mostly made up of McClellan's troops, is defeated by *Lee* and *Jackson* at SECOND BULL RUN (MANASSAS). Lincoln reappoints McClellan to full command, while Lee and Jackson advance to invade Maryland.

September 17, 1862: *McClellan* checks *Lee* in drawn battle at ANTIETAM in Maryland, but allows him to escape across the Potomac and resume his position in northern Virginia. Lincoln therefore replaces McClellan with *Ambrose Burnside* on November 7.

September 23, 1862: Lincoln publishes PROCLAMATION promising that on January 1, 1863, he will emancipate slaves in all states or portions of states then in rebellion against the United States government.

December 13, 1862. *Burnside*'s Army of the Potomac is defeated in futile assault on *Lee*'s fortified lines at FREDERICKSBURG. A constitutional crisis results in Washington, where Republican radicals seek closer control over Cabinet and President.

December 31, 1862–January 3, 1863: Armies of *Bragg* and *Rosecrans* clash in inconclusive, but bloody, battle at MURFREESBORO in Tennessee.

## War Events, 1863

January 1, 1863: Lincoln signs EMANCIPATION PROC-
LAMATION.

January 25, 1863: Lincoln replaces *Burnside,* unsuccessful
commander of Army of the Potomac, with Major General *Joseph Hooker. Grant* sets out downriver from Memphis to take VICKSBURG, chief Confederate stronghold on Mississippi River.

May 2–6, 1863: *Hooker* defeated by *Lee* and *Jackson* at
CHANCELLORSVILLE. As a result, Lee determines
to invade Pennsylvania.

June 28, 1863: *George Meade* replaces *Hooker* in command of
Army of the Potomac.

July 1–3, 1863: BATTLE OF GETTYSBURG, first real
victory of Army of Potomac over *Lee.* Ineffective pursuit
allows Lee to retreat to northern Virginia.

July 4, 1863: VICKSBURG surrenders to *Grant,* resulting
in Union control of Mississippi, splitting the Confederacy.

July 13–15, 1863: Three-day riot against the draft in New
York.

September 20–21, 1863: Confederates under *Bragg* score victory over *Rosecrans* at CHICKAMAUGA (Tennessee),
which is in part redeemed by Federal General *George
Thomas* in command of right wing. Union army retreats
to Chattanooga where, with Confederates posted on sur-
rounding hills, it seems likely to be starved into surrender.

October 23, 1863: *Grant* arrives in Chattanooga to take
charge, shortly re-establishes supply lines, and prepares
to advance on Bragg.

November 19, 1863: Lincoln delivers GETTYSBURG AD-
DRESS.

November 25, 1863: *Grant* defeats *Bragg* at CHAT-
TANOOGA, throwing Confederate army into confusion and opening route to Georgia.

## War Events, 1864

March 2, 1864: *Grant* created Lieutenant General, is given
charge of all Union armies. He sets *Sherman* in motion
towards Atlanta, Georgia, and himself joins the Army of
the Potomac in order to take Richmond.

June 7, 1864: Lincoln nominated for second term, but
Union casualties mount before Richmond.

July 11–12, 1864: Confederate General *Jubal Early* raids
Washington, occupies Silver Spring, Maryland, and
skirmishes at Seventh Street.

August 31, 1864: McClellan nominated as Democratic presidential candidate.

September 2, 1864: ATLANTA occupied by *Sherman.*

September 20, 1864: Union General *Philip Sheridan* defeats
*Early* and proceeds to drive Confederates out of Shenandoah Valley.

November 8, 1864: *Lincoln* re-elected for second presidential term.

November 15, 1864: *Sherman*'s army sets out from Atlanta to
march through Georgia to Savannah.

December 15–16, 1864: *Thomas* annihilates Confederate
army under *John B. Hood* in BATTLE OF NASH-
VILLE (Tennessee). This being the army which under
Johnston had defended Georgia, Sherman no longer has
to reckon with serious opposition.

December 22, 1864: *Sherman* enters SAVANNAH.

## Events, 1865

January 31, 1865: Congress passes THIRTEENTH
AMENDMENT banning slavery.

March 4, 1865: Lincoln's second inauguration.

March 29–31, 1865: *Grant* sets in motion flanking movement
to cut Richmond's last supply lines.

April 2, 1865: *Lee* warns *Jefferson Davis* that the Confederate
government and army must abandon Richmond.

April 4, 1865: Lincoln visits conquered Richmond.

April 9, 1865: *Lee* surrenders to *Grant* at APPOMATTOX.

April 13, 1865: *Grant* and his wife arrive in Washington, and Mrs. Lincoln invites them to a theater party the following evening which they first accept, then refuse. Lincoln decides to go in order not to disappoint the public.

April 14, 1865: *John Wilkes Booth* assassinates Lincoln at FORD'S THEATRE, while Booth's fellow conspirators attempt to kill the Vice President and Secretary of State, the two constitutional successors to a President who died in office.

# Index